***FREEDOM'S WITNESS***

West Virginia University Press 26506
Copyright 2013 by West Virginia University Press. All rights reserved.

First edition published 2013 by West Virginia University Press
Printed in the United States of America

21 20 19 18 17 16 15 14 13      9 8 7 6 5 4 3 2 1

ISBN Information for all editions:
Cloth:   978-1-935978-60-2
PB       978-1-935978-61-9
EPUB     978-1-935978-62-6
PDF      978-1935978-95-4

Library of Congress Cataloging-in-Publication Data
Turner, Henry McNeal, 1834-1915.
  Freedom's witness : the Civil War correspondence of Henry McNeal Turner / [edited by] Jean Lee Cole. -- First edition.
    p. cm
  ISBN-13: 978-1-935978-60-2 (cloth : alkaline paper)
  ISBN-10: 1-935978-60-8 (cloth : alkaline paper)
  ISBN-13: 978-1-935978-61-9 (paperback : alkaline paper)
  ISBN-10: 1-935978-61-6 (paperback : alkaline paper) [etc.]
  1. Turner, Henry McNeal, 1834-1915--Correspondence. 2. United States--History--Civil War, 1861-1865--Chaplains. 3. United States. Army--Chaplains--Correspondence. 4. African American clergy--Correspondence. 5. African Methodist Episcopal Church--Clergy--Correspondence. 6. United States--History--Civil War, 1861-1865--Personal narratives. 7. United States. Army--African American troops--History--19th century. 8. United States--History--Civil War, 1861-1865--Participation, African American. 9. Virginia--History--Civil War, 1861-1865--Campaigns. 10. United States--History--Civil War, 1861-1865--Campaigns. I. Cole, Jean Lee. II. Title.

E635.T87 2013

973.7'78092--dc23

[B]

2012049842

Cover design by Than Saffel with Ashley Muehlbauer.
Top cover image: Portrait of Henry McNeal Turner in *Harper's Weekly*, December 12, 1863, 796. Bottom cover image: Black soldiers, Ordnance Wharf, City Point, Virginia, 1864. United States Army Military History Institute.

# Freedom's Witness

## The Civil War Correspondence of

## Henry McNeal Turner

EDITED BY *Jean Lee Cole*

WITH A FOREWORD BY AARON SHEEHAN-DEAN

MORGANTOWN

2013

# Contents

vii    ***Note on the Text***
ix    ***Foreword*** by Aaron Sheehan-Dean
1    ***Introduction***

33    *Chapter One*
       **Emancipation and Enlistment**
       (March 22, 1862–April 18, 1863)

119    *Chapter Two*
       **Petersburg**
       (June 25, 1864–December 17, 1864)

163    *Chapter Three*
       **Fort Fisher**
       (January 7, 1865–February 18, 1865)

191    *Chapter Four*
       **Freeing Slaves, Meeting Sherman**
       (February 25, 1865–June 10, 1865)

251    *Chapter Five*
       **Roanoke Island**
       (June 24, 1865–August 5, 1865)

273    **About the Contributors**

## Note on the Text

### By Jean Lee Cole

*Freedom's Witness* MAKES ACCESSIBLE to students and general interest readers the early writings of Henry McNeal Turner. It includes the vast majority of Turner's writings published between 1862–1865 in the *Christian Recorder*, the denominational newspaper of the African Methodist Episcopal Church, based in Philadelphia, Pennsylvania, and focuses on those writings that demonstrated Turner's involvement in and thinking about the Civil War and emancipation, his involvement with the A.M.E. Church, and his personal experiences in the war. Turner had a decades-long relationship with the *Christian Recorder*, and also published in a variety of other publications, including two he founded in the years surrounding the turn into the twentieth century: the *Voice of Missions* and the *Voice of the People*.

Portions of three letters have been previously published: excerpts from the first letter in this collection appeared in *A Grand Army of Black Men: Letters from African-American Soldiers in the Union Army, 1861–1865*, edited by Edwin Redkey (Cambridge University Press, 1992), and the first two columns in Chapter 3 were also edited by Redkey and published as "'Rocked in the Cradle of Consternation:' A Black Chaplain in the Union Army Reports on the Struggle to Take Fort Fisher, North Carolina, in the

Winter of 1864–1865" in the journal *American Heritage* (December 1980).

The columns are, whenever possible, reproduced in their entirety in order to capture the breadth of Turner's interests and concerns, as well as the richness of African American life in Washington and in the military during this period. However, in Chapter One, some portions of individual columns, and some in their entirety, have been omitted. Nearly all of the omitted material concerns the minutiae of everyday church business; the content and extent of all exclusions are described in the footnotes.

Even though Turner's letters were hastily written and hastily edited, they required only minimal editing for publication in book form. This edition retains Turner's exact wording wherever possible; the very few editorial emendations required for grammar or sense have been indicated either with square brackets or in footnotes. Inconsistencies regarding spelling and capitalization (e.g., capital vs. Capitol, secesh vs. Secesh) have been rectified, and some punctuation has been regularized to facilitate reading by a twenty-first-century reader.

Scholars and researchers are encouraged to consult the *Recorder* itself. The most complete archive, held by the Mother Bethel A.M.E. Church in Philadelphia, is available on microfilm; a roughly edited full-text electronic version is available through Accessible Archives. For this edition, the microfilm copy was used as the source text; all transcriptions were checked against the microfilm for accuracy.

# *Foreword*

by Aaron Sheehan-Dean

THE U.S. CIVIL WAR, like nearly all wars, presents the spectacle of an event of purely human creation, quickly generating its own trajectory and spin, pulling and pushing people to take actions they might have fiercely resisted or never imagined only a short time before. The process of emancipation, so unanticipated and even undesired by many white Americans, represents one such action. The problem of slavery that caused the war pressed itself on the Lincoln administration in the form of runaway slaves, who, by hundreds of thousands, used the cover of war to flee bondage. Even as President Lincoln, Congress, and Union officers fumbled toward a response, black Americans embraced the coming of Jubilee. More than that, some saw the opportunity to affirm their place in the nation through military service. As Frederick Douglass wrote, "once let the black man get upon his person the brass letters U.S., let him get an eagle on his button, and a musket on his shoulder and bullets in his pockets, and there is no power on earth which can deny that he has earned the right of citizenship." By the end of the conflict, nearly 200,000 black men fought in the Northern ranks, equivalent to over 20 percent of the whole Confederate military.

Foremost among those who thrilled to the revolutionary potential of the conflict was Henry McNeal Turner. An up-and-coming minister in the African Methodist Episcopal Church, Turner was appointed the first black chaplain in the U.S. Army, a post that gave him the opportunity to observe the radical transformation of the conflict after 1863. As a columnist for the *Christian Recorder*, Turner provided a unique and revealing perspective on the war, the army, the experiences of black soldiers, and the reception of that army and those soldiers by black and white southerners. His observations alone are valuable, but Turner's columns also included his opinions of what saw. These are often sharp, sometimes contrary, but always thoughtful and well reasoned. Whether in wartime Washington or on the march through North Carolina, Turner had a keen eye and ear for local detail and the ability to contextualize what he saw within larger frameworks.

One of the problems that created the war and complicated its fighting was Americans' tendency to accumulate multiple, sometimes conflicting, loyalties to the concrete and imagined communities of which they were a part—families, hometowns, congregations, states, races, regions, and nations. Although most historians have focused on the obvious clash between Southern and American identities, everyone who lived through the war felt the strain among their various loyalties. Turner's columns show us how he, and blacks both in the North and South, balanced obligations to God, to their respective churches, to other African Americans, to the Union Army, and to the United States. Later in life, Turner resigned himself to the seeming futility of improving the condition of blacks within the United States, but his wartime experiences revealed an important moment when he believed, like many of his peers, that doing God's work would improve the spiritual, physical, intellectual, social, and political lives of black Americans.

Another value of Turner's writing is his honesty. Unlike some more political writers who tried to overlook the unavoidable burdens that enslavement had pressed onto black southerners, Turner offers sometimes startling assessments of the plight of enslaved people. Writing from Roanoke Island, North Carolina after the end of active fighting, Turner wrote that the Freedpeople "want instruction in ordinary affairs, viz: economy, industry, and thriftiness of every species." But unlike white Southerners and many white Northerners who blamed this lack of knowledge on blacks' innate incapacities, Turner understood ignorance as a deliberate effect of slavery. "It is not natural," he wrote, "that a people who have been held as chattels for two hundred years should thoroughly comprehend the limits of freedom's empire: the scope is too large for minds so untutored to enter upon at once."[1] Turner's honesty came neither from a cynical stance nor from the lofty plateau of what would later be called the "talented tenth." Instead, the Turner in these columns appears as a decided humanist. Black people in freedom, just like white people, would respond to their own best or worst instincts. They would, he wrote, "serve God or the devil."[2]

Turner's observations are by no means all dour. His chronicle of life in wartime Washington—principally the black Washington that is absent from so many accounts of the wartime city—bristles with the energy and drive of that community. The city possessed vibrant intellectual, social, and spiritual networks of the kind that sustained black Americans in the dark years that followed Reconstruction.[3] Like other Southern urban centers, Washington held a diverse population of enslaved and free black people, some confined to menial jobs while others achieved meaningful education, ran their own businesses, and engaged in civic pursuits. Turner's observations and experiences in Civil War-era Washington reflect the origins of a persistent dilemma in black American life about the nature, means, and mechanisms of communal uplift. Most historians frame this story around the turn-of-the-century contest between Booker T. Washington's enthusiasm for manual labor and basic education and W. E. B. Du Bois's championing of political activism and higher education. Turner, anticipating both these attitudes, wanted broad, basic education for Freedpeople, but also asserted their "claim for their superior ability." He believed that blacks had no limits to their potential, and during and after the war Turner dedicated himself to ridding the country of the artificial limits imposed by whites.

Turner served as chaplain at an important moment in a key theater of the war. Eastern Virginia, where the 1st Regiment United States Colored Troops (U.S.C.T.) was stationed in 1864, encompassed the efforts of several Union campaigns to reach Richmond, Virginia. These attacks failed, but they entailed serious fighting and Turner offers close and observant descriptions of the process and its effect on the men. Frustratingly, he was away from his regiment on July 30, 1864, when Union engineers detonated an enormous mine under the Confederate lines. What could have been a major breakthrough quickly collapsed as Union troops—including several unprepared black units hastily put into position just before the attack—funneled into "the crater" and were shot down by Confederates along its rim. As in previous engagements with black soldiers, Confederates offered no quarter and black men were shot down after or while surrendering. Despite his absence, Turner would surely have heard first-hand testimony and read about this event. Added to memories of similar treatment at Fort Pillow, Tennessee and other locations, the Battle of the Crater encouraged a retaliatory attitude among black troops. Turner describes black soldiers refusing to accept the surrender of Confederates, a reflection of the unrelieved violence and bitter yearning for revenge that characterized much of the war in 1864.[4] Beyond the battle at Fort Fisher, which Turner describes vividly, he moved farther south into North Carolina and compiled trenchant observations about the reaction of white and black Southerners to the collapse of slavery. Although these combatants were less violent to each other than the soldiers Turner traveled with, his portrait of an increasingly prostrate and vengeful white South augured poorly for the possibilities that he believed inhered in emancipation.

Despite his hopes and despite his valiant efforts to construct meaningful freedom for African Americans, Turner had good reason to be skeptical. As biblical stories told, change came slowly and without warning. Turner had read and no doubt preached about the Israelites and their deliverance, but he knew too their continued suffering. The awkward balance he maintained—between celebrating a people breaking free of bondage and the tempering effects of his own deep reading in religion and history—Turner offers us a realistic and human portrait of a divided and uncertain people trying to fashion a new world. Given the value of Turner's wartime writings, it is hard to explain why they have not been republished. A few justly famous African American authors—such as Frederick Douglass, Harriet Jacobs, and James Gooding—tend to monopolize our attention, but Turner ranks among them for the vibrancy of his prose and for the reach of his experience. Jean Lee Cole's double accomplishment here both remedies the problem of access and provides the appropriate context within which readers new to Turner or to the Civil War can understand his writing. We should be grateful to her for restoring these texts to us and to Turner for creating such a vivid and insightful record of one of our nation's most tumultuous periods.

*Aaron Sheehan-Dean*
*West Virginia University*

## Notes

1. July 22, 1865.
2. December 6, 1862.
3. Turner's D.C. resembles Ida B. Wells's Memphis as described in James West Davidson, *"They Say:" Ida B. Wells and the Reconstruction of Race* (New York: Oxford University Press, 2009).
4. June 30, 1865.

Portrait of Henry McNeal Turner in *Harper's Weekly*, December 12, 1863, 796.

# Introduction

*"I have seen war wonders":*
*The Civil War Writings of Henry McNeal Turner*

HENRY MCNEAL TURNER (1834–1915) embodied the tumultuous spirit of his age. Born free but poor in South Carolina, he labored alongside slaves as a young boy. By the age of thirty, he had risen through the ranks of the Methodist Church and was appointed one of the first black chaplains of the Union Army during the Civil War. After the war, he gained prominence, first as a politician in Georgia during Reconstruction, then as bishop of the African Methodist Episcopal (A.M.E.) Church. At the end of the nineteenth century, he embraced emigration as the solution to the problem of the "color line," the system of racial discrimination and segregation that became entrenched in American society by the end of the nineteenth century. A controversial figure in his own time, he has been remembered primarily for the emigrationist views he embraced late in life.[1] As the idea of emigration fell out of favor among black intellectuals and politicians during the twentieth century, his accomplishments have been largely forgotten. This volume attempts to reintroduce Turner to the historical—and literary—record, and to reestablish him as a key figure in the development of African American history and culture.

In a tribute published in the African American journal *Crisis* upon Turner's death, W. E. B. Du Bois described him as "the last of his clan: mighty men, physically and mentally, men who started at the bottom and hammered their way to the top by sheer brute strength."[2] Turner's intelligence, drive, and refusal to capitulate to those who would deter him characterized nearly every aspect of his life, beginning in his childhood. Threatened with whippings by whites to whom he was apprenticed in South Carolina, he ran away; denied schooling due to his race, he educated himself; he convinced skeptical whites of his intelligence by reciting long passages of scripture from memory and by sermonizing extemporaneously on a text given to him on the spot. By his late teens, he had become an itinerant minister in the Methodist Episcopal Church, where both whites and blacks flocked to hear the fiery young preacher.[3]

But while Turner was gratified by his success, he chafed at the limitations imposed on him by church leadership. By the age of nineteen, Turner had attained the rank of licensed minister—the highest rank allowed to blacks within the Methodist Episcopal denomination. Turner also was deeply troubled by the alignment of Southern Methodism with slavery. In 1866, he wrote, "You could not preach the pure gospel. . . . God's word had to be frittered, smeared, and smattered to please the politics of slavery."[4] The consequences for preaching "pure gospel" could be severe. Black preachers were whipped, beaten, and even executed for preaching in ways that were perceived as attempts to undermine the authority of slave owners or the slave system—or simply for preaching at all.

Thus, when he encountered members of the African Methodist Episcopal Church on a trip he made through Georgia, Alabama, and Louisiana in 1857, Turner found much to attract him to the denomination. The church had been established in 1816 by Richard Allen, a former slave who broke away from the St. George's Methodist Episcopal Church in Philadelphia due to its discriminatory treatment of its black members. Though dismayed by the behavior of white Methodists, Allen nevertheless believed in the principles of Methodism, as defined by John Wesley. In Allen's view, "there was no religious sect or denomination which would suit the capacity of the colored people as well as the Methodist; for this plain and simple gospel suits best for any people; for the unlearned can understand, and the learned are sure to understand." For Allen, "plain doctrine" and "good discipline" were keys not only to salvation but to black uplift. As the historian Clarence Walker observes, "What Allen wanted his church to do was instill the Yankee virtues of industry, thrift, and self-reliance. . . . The church, in short, would be the agency in which the Negro's 'character' was shaped or formed."[5]

While the A.M.E. Church had existed in South Carolina before the Civil War, it was disbanded in 1822 after several of its members were implicated in the slave rebellion plotted by Denmark Vesey, a co-founder of the church. Thus, it was not until Turner encountered the St. James Church in New Orleans, pastored by another young black divine, Willis H. Revels, that Turner learned of its existence. The A.M.E. Church's beliefs—in black uplift, the centrality of literacy in particular and education in general in that uplift, and the interconnectedness between religious, social, and political organization—all aligned with Turner's. John Dittmer writes that Turner, throughout his career, "saw his mission as both spiritual and political."[6]

After joining the A.M.E. Church, Turner continued his education, led several small congregations in St. Louis and Baltimore, and rose quickly to the position of pastor of Israel Church, a large congregation in Washington, D.C. He ably fulfilled his pastoral duties. Serendipitously, the church, he related some years later, "was only a couple of hundred yards from the United States Capitol, where mighty speeches were being made in the United States Congress"; as he frequented the congressional galleries, he became acquainted with influential politicians, including Charles

Sumner and Benjamin Wade.[7] Perhaps it was due to his interest in politics in addition to his able leadership of his congregation that led him to become the "Washington Correspondent" for the newly reestablished newspaper of the A.M.E. Church, the *Christian Recorder*.

The *Recorder*, which had languished due to lack of funds a few years after being established in 1852, was revived in 1861 under the energetic editorship of Elisha Weaver, who brought the paper to national prominence and transformed it into a publication not just for the A.M.E. Church, but also for a national African American readership. It is most likely that because of its religious affiliation, the newspaper has not received the same level of scholarly attention as abolitionist journals, in particular, Frederick Douglass's *North Star* and *Frederick Douglass' Paper*. In fact, however, it was the longest-lived African American newspaper and very likely was read at least as widely, if not more so, than Douglass's newspapers.[8] Through its nationwide network of "agents" (primarily A.M.E. ministers), the *Recorder* was distributed from north to south and from coast to coast, and became one of the primary sources of Civil War news, along with the secular *Anglo-African*, published in New York and edited by Thomas and Robert Hamilton.[9]

A four-page weekly, the *Recorder* did not just contain news. Nor did it solely deal with ecclesiastical concerns. In fact, it presented a variety of content, including editorials and news items contributed by the newspaper's regional "corresponding editors" and individual readers, church news, and digests of national and world news on the first two pages, and fiction, pieces on popular science, poems and lessons for children, and ads dominating the third and fourth. It published the earliest-known novels written by African Americans, *The Curse of Caste* by Julia C. Collins (serialized in 1865, with installments often on the same page on which Turner's columns also appeared) and several by Frances Watkins Harper.

Elizabeth McHenry persuasively argues that publications like the *Recorder* and the *Anglo-African* "regarded the need for self-representation as central to the future of black Americans in the United States and saw their columns as places where black voices would find a receptive audience."[10] Items for the *Recorder* and for other African American newspapers were written by blacks *for* blacks—unlike the most widely studied genre of nineteenth-century African American literature, the slave narrative, which was written for a largely white audience, and often not actually written by blacks, but ghostwritten (or "edited") by white abolitionists. By presenting African Americans as authors, speakers, and commentators on the world around them, for a black audience that was assumed to be thoughtful, engaged, and literate, black periodicals created a space for African American discourse outside of what Lawrence Hogue has described as a "white/black binary of signification that defines whites as normative and superior and that represents blacks as victim, as inferior, as devalued Other."[11]

In contrast to the slave narrative, which is fundamentally structured on this "white/black binary," positing whites as masters, owners, and disciplinarians, in contrast to the powerless, victimized, persecuted slave, writers in black periodicals presented themselves as independent subjects outside white control and outside the white gaze. News items about church activities, including debating societies like the Israel Lyceum, which Turner organized at his church, contraband relief societies, and religious conferences, demonstrated a lively and cohesive African American community with vibrant, charismatic black leaders. Poetry and fiction, as well as items about popular science, the domestic arts, history, and world news expanded African American discourse beyond abolition, slavery, and race relations—though certainly the act of engaging in these broader discourses was a statement in itself about the assumed intellectual inferiority of blacks.[12]

Perhaps the most important of the contributions to the *Recorder* during the Civil War period were the regular "correspondences" from readers as far-flung as Rhode Island and Oswego, New York, Florida, and Louisiana, and as far west as Iowa, Kansas, and California. These correspondents, whom one might describe as a hybrid between a writer of a "letter to the editor" and a regular newspaper columnist, came from all walks of life, were both male and female, and engaged a wide array of subjects. Eric Gardner writes that while the *Recorder's* correspondents wrote for the express purpose of conveying "the news," this "*news* was a locus for multigeneric individual and communal dialogue whose subjects varied significantly, from the personal and familial . . . to items of local interest . . . to commentary on national issues."[13] Turner was just one of a number of writers who created authorial personae that allowed readers to imagine black subjectivity in a variety of forms, yet contained in a single publication. In a fundamental way, the *Recorder* and other African American periodicals helped define the outlines of what Carla Peterson has called the "ethnic public" sphere of African American society—a sphere that was wider than the domestic sphere of the family as well as localized ethnic communities, but distinct from the national public sphere[14]—that is to say, they created a distinctly *African American* community.

Turner came to prominence in both the A.M.E. Church and as a correspondent for the *Recorder* just as the war was getting underway. Unlike many blacks, who were jubilant at the news of the fall of Fort Sumter, Turner was initially horrified by the outbreak of war and by the bloodshed it promised. On May 13, 1861, he wrote in his diary that in both "north and south" "surely they have forgot that there is a hell, and that all the wicked will there be turned, with the nations that forget God."[15] Yet he concurred with nearly all blacks who were deeply disappointed in Lincoln's reluctance to make the abolition of slavery central to the war effort. Although Lincoln himself opposed slavery, he knew that emancipation would create serious complications with slave states that had remained in the Union; also, he understood that freeing the slaves was not a cause many Northern soldiers found worth fighting for. As a result, he initially chose to characterize the war as being one to "save the Union" rather than one to "free the slaves." In an August 22, 1862, letter to the abolitionist and newspaper editor Horace Greeley, Lincoln made this clear:

> My paramount object in this struggle is to save the Union, and is not either to save or to destroy slavery. If I could save the Union without freeing any slave I would do it, and if I could save it by freeing all the slaves I would do it; and if I could save it by freeing some and leaving others alone I would also do that. What I do about slavery, and the colored race, I do because I believe it helps to save the Union; and what I forbear, I forbear because I do not believe it would help to save the Union.

Yet even as he wrote this letter, he privately believed that emancipation would be essential to saving the nation. He eventually devised a plan to announce the emancipation of slaves in rebellious states, while allowing slaveholders in Union states to retain their "property." Secretary of State William Seward advised that if Lincoln were to issue a declaration of emancipation after the Union had achieved a significant military victory, it could be offered as an incentive for rebel states to rejoin the Union. This opportunity came after the Battle of Antietam (September 17, 1862), which was declared a Union victory despite the staggering number of casualties suffered by both sides. At this time, Lincoln issued his Preliminary Emancipation Proclamation, which warned the Confederate states that if they were still in a state of insurrection on January 1, 1863, any slaves in those states would be freed once the Union armies reached them.

Of course, neither Turner nor the rest of the American public was aware of much of this political maneuvering. A more visible factor that made emancipation an attractive—or plausible—strategy in the execution of the war was the growing tide of black slaves seeking refuge along the front lines of the Union Army. Initially, Union commanders returned many of these slaves to their Confederate owners, following the directives of the Fugitive Slave Law enacted in 1850. However, as the war progressed, and especially, once the Union Army penetrated the South, both soldiers and commanders became increasingly uncomfortable with the law. Eventually, the army adopted the so-called "contraband" policy devised by the abolitionist Union general Benjamin Butler, who, when confronted with several fugitive slaves in May 1861, justified the confiscation of slaves as "contraband of war"—that is, as enemy property—as a way of depriving the Confederacy of resources. As the war progressed, hundreds of thousands of slaves fled to Union lines to offer themselves up as contrabands. While some contrabands were employed as Union labor, they increasingly sapped the Union Army of resources, as the army was expected to protect contraband property. Emancipation thus became a way to free the army of the burden of protecting the contrabands, while also providing a path to the eventual enlistment of black soldiers.

When the Preliminary Emancipation Proclamation was declared in September 1862, Turner wrote, "All can now see that the stern intention of the Presidential policy is to wage the war in favor of freedom, till the last groan of the anguished heart slave shall be hushed in the ears of nature's God." When the Emancipation Proclamation took effect, Turner declared even more forcefully, "The first day of January 1863 is destined to form one of the most memorable epochs in the history of the world." According to the historian James Campbell, by this time Turner had "glimpsed in the carnage a kind of ritual expiation that would wash away the stain of slavery and enable Americans of all races to live together in harmony."[16] He also saw an immediate need for blacks to act—first, by helping the contrabands who would be definitively and permanently emancipated, and second, by volunteering to fight for the Union.

Turner believed that if blacks were to be recognized as free citizens of the United States, they must be willing to fight. If they were to be free to work, to play, to travel, then, he wrote, "I tell you what we will have to do; if this nation don't mind, we will have to settle this American war." Blacks, of course, had aided in the war effort from the outset—as laborers, personal servants, nurses, informants, and even as guards. But even though several black regiments had been formed prior to emancipation, white commanders were reluctant (if they did not refuse outright) to use black soldiers in combat: it was believed by many, to use the vulgar phrase of the day, that "The niggers won't fight." Some believed that blacks were simply too cowardly to engage in battle; even the more thoughtful believed that it was impossible to produce black soldiers in a culture shaped by an assumption of white supremacy (and thus, black inferiority). As Edwin S. Redkey put it, "Most whites . . . reasoned that blacks could not be relied on to fight their 'superiors,' the white troops of the Confederacy."[17]

At the same time, the question within the black community was not about whether blacks would fight, but whether or not they *should*. Time and again, within the pages of the *Recorder* and other African American publications, blacks argued that they should not fight unless they could be guaranteed equal pay, equal treatment, and equal opportunities for advancement—none of which the government was willing to grant.[18] The ambivalence felt within the black community initially resulted in tepid enlistment numbers. Turner found himself having to persuade both blacks and whites of the value of black soldiers. His success at doing so brought him to the attention of Washington politicians, who were instrumental in recommending his appointment as chaplain for the troops he helped recruit, the 1st Regiment, United States Colored Troops (U.S.C.T.);[19] he was duly commissioned late in 1863. As one of only 14 black chaplains of the 2,300 chaplains that served in the Union Army, Turner and his fellow blacks constituted less than 10 percent of the chaplains serving the black regiments. They also were virtually the only black officers to serve in the Civil War.[20]

Turner's regiment initially was organized to provide support rather than to engage in combat. The Emancipation Proclamation, in fact, stipulated that such troops should not be used in active combat, but rather "to garrison forts, positions, stations, and other places, and to man vessels of all sorts in said service." But after several key battles—in particular, the assaults on Fort Wagner, South Carolina, and Port Hudson, Louisiana, in July 1863—some white commanders became convinced that black troops could be relied upon to fight, and fight well. As Turner's correspondence shows, Generals Wild, Butler, and Terry entrusted black troops with significant "strategetical" roles (to use Turner's characteristic term) in the battles of Wilson's Landing, Fort Fisher, and in the capture of Wilmington, North Carolina, in the winter of 1864–65. Union commanders' willingness to deploy black troops varied widely, and some commanders—most famously, William Tecumseh Sherman—never approved of using black soldiers in combat.

Certainly, relations between black and white soldiers and officers were often deeply fraught. The white and black regiments (there were no integrated regiments, although some free blacks succeeded in enlisting in white companies) competed with each other for resources, respect, and recognition. White troops were often motivated to volunteer for dangerous engagements simply to prevent black troops from getting credit. Turner himself noted of white soldiers during the Second Battle of Fort Fisher, "I thought they could never stand it; neither do I believe they would have stood, but for the fact that they knew the black troops were in the rear, and if they . . . failed, the colored troops would take the fort and claim the honor." At Fort Wagner, Fort Pillow, and the Battle of the Crater, among many examples, black troops knew their missions were desperate, if not impossible—but followed orders to avoid being labeled cowards.

On a more basic level, black troops deeply resented the fact that they received less than half the regular pay of white soldiers. In many cases, they received no pay at all. They also were subject to verbal and physical abuse from white troops and officers, and suffered from the same kinds of discrimination serving in the military that they experienced in civilian life. As a black officer, Turner found himself in an unusual position: elevated in a position above the white rank-and-file soldiers, but unable to presume basic privileges offered to white officers. In a January 1865 column, he described the reaction of a young black boy waiting at his table: "He was so much surprised at seeing me, a colored man, eating with white officers, that he did nothing but stand and look at me. I suppose that he never saw such a sight before." Yet in his very next entry, he is denied lodging, a privilege expected by officers, in Beaufort, North Carolina, and he hinted throughout the columns that finding housing was a constant worry during his travels.

Turner proved himself more than capable of handling these challenges. One soldier wrote, "Mr. Turner has always been the idol of our men, he goes with us every where; in cold or heat, battle or sickness, he is always there."[21] As chaplain, Turner comforted and nursed the wounded (sometimes serving as the de facto lead medical officer), held religious services of various types, wrote letters, and carried messages. In his biography of Turner, Stephen Ward Angell wrote that above all, his "zeal to evangelize the unconverted" was only "matched by his enthusiasm to teach African American soldiers to read."[22] Like the black troops generally, Turner and the other black chaplains joined the military in order to demonstrate African Americans' willingness to fulfill the duties of citizenship and ultimately to demonstrate their humanity. But the chaplains had also enlisted in a different kind of war—the war for souls—that the Civil War represented for the A.M.E. Church and for other Protestant denominations. Most immediately, Turner sought to convert his own soldiers; as he wrote in his October 8, 1864, column, "We are regularly fortifying ourselves as securely against the devil and his subalterns, or angels, as we are against the rebels." But he also ranged further afield, into the Southern territories that fell to the Union in the final months of the war.

As Walker puts it, "Emancipation made the South a missionary field." At the April 1863 A.M.E. Church's annual conference in Baltimore, it was decided to send church ministers to the South Carolina coast as missionaries, since the Union had overtaken this region. These ministers, Walker writes, "were the vanguard of an 'army' that would spread across the South gathering black souls for the glory of God and the A.M.E. Church." The A.M.E. Church was especially motivated to send ministers and teachers because they believed that the newly freed slaves would benefit most if they were taken under the wing of fellow blacks. While they recognized the real good being done by white educators and religious leaders, they believed that "black teachers could accomplish this great work faster."[23]

Ironically, but perhaps not unexpectedly, the A.M.E. Church ministers, missionaries from other denominations, and military chaplains frequently clashed with each other as they competed for members. Walker writes that "Antagonisms between men of God took a variety of forms: racial, intraracial, interdenominational, denominational, sectional, and political." As an A.M.E. Church pastor as well as a correspondent for the official A.M.E. Church newspaper, Turner duly relayed his views not just on the battles he witnessed on the field, but between congregations. Most significant of these was the competition between A.M.E. Church ministers from the North, many of whom were present in the South under the auspices of military chaplaincy, and the leaders of the M.E. Church and A.M.E. Zion Church, both of whom were already established in the South. Turner recounts several instances, at times in concretely militaristic terms, where he would overtake a congregation, or even a physical church building, and claim it for the

A.M.E. Church. In the case of a former Methodist church in Edenton, North Carolina, for example, he "proposed to send Reverend John Hames with one division to engage them and draw their fire, so as to ascertain their strength and discover their topography. Afterwards I would come with the remainder of the corps and carry every thing by storm." Though his columns record no physical violence between leaders of these groups, the rhetoric could become heated: in the April 1, 1865, *Recorder*, he described his attempts to mediate between William H. Hunter, of the A.M.E. Church and chaplain of the 4th U.S.C.T., and James Walker Hood, of the A.M.E. Zion Church, writing, "I heard and saw enough to sicken any man." Turner, speaking for himself, professed his preference "for unity, at all hazards," and on repeated occasions pleaded for the different denominations to come together, perhaps simply renaming itself the "United Methodist Episcopal Church."[24]

Reginald F. Hildebrand argues that the fights between black denominations was not just about competing for new members, but also about what the very idea of freedom meant. Because they had always been included as members of the church, and, within the black denominations, even held positions of power and self-determination, he writes, "The church was one of the few areas in which blacks were relatively free to define an aspect of freedom in ways that made sense to them."[25] For some, this meant demanding full political and social equality. Others, like Turner, doubted that blacks could achieve complete equality in a system that had been so long based on assumptions of racial difference and white supremacy. His desire for "unity, at all hazards" indicates his desire for racial solidarity; but by removing the word "African" from the new name he would give a unified denomination, he also demonstrates his desire to define the church primarily as a Methodist Church, rather than distinguishing it as an "African," rather than "white," denomination. Turner never succeeded in unifying the different Methodist denominations. But he certainly was instrumental in the A.M.E. Church's campaign for souls; by 1876, the church membership had expanded sixfold, in large part due to the influx of new members from the South.

After the war ended, the 1st U.S.C.T. was deployed to the Freedmen's Colony on Roanoke Island, North Carolina, the site of the first English settlement in North America in 1587. According to the historian Patricia C. Click, the Roanoke Island colony was one of a hundred or so camps for freed slaves established by the federal government by the end of the Civil War.[26] Here, Turner faced new challenges. Before emancipation Turner had written, "The deep concern now with thousands is, what the President is going to do with the negroes? . . . if he is freed, what is he going to do for a livelihood, and where is he going to locate?" In Roanoke, he and his superiors confronted this very question. "They need instruction in every thing," he lamented in June 1865; they "are without money, land, home, and houses; and many, to all noble purposes of life, are insensible. They want instruction in ordinary affairs, viz: economy, industry, and thriftiness of every species." Turner was overwhelmed by the magnitude of the task. He wrote, "the duties devolving upon me are so weighty and responsible that I can rarely find enough of spare moments to write any thing." Though he claimed in late June that he was "at a loss for a starting point" to describe how much had changed since the arrival of the 1st U.S.C.T, the regiment could not have accomplished much in the few short months they were stationed there. The columns Turner published in the *Recorder* during this time are more significant in their description and assessment of the challenges facing the South than in recording actual progress.

After the 1st U.S.C.T was disbanded in September 1865, Turner was assigned to Georgia under the authority of President Johnson, who appointed him chaplain of the Freedmen's Bureau there, and by the A.M.E. Church bishop Daniel Payne, who simultaneously wanted him to oversee the state's churches. After experiencing discriminatory treatment at the bureau, and perhaps sensing the capitulation to Southern white interests that would take place during Reconstruction, he resigned his government post after serving for only a few weeks. He then turned his attention to his ministerial duties. Under Turner, the A.M.E. Church in Georgia experienced what the historian James Campbell described as "spectacular growth," adding ten thousand members within just three months.[27] At the same time, he became a highly visible political figure. He was a key organizer of the state Republican Party and was elected to the state legislature in 1868. Turner initially was sanguine about the future of blacks in the newly reunified country, but soon became disillusioned when he realized that President Johnson—and politicians generally—were more interested in normalizing relations between the Southern states and the federal government than in extending civil rights to African Americans. Turner's political pragmatism and willingness to compromise, moreover, were appreciated by neither Democrats nor Republicans. In 1871, he described his political career to his congregation thus: "I have been the constant target of Democratic abuse and venom, and white Republican jealousy."[28]

By the end of Reconstruction Turner had given up on the possibility of blacks' achieving full equality with whites. In 1880, he wrote, "I am down on the whole nation. I think my race has been treated by it with the kindness that a hungry snake treats a helpless frog. I am as near a rebel to this Government as any Negro ever got to be."[29] Turner's experiences had convinced him that most whites would never consider blacks their political, much less social, equals. As a result, he abandoned politics altogether and focused his energies on his church work, believing that if the American government had absconded its responsibilities to black Americans, the black church could provide necessary secular leadership. He quickly moved up the ranks of the A.M.E. Church leadership, and was elected bishop in 1880.

Turner's election to the bishopric was controversial. For one thing, he represented the views of members from the newly reincorporated Southern states (which included many newly freed slaves), which often conflicted with the Northern black elite who had dominated the A.M.E. Church before the Civil War. Moreover, Turner, himself born in the South and largely self-educated, was famously lacking in the kinds of social graces and sophisticated tastes that characterized what Du Bois would dub the "Talented Tenth." Once elected, Turner alienated himself further from the other leaders of the church by actively espousing emigration as the solution to the race problem in America. During the war, Turner emphatically rejected the establishment of colonies in Africa—most notably, Liberia, which became an independent nation in 1847; he described African emigration in his Civil War–era writings as simple "foolishness." However, his experiences during Reconstruction showed him that it would be difficult, if not impossible, to eradicate the legacy of white supremacy and slavery in United States in the minds of either whites or blacks. Living in the South, he witnessed the dramatic increase in lynchings, racial violence, and the erosion of black civil rights, and came to believe that it would take a new nation led by blacks, for blacks, to truly understand independence and democracy. Accepting an honorary vice presidency of the American Colonization Society in 1876, he wrote that he had decided on emigration as a solution because "My race cannot long remain in the land of its centuries of thralldom unless it be in a state of serfdom or ward-espionage."[30]

The A.M.E. Church had rejected colonization practically from its inception, because many of its (white) advocates believed blacks should be removed to Africa because they were unassimilable to American culture.[31] But for Turner, as well as for others who would follow his steps in the late-nineteenth-century back-to-Africa movement, the establishment of a successful black nation came to represent black self-sufficiency and racial solidarity rather than a capitulation to racist assumptions of black inferiority. "Nothing less than a nation owned and controlled by the Negro will amount to a hill of beans," he said. Turner, wrote Campbell, "maintained that blacks would earn white respect, and recover their own self-respect, only when they demonstrated their capacity to maintain a nation of their own."[32] Turner thus presented emigration as a solution to the "problem of the color line" distinct from both Booker T. Washington's accommodationism and the more militant demands for full civic and political equality articulated by Du Bois, strategies that were both flawed, in Turner's view, because they depended on cooperation with whites. Redkey writes that "He urged neither integration nor accommodation with white society," but rather, complete independence of blacks *from* white society.[33]

While Turner's views were dismissed and even mocked by the Northern black intellectuals, emigration was popular among poor, Southern blacks.[34] Turner also was instrumental in laying the groundwork for later black separatist movements in the twentieth century—in particular, the focus on an independent Liberia as "a central pillar of black nationalist thought."[35] In the end, Turner's historical legacy was a mixed one. Although he was recognized as an influential leader within the African American community, and instrumental in the A.M.E. Church's expansion in the South after the Civil War, he never attained the mainstream visibility of his contemporaries, Frederick Douglass, Martin Delany, Booker T. Washington, and W. E. B. Du Bois. His commitment to the A.M.E. Church as his domain may have limited his reach; his contradictory views and actions also make it difficult to provide a succinct, holistic assessment of his life. Willing to compromise—even with virulently racist Southern politicians—he nevertheless refused to apologize for being black; by championing emigration, he formed uneasy alliances with those who actively sought to rid the United States of its African American citizens. He ridiculed Washingtonian accommodationists and Du Boisian integrationists alike for capitulating to white expectations and standards for black behavior, yet continued to advocate education and Christianity as avenues for black uplift. Despite all this, what underlies all of Turner's work, according to the biographer Stephen Angell, is his "defense of human rights as an absolute moral obligation" and his "strongly worded affirmations of the dignity of African Americans."[36]

\* \* \*

In April of 1865, the final month of the Civil War, Turner wrote in amazement, "I have seen war wonders." Turner's Civil War correspondence has been described by Angell as an "an intimate, valuable record"; that is, as an eyewitness account.[37] But Turner's emphasis on the war's "wonders" points to an aspect of his writing that has been largely ignored: its significance as a work of imagination, an example of literary style, and an opportunity for ministry. In these columns, we can see Turner experimenting with several different stylistic modes. As the *Recorder*'s "Washington Correspondent," he initially writes as a journalist, an observer of events, even referring to himself (sometimes with a wink to his readers) in the third person. As he came to be seen as a personage in his own right, the columns become more journal than journalism, more exhortation than reportage. Throughout, Turner exhibits a sheer love of language, as well as a deep concern for the future of black America. His columns are an assertion of a distinctly black notion of free selfhood, rooted in black oral and sermonic traditions, that form a counterpoint to the more genteel, sentimental mode that dominated African American writing of the time.

From the start, Turner's boisterous, and at times bombastic, diction and syntax leap off the page. He is a lover of syllables and lists, of hyperbole and excess; his sentences spill over the rules of grammar. He respects few rules of literary decorum. As an example, one might recall his description of atrocities committed by Confederate soldiers: "the diabolical flagitiousness of the villainous perpetrations done by the snake-hearted squatter-smatters of that hydrophobic dropsy-headed oligarchy—is sufficient to shudder a nervous being, but such vile imps of creation God will judge and reward." The words must literally be spit out of one's mouth, conveying the spluttering disgust Turner clearly feels toward the soldiers. At the same time, the phrasing is rhythmic, and almost musical—the "diabolical flagitiousness" paralleling, rhythmically, the soldiers' "villainous perpetrations," and multiplied by the "hydrophobic dropsy-headed oligarchy." He mixes biblical, legal, political, and scientific language with down-home slang, along with words that have no meaning at all. And why not? "Good nonsense is not unfrequently appreciated as our most interesting literature," he claimed. One can see in his writing the effect of his unconventional education: he learned to read largely at the hands of the lawyers who employed him as a teenager, who, according to Angell, educated him in "arithmetic, astronomy, geography, history, law, and theology"; he did not study grammar until he undertook formal schooling in Baltimore in 1858—only a few years before he began writing for the *Recorder*.[38] Here, we can see a writer reveling in and stretching the limbs of his own literacy.

As a stylist, however, Turner also owes much to the Methodist divines who traveled the South Carolina up-country surrounding Abbeville, where he spent much of his youth. He essentially learned at the knee of these black preachers, some illiterate, some learned, who depended heavily on memorization—and improvisation—to "hold their audiences spellbound by their colorful, insightful, and often quite detailed expositions of Scripture."[39] The improvisational aspects of black sermonizing, argues Angell, came from Africa, evidenced in West African griot storytelling traditions, but also in African-influenced dances and songs, like the ring shout and the spiritual, that came to infuse African American religious practice.[40] Conjoined with the evangelical aim of bringing souls to Christ, the preacher used his (and in a few cases, her) charisma, passion, creativity, and sheer vocal power to inspire and ultimately convert the congregation into new life. James Weldon Johnson wrote in 1927 that the black preacher

> knew the secret of oratory, that at bottom it is a progression of rhythmic words more than it is anything else. Indeed, I have witnessed congregations moved to ecstasy by the rhythmic intoning of sheer incoherencies.... His discourse was generally kept at a high pitch of fervency, but occasionally he dropped into colloquialisms and, less often, into humor. . . . His imagination was bold and unfettered.[41]

The importance of orality, rhythm, and music are distinctive stylistic characteristics of the sermon, a form that has contributed to African American expression as much as the blues or jazz.[42]

In terms of its content, the sermon also brings much to bear on Turner's writings for the *Recorder*. The preacher's call for members of the congregation to recognize their sin has its roots in the jeremiad; his demand for both individual and communal transformation are prophetic. Depending on biblical examples, most importantly, the story of Exodus from the Old Testament and Christ's resurrection in the New Testament, and by linking those examples concretely to lived experience, the preacher exhorted his followers to look to the past, but also act in the present and future. Dolan Hubbard writes, "The preacher stands between the people and God; his sermon moves people to act more justly in the world as it moves them closer to God." The sermon thus establishes connections between history, the Bible, and lived experience, fulfilling both sacred and secular functions.[43]

We can see examples of this kind of preacherly exhortation most clearly in Turner's columns early in the war, most particularly in his July 12, 1862, column ("The Plagues of this Country"). Here, he likens President Lincoln to the pharaoh, who refuses Moses' calls to free the Israelites and subsequently is visited by ten plagues that eventually drive him to acquiesce. Following the biblical story, Turner relates various setbacks suffered by the Union early in the war to five of the plagues, and then, in a prophetic threat to Lincoln, writes, "I tell old mystic Egyptian to-day, *my people must go free*. The sixth plague . . . is just ahead. . . . the great revolution which is to rack the earth and convulse the nations about the year 1866, is the liberation of the oppressed." Throughout his columns, he stresses the providential nature of the war, echoing a common theme of the black sermon, "that God is at work in all history."[44] Finally, he calls upon blacks themselves to act—as people of God, and as free citizens. In the final column reproduced in this volume, he describes American blacks as "a race upon whom are fixed the eyes of the world." This reference to Jesus' Sermon on the Mount (Matt. 5) is at the same time an allusion to John Winthrop's 1630 sermon "A Model of Christian Charity," a foundational document in the formation of American polity, where Winthrop declared to his followers that in establishing a Puritan colony in North America "we must consider that we shall be as a city upon a hill. The eyes of all people are upon us." Like Winthrop and Jesus Christ himself, Turner called upon his readers-*cum*-congregation to act on their faith, and realize their own world for the benefit of the "unborn millions."

Turner's columns present a counterpoint to the prevailing style of African American belles-lettres of the day: a refined, genteel mode of discourse that employed elevated language, appealed to readerly sympathy, and adopted Anglo-American literary forms.[45] Embodied most visibly in the forms of the slave narrative, the spiritual autobiography, and sentimental fiction, this mode also dominated the *Recorder*—unsurprising, perhaps, because of the A.M.E. Church's belief in the correspondence between intellectual and spiritual uplift. Dickson D. Bruce writes that the "most clearly established traditions" of African American letters of this period were "religious, moralistic, and genteel"; many writers—and readers—also valued writing that displayed qualities of "exemplary accomplishment."[46] Writers such as Charlotte Forten, Frances Ellen Watkins Harper, and perhaps most of all, Frederick Douglass exhibited all of these qualities; while Turner's writings were certainly religious and moralistic, they were often more folksy than genteel, and also demonstrated a striving for, rather than an exhibition of, literary accomplishment.

Yet the power of Turner's writing cannot be denied. Melbourne Cummings writes that "his blunt, open manner, his colorful, sometimes coarse language, and his ability to attach racial oppression and the evasive, ambiguous prattle of both Black and white spokesmen" appealed to his readers.[47] In many ways, it reflected the strength of his character. After Turner's death in 1915, the Reverend J. A. Jones wrote, "To be bent was not in his makeup. At one time, while on the platform or in the pulpit, he would 'shock the sensibilities' of the 'refined,' and in the next sentence he would entrance them with flights of eloquence and profundity of logic. He was easily the most magnetic Bishop that has occupied the Episcopal bench for the last forty years."[48] In his unbending assertion of black selfhood and sheer magnetism, Turner can be placed on a trajectory of militant dissent against white supremacy that begins with David Walker's *Appeal to the Coloured Citizens of America* (1828) and continues through Marcus Garvey and Malcolm X.

Given all this, one wonders, why has he been forgotten?—or at least, why has he been left behind by scholars of African American history and literature? Stephen Angell writes that "black churches have kept Turner's memory alive in their midst, while white Americans have all but forgotten about him."[49] One clear reason is that he chose to publish almost exclusively in newspapers, first in the *Recorder*, then, in other A.M.E. Church–related organs he edited; as a result, his audience was largely restricted to A.M.E. Church members and those with an interest in the church. He never published anything in book form, aside from several introductions to other authors' works. While the publications for which he wrote were long-lived—*The Voice of Missions*, which he founded in 1893, is still published today—as periodicals, they are by nature intended to be ephemeral. Though he must have kept a voluminous correspondence, especially once he was elected bishop of the A.M.E. Church, his letters were never collected. He appears to have been so preoccupied with his day-to-day work that he paid little attention to preserving his legacy.

Speaking in particular of Turner's Civil War–era correspondence, their publication within the columns of a newspaper, and their sheer "news value" may also have obscured their literary worth; as Elizabeth McHenry writes, literary scholars in general and African American literary historians in particular have until recently failed to recognize "treatises, declarations, letters, appeals, and, perhaps most significantly, journalism of every variety" as forms of literature.[50] But their inclusion in a religious publication may have made them even easier to ignore. Joycelyn Moody, writing about nineteenth-century spiritual autobiographies by African American women, notes the "sometimes implicit, sometimes explicit condemnation" of writing that expresses one's faith in God. This condemnation and suspicion of religious discourse, of course, is not restricted to African American writing but is pervasive throughout the academy. "Faith in the mystical need not be seen as an indication of imbecility," Moody argues; unfortunately, it often is.[51]

Finally, Turner may actually have ensured that he would be forgotten by alienating the very people who would have recorded his legacy. As his emigrationist beliefs became further entrenched and, at the same time, further removed from the mainstream of black political thought, his writings became increasingly vitriolic.

He ridiculed those who chose to remain in the United States, calling them "human dogs," "scullions and lick-spittles." Even though he never did emigrate to Africa, he called the United States a "sham of a nation," and famously described the American flag as "a rag of contempt instead of a symbol of liberty."⁵² The colloquial language that charms in his early columns for the *Recorder* became simply vulgar later in his life, and his wry sense of humor gradually soured into bitter irony and invective, as Turner lost hope in the possibility of achieving racial equality in the United States. While Turner continued to appeal to his less educated followers, black leaders and intellectuals found it increasingly easy to dismiss him as intemperate, irrational, unhinged.

While no apologies can be made for Turner's faults, this volume is an attempt to restore him to the historical record as a vital presence, an indefatigable defender of black humanity and civil rights, and an innovative stylist. In these columns, Turner displays the qualities that made him so successful an evangelist and a leader; he also testifies to a distinctly African American mode of perception and creativity. He is a quintessential example of what literary historian Dickson Bruce has described as an "authoritative voice," a "'black' voice with a special authority that was the product of its own blackness."⁵³ His muscular, virile spirituality contrasts with the sentimental, confessional mode that has received more scholarly attention, and points toward the vibrant vernacular preacher figures represented in James Weldon Johnson's *God's Trombones* (1927), Zora Neale Hurston's *Jonah's Gourd Vine* (1934), and James Baldwin's *Go Tell It On the Mountain* (1953).

\* \* \*

The columns Turner wrote for the *Recorder* during the Civil War have never been published in book form. *Army*

*Correspondence* thus adds significantly to the short stack of African American eyewitness accounts of this momentous, some would say definitive, national event. Most important of these is Edwin S. Redkey's *A Grand Army of Black Men: Letters from African-American Soldiers in the Union Army, 1861-1865* (Cambridge University Press, 1992), a compilation of over one hundred letters originally published in the *Christian Recorder,* the *Anglo-African,* and *Pine and Palm,* including one from Turner. A large number of letters written by and about African American soldiers in an official capacity and held in the National Archives have been reprinted in *The Black Military Experience,* edited by Ira Berlin, Joseph P. Reidy, and Leslie S. Rowland (Cambridge University Press, 1982).

Turner was only one of many regular correspondents to the newspapers, but very few of these correspondents have had their works collected and published. The letters of Corp. James Henry Gooding, who served in the 54th Massachusetts, were edited by Virginia M. Adams and published in the book, *On the Altar of Freedom: A Black Soldier's Letters from the Front* (University of Massachusetts Press, 1991); those written by George E. Stephens, who also served in the 54th Massachusetts, published in *A Voice of Thunder,* edited by Donald Yacovone (University of Illinois Press, 1998); and Thomas Chester's correspondence for the white-owned *Philadelphia Press* has been published in *Thomas Morris Chester, Black Civil War Correspondent,* edited by R. J. M. Blackett (Da Capo Press, 1991). A rare account of the war—and the United States Colored Troops—from a woman's perspective, was published in 1902: Susie King Taylor's *Reminiscences of My Life in Camp with the 33rd U.S. Colored Troops, Late 1st South Carolina Volunteers,* which was edited and reissued by Patricia W. Romero and Willie Lee Rose under the title, *A Black Woman's Civil War Memoirs* (Markus Weiner Publishers, 1988).

## Sources for Further Study

Angell, Stephen Ward. *Henry McNeal Turner and African-American Religion in the South.* Knoxville: University of Tennessee Press, 1992.

Bailey, Julius H. *Race Patriotism: Protest and Print Culture in the A.M.E. Church.* Knoxville: University of Tennessee Press, 2012.

Barrett, John G. *The Civil War in North Carolina.* Chapel Hill: University of North Carolina Press, 1963.

Berlin, Ira, Joseph P. Reidy, and Leslie S. Rowland, eds. *The Black Military Experience.* Cambridge: Cambridge University Press, 1982.

Bruce, Dickson D. *The Origins of African American Literature, 1680–1865.* Charlottesville: University Press of Virginia, 2001.

Campbell, James. *Songs of Zion: The African Methodist Episcopal Church in the United States and South Africa.* Chapel Hill: University of North Carolina Press, 1998.

Click, Patricia C. *Time Full of Trial: The Roanoke Island Freedmen's Colony, 1862–1867.* Chapel Hill: University of North Carolina Press, 2002.

Ernest, John. *Liberation Historiography.* Chapel Hill: University of North Carolina Press, 2004.

Gardner, Eric. *Unexpected Places: Relocating Nineteenth-Century African American Literature.* Jackson: University of Mississippi Press, 2011.

Gragg, Rod. *Confederate Goliath: The Battle of Fort Fisher.* Baton Rouge: Louisiana State University Press, 1994.

Haywood, Chanta M. *Prophesying Daughters: Women Preachers and the Word, 1823–1913.* Columbia: University of Missouri Press, 2003.

Hubbard, Dolan. *The Sermon and the African American Literary Imagination.* Columbia: University of Missouri Press, 1994.

Johnson, James Weldon. *God's Trombones: Seven Negro Sermons in Verse.* New York: Viking Press, 1927.

McHenry, Elizabeth. *Forgotten Readers: Recovering the Lost History of African American Literary Societies.* Durham: Duke University Press, 2002.

Moody, Joycelyn. *Sentimental Confessions: Spiritual Narratives of Nineteenth-Century African Women.* Athens: University of Georgia Press, 2001.

Redkey, Edwin S. *Black Exodus: Black Nationalist and Back-to-Africa Movements, 1890–1910.* New Haven: Yale University Press, 1969.

———. *A Grand Army of Black Men: Letters from African-American Soldiers in the U.S. Army 1861-1865*. Cambridge: Cambridge University Press, 1992.

Smith, John David. *Black Soldiers in Blue: African American Troops in the Civil War Era*. Chapel Hill: University of North Carolina Press, 2002.

Turner, Henry McNeal. *Respect Black: The Writings and Speeches of Henry McNeal Turner*. Ed. Edwin S. Redkey. New York: Arno Press, 1971.

Walker, Clarence E. *A Rock in a Weary Land: The African Methodist Episcopal Church during the Civil War and Reconstruction*. Baton Rouge and London: Louisiana State University Press, 1982.

Williams, Gilbert Anthony. *The Christian Recorder, Newspaper of the African Methodist Episcopal Church: History of a Forum for Ideas, 1854-1902*. Jefferson, North Carolina: McFarland, 1996.

## Notes

1. Edwin S. Redkey published a collection of Turner's writings, *Respect Black: The Writings and Speeches of Henry McNeal Turner* (New York: Arno Press, 1971), which contains none of Turner's writings from the Civil War period. The majority of the works published in that volume are expressions of Turner's emigrationist views.
2. W. E. B. Du Bois, "Editorial: Three Senior Bishops," *Crisis* (July 1915): 132.
3. Stephen Ward Angell, *Bishop Henry McNeal Turner and African-American Religion in the South* (Knoxville: University of Tennessee Press, 1992), 24.
4. Qtd. in Angell, *Bishop Henry McNeal Turner*, 20.
5. Qtd. in Clarence E. Walker, *A Rock in a Weary Land: The African Methodist Episcopal Church during the Civil War and Revolution* (Baton Rouge and London: Louisiana State University Press, 1982), 5, 7.
6. John Dittmer, "The Education of Henry McNeal Turner," in *Black Leaders of the Nineteenth Century*, ed. Leon Litwack and August Meier (Urbana and Chicago: University of Illinois Press, 1988), 253.
7. Turner, "Emancipation Day (1863)," in *Respect Black*, 2-3.

8. See Elizabeth McHenry, *Forgotten Readers: Recovering the Lost History of African American Literary Societies* (Durham: North Carolina, 2002), 137–38; Frances Smith Foster's introduction to *Minnie's Sacrifice; Sowing and Reaping; Trial and Triumph: Three Rediscovered Novels by Frances E. W. Harper* (Boston: Beacon Press, 1994), xi–xxxviii; and Mitch Kachun, "Interrogating the Silences: Julia C. Collins, 19th-Century Black Readers and Writers, and the *Christian Recorder*," *African American Review* 40, no. 4 (Winter 2006): 649–51, for more on the importance of religious periodicals and religious institutions in the establishment of African American literacy and literature. Eric Gardner's "Remembered (Black) Readers: Subscribers to the *Christian Recorder*, 1864–1865," *American Literary History* 23, no. 2 (Summer 2011): 229–59, offers preliminary evidence supporting the widespread readership of the *Recorder*.
9. According to Patrick Washburn, only thirty-eight African American newspapers had been published up to the end of the Civil War (Washburn, *The African American Newspaper: Voice of Freedom* [Evanston, Illinois: Northwestern University Press, 2006], 24–25). The vast majority of these newspapers were extremely short lived, due to a lack of funds, low literacy rates, and active suppression by whites.
10. McHenry, *Forgotten Readers*, 130.
11. Lawrence Hogue, *The African American Male, Writing, and Difference*, x. More specifically, John Ernest writes that African American newspapers "were essential to the effort to establish a community defined by something other than anti-slavery concerns" (John Ernest, *Liberation Historiography: African American Writers and the Challenge of History, 1794–1861* [Chapel Hill: University of North Carolina Press, 2003], 279). For more on the specific role played by the *Recorder* in African American society, see Gilbert Anthony Williams, *The Christian Recorder, Newspaper of the African Methodist Episcopal Church: History of a Forum for Ideas, 1854–1902* (Jefferson, North Carolina: McFarland, 1996) and Julius H. Bailey, *Race Patriotism: Protest and Print Culture in the A.M.E. Church* (Knoxville: University of Tennessee Press, 2012).
12. In addition to publishing some of the earliest examples of African American fiction, the *Recorder* also published poetry in every issue.

Eric Gardner has collected and republished some of this work, with valuable commentary, in "African American Women's Poetry in the *Christian Recorder,* 1855–1865: A Bio-Bibliography with Sample Poems," *African American Review* 40, no. 4 (December 2006): 813–31; and in "'Yours, for the cause': The *Christian Recorder* Writings of Lizzie Hart," *Legacy* 27, no. 2 (2010): 367–91. He also analyzes a variety of African American periodicals, including the *Recorder,* in *Unexpected Places: Relocating Nineteenth-Century African American Literature* (Jackson: University of Mississippi Press, 2009).

13. Gardner, "'Yours, for the Cause,'" 369–70.
14. Carla Peterson, *Doers of the Word: African-American Women Speakers and Writers in the North (1830–1880)* (New York: Oxford University Press, 1995), 8.
15. Howard University, Moorland-Spingarn Research Center, Manuscript Division, Henry McNeal Turner Papers, Collection 106-1, Folder 2.
16. James Campbell, *Songs of Zion: The African Methodist Episcopal Church in the United States and South Africa* (Chapel Hill: University of North Carolina Press, 1998), 80.
17. Edwin S. Redkey, A *Grand Army of Black Men: Letters from African-American Soldiers in the U.S. Army 1861-1865* (Cambridge: Cambridge University Press, 1982), 7.
18. McPherson, *The Negro's Civil War,* 29–30.
19. Dittmer, "Education of Henry McNeal Turner," 255; Angell, *Bishop Henry McNeal Turner,* 52.
20. David Stephen Heidler, Jeanne T. Heidler, and David J. Coles, eds. *Encyclopedia of the American Civil War: A Political, Social, and Military History* (New York: W. W. Norton, 2002), 405. Although Turner often is described by historians as the first black chaplain appointed in the U.S. army, it is not clear that he was, indeed, the first. Stephen Angell argues that because several chaplains were appointed at virtually the same time, the distinction between them is "of little importance" (Angell, *Bishop Henry McNeal Turner,* 286, n. 72). Martin Delany was one of the few black officers to serve in the army who was not a chaplain.
21. William H. N. Brown, Co. C., 1st U.S.C.T., "Letter from Roanoke Island, N.C.," *Christian Recorder* 5, no. 29 (July 22, 1865): 1.

22. Angell, *Bishop Henry McNeal Turner*, 56.
23. Walker, *Rock in a Weary Land*, 82, 49–52. Altogether, Walker claims, seventy-seven A.M.E. ministers were sent to the South.
24. Walker, *Rock in a Weary Land*, 82–83; *Christian Recorder* (April 1, 1865); *Christian Recorder*, July 1, 1865.
25. Reginald F. Hildebrand, *The Times Were Strange and Stirring: Methodist Preachers and the Crisis of Emancipation* (Durham, North Carolina: Duke University Press, 1995), xvii.
26. Patricia C. Click, *Time Full of Trial: The Roanoke Island Freedman's Colony, 1862–1867* (Chapel Hill: University of North Carolina Press, 2002), 3.
27. Campbell, *Songs of Zion*, 59.
28. Redkey, *Respect Black*, 31.
29. *Christian Recorder*, March 25, 1880; qtd. in Redkey, *Respect Black*, 49.
30. Letter to the *African Repository* 52, no. 3 (July 1876); qtd. in Redkey, *Respect Black*, 42.
31. Walker, *Rock in a Weary Land*, 16–17.
32. Campbell, *Songs of Zion*, 82.
33. Edwin S. Redkey, "Bishop Turner's African Dream," *Journal of American History* 54, no. 2 (September 1967): 290. Melville Cummings implies that Turner's views may have been "overshadowed" because Washington's and Du Bois's were "more palatable" ("The Rhetoric of Henry McNeal Turner," *Journal of Black History* 12, no. 4 [June 1982]: 257).
34. Redkey, ed., *Respect Black*, vii; Redkey, "Bishop Turner's African Dream," 287–88.
35. Campbell, *Songs of Zion*, 82. See pp. 80–88 for an assessment of Turner's views on emigration and their impact on the A.M.E. Church and later social movements.
36. Angell, *Bishop Henry McNeal Turner*, 253.
37. Angell, *Bishop Henry McNeal Turner*, 53.
38. Angell, *Bishop Henry McNeal Turner*, 18.
39. Stephen W. Angell, "Black Methodist Preachers in the South Carolina Upcountry, 1840–1866: Isaac (Counts) Cook, James Porter, and Henry McNeal Turner," in *"Ain't Gonna Lay My 'Ligion Down": African American Religion in the South*, ed. Alonzo Johnson and Paul Jersild (Columbia: University of South Carolina Press, 1996), 88.

40. African-derived cultural forms such as the ring shout and the spiritual were incorporated into black Christian religious practices, particularly in the South, and became a source of embarrassment to many Northern church leaders (in particular, Bishop Daniel Payne), who sought a more "dignified," "regularized" worship that conformed to European traditions. See Campbell, *Songs of Zion*, 38–43; Angell, "Black Methodist Preachers," 87–109.
41. James Weldon Johnson, *God's Trombones: Seven Negro Sermons in Verse* (New York: Viking Press, 1927), 5.
42. Dolan Hubbard argues that the sermon should be considered part of a historical continuum that extends from African cultural forms to jazz. See Hubbard, *The Sermon and the African American Literary Imagination* (Columbia: University of Missouri Press, 1994), Chapter One.
43. Hubbard, *The Sermon and the African American Literary Imagination*, 17. For more on the jeremiad and prophecy in the African American sermon, see, respectively, David Howard-Pitney, *The Afro-American Jeremiad: Appeals for Justice in America* (Philadelphia: Temple University Press, 1990); and Chandra Haywood, *Prophesying Daughters: Women Preachers and the Word, 1823–1913* (Columbia: University of Missouri Press, 2003).
44. Hubbard, *Sermon and the African American Literary Imagination*, 15.
45. For an example of this dominant mode of discourse, see Julia C. Collins's *The Curse of Caste: Or, the Slave Bride*, which was serialized in the *Recorder* at the same time that Turner's columns appeared in the newspaper.
46. Dickson D. Bruce, *The Origins of African American Literature, 1680–1865* (Charlottesville: University Press of Virginia, 2001), 259, 262.
47. Cummings, "The Rhetoric of Henry McNeal Turner," *Journal of Black Studies* 12, no. 4 (June 1982): 262.
48. Jones, "Bishop H. M. Turner as a Forceful Character," *Christian Recorder* (July 8, 1915): 3.
49. Angell, *Bishop Henry McNeal Turner*, 5.
50. McHenry, *Forgotten Readers*, 12.
51. Joycelyn Moody, *Sentimental Confessions: Spiritual Narratives of*

*Nineteenth-Century African Women* (Athens: University of Georgia Press, 2001), xi.
52. Redkey, *Respect Black*, 80, 137, 83, 60.
53. Bruce, *Origins of African American Literature*, x. It is interesting—and revealing—that Bruce does not include any discussion of Turner or other contributors to religious periodicals in his otherwise groundbreaking work.

*Chapter One*

# *Emancipation and Enlistment*

### March 22, 1862–April 18, 1863

TURNER'S FIRST LETTER TO the *Christian Recorder* was published on March 22, 1862, just over two years after Elisha Weaver relaunched the newspaper. He wrote to Weaver in response to President Lincoln's March 6 message to Congress, where he recommended the passage of a joint resolution that would provide financial compensation to any state that would "adopt gradual abolishment of slavery." Turner was skeptical of this "Message"; while many believed that it was a cause for "hope for a brighter day"—that is, full emancipation—he believed it was nothing more than an "ingenious subterfuge," a sop to the abolitionists that would in fact accomplish little. In fact, Lincoln's message almost immediately bore fruit: the District of Columbia Emancipation Act was passed in April 22, an event that Frederick Douglass described to the abolitionist senator Charles Sumner as feeling like "a dream."

Soon after the District of Columbia Emancipation Act was passed, Turner relocated to Washington from Baltimore and was installed as pastor of the Israel A.M.E. Church.¹ Washington at this time was experiencing explosive growth due to the war; the historian Shelby Foote relates that the "ante-bellum population of 60,000 . . . nearly quadrupled under pressure from the throng of men and women rushing in to fill the partial vacuum created by the departure of the Southerners who formerly had set the social tone." Turner found himself engaged in a tone-setting exercise of his own, writing in his diary that he found "this church very much delapidated [sic] both in a spiritual and temporal point of veiw [sic]."² During his first months as pastor, he led services on weeknights and several times each Sunday. He also initiated renovation projects to the church building, established a speaker series that featured prominent African American citizens (including Robert Smalls, one of the best-known African Americans to serve in the U.S. Navy), started up the Israel Lyceum, a debating society for young male members of the church, and organized aid for the contrabands—the name given to slaves who were received as "contraband" by the Union troops as they overtook Confederate territory. The contrabands, in particular, excited Turner's deepest sympathies. From these "homeless, shoeless, dressless, and moneyless" refugees of the war he heard stories of "horrid, hideous, shocking and inconceivable scenes of suffering"; some, he was told, killed their own children to prevent them from being killed by their masters, while others narrowly escaped being executed themselves.

---

1. In a December 12, 1862 journal entry, Turner wrote that he had been appointed pastor "7 months" previous, which would mean that Turner probably would have still been in Baltimore when the District of Columbia Emancipation Act was passed.
2. Shelby Foote, *The Civil War: A Narrative: Fredericksburg to Meridian* (Vol. 2), 152; Henry McNeal Turner Diary, Howard University, Moorland-Spingarn Research Center, Manuscript Division, Henry McNeal Turner Papers, Box 106-1, Folder 2.

Turner also spent hours attending the legislative sessions of Congress, located several hundred yards away, in the yet-to-be-completed Capitol Building. Perhaps his familiarity with congressional debates and the views aired by his representatives led him to change his views about Lincoln. By the time Lincoln issued the Preliminary Emancipation Proclamation on September 22, 1862, Turner's skepticism had turned into admiration. To those who doubted Lincoln's sincerity, Turner responded:

But suppose the president did not deliver his proclamation in good faith? What need I care? Or suppose he was driven to it by force of circumstances. What of it? That is nothing to cavil over. Let us thank God for it, for to him be the glory forever and ever. . . . Mr. Lincoln loves freedom as well as any one on earth, and if he carries out the spirit of his proclamation, he need never fear hell. *God grant him a high seat in glory.*

Once the proclamation did, indeed, go into effect in January 1863, Turner quickly embraced the idea of arming black soldiers (an idea that his contemporary, Frederick Douglass, had strongly advocated from the outset of the war in 1861). He lamented war's violence, for "it only shows how low down in the scale of moral depravity we are. . . . The pugnacity of a man does not establish his greatness." At the same time, he was willing to entertain the possibility that wars were a necessary expression of God's providence. In the same column, he wondered if "Christ foresaw that feuds would breed and fester, and that men's growing virulence would lead them on to dreadful collisions out of which they should purgatorially emerge from their own throttled and ruptured combats with lessons experimentally learned, which should gradually advance them to a higher degree of conception of their rights and wrongs."

During the months following emancipation, lawmakers and military leaders also were undecided about whether and how black

Fig. 1. The U.S. Capitol Building under construction, 1862. National Archives.

regiments should be used. Turner mentions several of the debates surrounding black enlistment that occupied Congress in early 1863, at one point noting a shocking proposal to "try" black regiments against Indians (most likely, the Sioux in the West who were engaged in the Dakota Wars). If they were successful against the Indians, then they would be used against the Confederates.[3] Turner, viewing blacks and Indians as "co-sufferers," was horrified by this idea. "O Indian," he wrote, "how could I slay thee; how could I cut thy throat, or put the dagger to thy heart?" Turner argued instead that blacks should be used in combat, against pro-slavery forces. "Let me front my enemy and then demand my courage," he declared.

Turner also argued for black leadership of black troops—in fact, he advocated black soldiers' "entire separation from soldiers of every other color," so that "if we deserve any merit it will stand out beyond contradiction." In addition to heightening racial tensions, he foresaw that having whites and blacks fighting together would result in the manipulation of accounts to minimize the bravery of black troops or to discredit them altogether. Turner's views, unsurprisingly, failed to carry the day. When the Bureau for Colored Troops was established on May 22, 1863, it stipulated that all black regiments would be commanded by white officers.

Despite his disagreement with the government on this point, Turner threw himself into recruiting with zeal; due in large part to his efforts, the 1st U.S.C.T., as its name implied, was the first to be mustered in by the bureau on June 30, 1863. Once Turner's

---

3. In August 1862, hundreds of white settlers were massacred by the Sioux in Minnesota, leading to the trials of hundreds of Sioux warriors and the eventual execution of thirty-nine of them on December 26, 1862. Following the mass execution, Gen. John Pope, commanding the Department of the Northwest, agitated loudly for additional troops to "exterminate the Sioux." C. M. Oehler writes that Pope "made his appeals for men heard above the Civil War tumult" (*The Great Sioux Uprising* [New York: Oxford University Press], 227).

efforts as a recruiter kicked into high gear, he was unable to continue as the *Recorder*'s Washington correspondent.[4] We thus must rely on secondhand reports for descriptions of this work. One "Lancaster," who substituted as a correspondent, explained in the June 20 issue that the "invaluable correspondent of this city, H.M.T., has become so carried away with shoulder straps, Sharp's rifles, Parrot guns, Uncle Sam's purse, &c., that he cannot find time to inform you and your numerous readers of what is going on in this city."[5] Even his sermons apparently took on a military flavor; as one substitute correspondent described it, he pursued his argument like "a skillful military tactician," arraying his "columns of common duty," deploying the "bright bayonets of facts," and, as a last resort, launching the "flying artillery of theology's jurisprudence."[6]

Turner also was too preoccupied with events on the ground to provide written responses to several key events affecting black enlistment. Perhaps most importantly, we lack his response to the New York City draft riots of July 1863, when mobs made up largely of working-class Irish men protesting the ending of slavery as a war aim lynched dozens—perhaps over one hundred—black New

---

4. He wrote several essays for the *Recorder* during the fall and winter of 1863–64, but would not continue his regular column until after joining his regiment in Virginia in May 1864. These essays—one promoting Wilberforce University, which had just been reincorporated in July 1863 after closing, due to lack of funds, in 1862; another on the value of republican government; and a response to Anglican bishop J. W. Colenso's treatise questioning the literal truth of the Pentateuch, appeared in the *Recorder* in August through November 1863. These essays are not included in this volume.

5. *Christian Recorder*, June 20, 1863.

6. Thomas H. Hinton, "Washington Correspondence," *Christian Recorder*, September 5, 1863.

Yorkers.[7] We also lack commentaries on several important battles involving black soldiers, including the Battle of Port Hudson, Louisiana (May 27), and the attack on Fort Wagner, South Carolina (July 18). In effect, there is a gap in Turner's correspondence of over a year, from April 1863 until June 1864. However, the columns in this chapter succeed in showing the breadth of Turner's activities before he was appointed chaplain. They also show his views on emancipation, his belief in the centrality of education in the mission of the A.M.E. Church, and his support of female leaders in the African American Methodist community.

\* \* \*

## "Turner on the President's Message"
(*The Christian Recorder*, March 22, 1862)

Mr. Editor:— The late Message of President Lincoln to Congress, relative to emancipation, has given rise to more speculations and created more surmises than any other document ever issued from the mansion halls of the White House; and likely no other message ever, for the moment, was productive of so surreptitious suspense since this nation had its name. Its annunciation seems to benumb the most active intellects, and paralyze the most flippant tongues.

Both Houses of Congress were thrown into a mazy wonder, as to how they would unwind the intricate strata of its apparent preternatural syllabication. Collegiate sons who had been reared on the bread of literature, and had prowled through the fields of classic lore, gleaning from every source language, constructibility, and

---

7. The Washington draft was instituted only a few weeks later, and correspondents to the *Recorder* responded with relief when riots did not erupt in the capital.

how its convoluted recticulations [*sic*] should be dismembered, were paradoxically magnetized from all appearance, or else logic, rhetoric, and analysis, were proving recreant to the noble trust for which they had been procured.

But passing on from Congressmen to the lower grades of society, we behold governors, state legislatures, mayors, city counsellors, police officers, political petit-maîtres, Irishmen, Germans, women, children, and, last of all in God's universe, the Ethiopian, all making terrible strides to get the paper. The newspaper boys are flitting up and down the streets as on India rubber toes and wiry springing heels, proclaiming, as they go, *President Lincoln on emancipation*! Silence, say the inmates of many houses (who never think of a paper). What's that? The boy shrills out again—*President Lincoln on emancipation*! Get the paper, get the paper! say the rich, poor, white, or colored, whoever he may be, for all must see. Accordingly, the paper is bought regardless of price; and the way they go at reading it!—every one is spell-bound, the children all come around with eager anxiety to see what is the matter, they look as though a death-warrant had arrived, the old folks are all breathless, the reader proceeds to chatter out the message,—listen—be quiet,—

"*Resolved*, The United States ought to co-operate with any State which may adopt gradual abolishment of slavery, giving to such State pecuniary aid to be used by such State in its discretion, to compensate for the inconveniences, public and private, produced by such a change of system."

But at this juncture the baby wakes up, and countermands the silence by a few sonorous yells (great confusion). Every solace is offered, and unless the irritated child soon learns the art of muteness, it is hurried away to some sphere where its interrupting loquacity breaks not the incorporate charm that enshrines every fibre of the mind.

The Ethiopian, too, with all his untutoredness, verges out of his dreary iceberg cavern as if touched by the thawing sun of a freer day. Laying hold of the Message, he grapples with Herculean strength in untwisting its most technical terminologies, hoping to congratulate in the person of the President a Moses waving a mace of independence, with a voice waxing louder and louder, exclaiming, *Let my people go,*—hoping to hear freedom's birth heralded in tones of volcanic mutterings,—hoping it (the Message) to be the Jesus of liberty coming to dethrone the Herod of tyranny,—hoping to hear the Jubilee trumpet, *Arise, ye slaves, and come to freedom!* but alas, alas, *not yet,* is the echo.

Newspaper correspondents, too, join the puzzled van, and drift down the deep current of—*I don't know what it means.* Several days pass by, and no one dares to comment upon it. The thing is too tender—too near the heart strings. The vitals of the nation are touched. The immortal negro is too precious—dearer than the thousands of the gallant sons of the nation, who have fallen the bloody victims of slavery's hellish caprice.

The generals, colonels, captains, lieutenants, and soldiers who have wallowed and died in human gore at Bull Run and other places, the carnage hand and devastating sweep of death, which racks the nation and convulses society, the widowed wives and orphaned children, are all insignificant and worthless when compared with the brave sons of Africa. Why, who would have thought, five years ago, that we were so valuable?

But what is the conclusion arrived at in relation to the true spirit of the Message? Sir, it is this:—A great many here have been blinded and made to believe that it portends hope for a brighter day; but I look at it as one of the most ingenious subterfuges, to pacify the humane and philanthropic hearts of the country that was ever produced, and I believe it will result to the North what Senator Douglas' Squatter Sovereignty did to South Carolina.[8] I have not time

---

8. Stephen A. Douglas, senator from Illinois, was the most vocal advocate for the belief that individual states had the right to regulate their own "domestic institutions" (i.e., slavery).

nor space to analyze the Message; but how some of our people can see so much in it to elate them, I cannot find out; for, after recommending it, it denies that Congress has any power to legislate on slavery—leaving it under the absolute control of individual states, with which control they have ever been invested. Before we raise our joys too high, mark this phrase,—*giving to such state pecuniary aid to be used by such state in its discretion.*—In that phrase there is a broad field, a wide space, an ocean of thought.

H.M.T.
Baltimore, March 16, 1862.

## *"Letter from Washington"*
(*The Christian Recorder,* June 21, 1862)[9]

Mr. Editor:—There is a very happy state of things in our churches in this city. Our promise for future success is very bright, and if the Lord will be with us, we trust to have a most glorious harvest in the ingathering of souls; souls whose existence must run counter with an never ending eternity. Quite an excitement has been in the city for several days, caused by the constant income of rebel prisoners, which draw on the street a large crowd of curious spectators. And what was equally, if not more curious, was the shaggy, paltry-looking rebel chaps brought in under the nomenclature of Confederate prisoners; for certainly a harder specimen of humanity never existed than they claimed to be the portraiture of. Some soft-headed misanthropists have puffed off a great deal of gas in order to prove that the negro is an emanation of the orang-outang, but I think if they were in Washington at the time when some of

---

9. The first page of the previous issue (June 14, 1862) is no longer extant. This issue may have contained the first "Washington Correspondence" column from Turner.

the rebel prisoners were coming in, the result of their anthropological investigation would have assigned many of them a place among the baboon species. And as for their uniforms, they are like Joseph's coat of many colors, but the most prominent color was dirt color. One very remarkable peculiarity, however, about their uniforms, which distinguished them from any I ever saw before, was the manner in which their uniforms were fringed and flounced. Many of them were fringed and flounced from head to foot, though it was threadbare fringe and ragged flounces. In consequence of so many wounded and sick soldiers being brought to the city, the government authorities have seized several churches and notified others that it is probable they too will be taken as temporary hospitals. It was thought at first that the disloyalty of some of the ministers was the cause of this seizure, but since, others have been taken which are known to be loyal. The matter is looked at from an entire benevolent stand-point. Some of our people are apprehensive that our church may be seized. The white friends here are very much put out with General McClellan about his slow movements before Richmond. They think he is waiting for them to evacuate their capital, otherwise he will not move for the next six months. . . .[10]

Last Monday night the members of Israel Church met, and authorized the trustees of said church to repair the basement of their church, which has for many years been standing in a useless condition. They intend to floor, plaster, and bench it in fine order, so as to be appropriated to the use of protracted meetings, lectures, and other demonstrations, which are not unbecoming to a Christian edifice. They farther resolved to repair the vestibule, enlarge the gallery, fresco the main audience room, which, when completed, will not only be a magnificent church, but hold at least twelve hundred persons, two hundred more than it now holds; while the improved basement will seat, when done, one thousand. The said

---

10. Three paragraphs of church news are omitted.

church has made quite an improvement on the Sabbath School. Five weeks ago it numbered about twenty scholars, now it numbers two hundred and fifty. The entire afternoon is devoted to the Sabbath School, which consists of children and adults.

Rev. James A. Handy, pastor of Union Bethel Church, is making quite an impression in the upper part of the city. The members of Union Bethel have, though a young man in the ministry, one whom they need to be proud of, as he is not only a very eloquent man, but one of unquestionable ability.

H.M.T.

Washington, June 16th, 1862.

## "The Plagues of this Country"
(*The Christian Recorder*, July 12, 1862)[11]

Mr. Editor:—There seems to be a very singular correspondence existing between the war in the United States and the Egyptian plagues. I suppose no one, in the face of so many evidences, will question the practicableness of the assertion, that this war is being waged through a providential interposition for the benefit of some portion of discarded humanity. For the last two hundred years many of the most pious and learned theologians have been preaching among the inhabitants of the earth about the year 1866. And that this catastrophical condition of things would be very transitory in its duration, and afterwards the earth, being refined by the agencies of this universal disaster, should emerge forth in all the purity of Eden's innocency.

These speculations are not yet at an end, though they had partially ceased to agitate the theological world till Miller's theory spread

---

11. The "Letter from Washington" from July 5, 1862, is omitted. Containing mostly church news, it also mentions the imminent visit to the United States of President Benson of Liberia.

consternation through America and a part of Europe, by proclaiming that the world would end in 1842.[12] When men of all grades and positions began to sift the Scriptures, either for the purpose of refuting or proving this theory; and strange to say that any of its most stern opposers sit down with every fibre of their soul prejudiced against it; but rose after an examination with favorable convictions. And since that time such gigantic minds as are possessed by Dr. Cross, of the Methodist Church, and Dr. Seiss, of the Lutheran Church in this country, in connection with the immortal Drs. Cumming and Elliot of England (especially the latter's *Horae Apocalypticae*), have been organizing a grand galaxy of premillenarians, the works, arguments, suggestions and sentiments of whom have been calling attention to some great issue just ahead. Though piles of infamy and derision have been heaped upon Miller and his theory, because he erred in his conclusions, so much so that all those who have not since looked at things in absolute contradiction to Miller, have been branded as a Millerite, yet my impression is that the world will yet see that Miller was not as big a fool as they supposed him.

Though Miller did certainly err in his assumption of fixed dates, and to precise definite periods, and there is where he lost his power. If Miller had took the grounds that Drs. Cumming and Cross did, by compiling his prophetic figures and chronological predictions to show that some great change in human affairs would soon take place, he would have retained a more durable influence, which would have diffused a spirit of inquiry among the common people of as great avidity as he did among the few learned.

But because there was not a literal fulfillment of his predicted

---

12. Millerism, based on the ideas of William Miller, a New York farmer and lay Baptist preacher, was a belief that the Bible foretold the Second Coming of Jesus Christ in 1843. As Turner indicates, it was just one of a number of millennialist movements popular in the nineteenth century, several of which Turner mentions later in the paragraph.

statements, two-thirds of the people who even claimed to think, without ever examining or comparing his views with the prophetic bearing of sacred writ, began at once to pour forth their denunciatory tirades upon him, with about as much consistency as the Roman inquisition did upon Galileo, for what with a little improvement was philosophically true. Now Miller saw, both from the indexes of prophecy and the prognostication of transpiring events, that the world was on the eve of some great mutation, which should rock nations and convulse societies in every human sphere. He saw that this dispensation of human affairs was fast receding, and that God was about to sever the distinctions which split the social order of humanity, by placing them upon a platform of more equality and unanimity. But the great error into which both Miller and others no less distinguished have fallen, is in attempting to define what this great consummation of things should be, which they thought the *sine qua non*, because every man being prone to think for himself who has mind enough to rise above the current of the fogyism of his day, have been actuated with a sufficiency of self-certainty to tell, so far as his own views extend, what this thing about to take place should be. Some have thought that the world was about to end, others that Christ was about to enthrone himself at Jerusalem and sway a scepter of universal righteousness, others that God was about to purify the earth with fire, and afterwards to refit it for the habitation of his saints, &c.; but all agree that it is for the bettering of oppressed humanity. Now how far truth may corroborate with any of the above statements must be seen by future generations.

But that the King of heaven has been appealing to the hearts of men to get ready for some dreadful issue, I think is verified in the many ministers whom God has recently raised up, and books which have been sent out to warn us of some great *fullness of time*.[13]

---

13. Gal. 4:4, a reference to Christ's Coming. "But where the fullness of the

Three years ago the northern lights, which frescoed the heavens, were terrific in their appearance—that the skies would at times seem to be turning with blood, and the hearts of men in every direction failing, from the dreadful foreboding anticipations which agitate a criminal conscience. The free people of color in every direction were hunted and pursued as rabbits, and particularly in the slave states denounced as an offensive nuisance, while church conventions and conferences broke up in wild confusion, political assemblies, legislative and congressional bodies, ended in partisan strife. The atmosphere of human society seemed to be charged with sectional divisibility, and all avowed obligations which bound man to man appeared to be severed. And then to crown this *hell-forged schism*, Jeff. Davis, elder brother to Pluto, was inaugurated in all his bestial vices to preside over a power organized for the purpose of crushing down the manliness of as loyal hearts as ever owed fealty to the God of heaven.

Abraham Lincoln and not Jeff. Davis becomes the Pharaoh of the mystic Egypt (American slavery). And however unwilling to comply with a dispensation of liberation, nature's God calls from heaven, echoed to by five million of mystic Israelites (abject slaves), in peals of vivid vengeance, *let my people go*. Moses and Aaron, in the garb of threats for the nations' heart-blood, stand before the mystic Pharaoh with a demand endorsed by the purposes of God, for their redemption; but, being refused, a series of plagues begins, commencing at Fort Sumter.

A proclamation calling forth seventy-five thousand men to protect an ensign which had long waved over an enslaved people, is issued; but with no contemplation of responding to Heaven's demand.

The first plague which staggered the nation's energies, was the killing of several soldiers in the streets of Baltimore; but partly

---

time was come, God sent forth his Son made of a woman, made under the Law. . . ."

recovering from that by the encouragement gained through the energetic achievements of General Butler, General McDowell was invested with the chieftainship of the Potomac Army. He, very forgetful of his mission, issued a proclamation that no negro should come within his military lines. This, of course, being endorsed by the President, else he would have soon altered it, as in the case of Frémont and Hunter, the second plague smote the American Egyptian in the Bull Run defeat.

Shortly after another partial recovery, General Frémont in the West heard a voice saying from heaven, *Let my people go*. He hearkened to the call by a corresponding proclamation, that rebels should be shot and their slaves set free; but the presidential Pharaoh hardened his heart and made void all his proceedings. And mystic Egypt was smitten by the third plague in the death of General Lyon, the fall of Lexington, and the demoralization of General Siegel's army. Shortly after General Frémont was removed and Halleck placed in his stead, he issues a proclamation, that negroes were disloyal, and merely came as spies into the Federal lines, and forbid their future entrance, and returned many back to their rebel masters. Again, as a penalty, the fourth plague smote this mystic Egypt in the destruction of lives, ships, and other property, and almost the demoralization of the entire nation by the coming out of the Merrimac from Norfolk. General Hunter soon after saw that it was no use to try to refuse the heavenly demands, and in one sweeping proclamation, over which angels rejoiced, declared the mystic Israelites free throughout South Carolina, Georgia and Florida; but the presidential Pharaoh hardened his heart, and in one gr[i]m mutter, furious enough to make hell grumble, precipitately hurled them back into the darkest caverns of oppression, ever felt by a fiendish nerve. Soon after, the fifth plague smites in the extermination of a Maryland regiment, the capturing of thousands of prisoners by Stonewall Jackson, the running of General Banks, and the perpetration of other cruelties too horrible, too brutal, too infernal to mention. And I tell old mystic Egyptian to-day, *my people must go free*. The sixth plague—the sixth phial or vial—or the sounding of the sixth trumpet is just ahead. What Miller and other prophet writers have been seeing, and the great revolution which is to rack the earth and convulse the nations about the year 1866, is the liberation of the oppressed. And I now predict that the time is near at hand. Miller saw it through the fog of a few future years, and could not describe it; but all the nations of Europe and America will be in war before five years, unless freedom's banner waves in majestic splendor over every hill and dale. If England and France ever interfere with this nation, it will be because God in his providence will compel them for the purpose of exterminating slavery. And mystic Egypt, with mystic Pharaoh at its head, may refuse compliance to Heaven's demand; but the inexpressible tortures inflicted upon ancient Egypt, the cruelties of Antiochus to the Jews, the devastation of Jerusalem by the Roman Generals Titus and Vespasian, the bloody streets of France in 1792, will all hardly bear a comparison to what will befall this nation.

H.M.T.
Washington, July 2, 1862.

## *"For the Christian Recorder"*
(*The Christian Recorder,* July 19, 1862)

Mr. Editor:—The weather is excessively warm here; but is something milder now than it was a few days ago. Several persons gave out on Monday by being overpowered with heat. The pastor of Israel Church was taken very sick on Sabbath morning just as he was commencing to preach, and had to be conducted home; but his health has considerably improved.

The 4th of July was a high day among all parties here. Our people who made ice cream, mineral water, and like things, severely suffered, while tongues and lips in every direction were seen very freely spinning out such confabulations as were adapted to their several tastes. One of the grandest affairs, however, that marked the progress of the day was the annual celebration of the grand Sabbath-school union. . . .[14]

Mr. Joseph E. Williams, who has gained considerable notoriety through the country, from being the projector of the Central American scheme, is still in Washington, perambulating the streets as large as if he contemplated the final achievement of his desires.[15] However much some of us may differ from the policy urged by Mr. Williams, I think that Mr. Williams is actuated by motives pure to the race he represents, and would not knowingly exert an influence which would detrimentally culminate in our injury.

I was in the Senate the other day, and had the pleasure of listening to Senator Lane pleading the cause of the colored man.[16] And, while listening to him enter into our feelings and sympathies so accurately, I could hardly credit the idea that it was a full-blooded white man speaking; and, indeed, the Senate is almost abolitionized. Yesterday two Senators hitherto known as exceedingly

---

14. Several paragraphs describing the Sabbath-school celebration have been omitted.
15. Williams was an African American advocate of Central American emigration, and had previously supported James Redpath's efforts to establish a colony in Haiti. See Kate Masur, "The African American Delegation to Abraham Lincoln: A Reappraisal," *Civil War History* 56, no. 2 (2010): 123–24.
16. James Henry Lane (1814–66), a vociferous advocate for the arming of black soldiers, recruited the 1st Regiment Kansas Volunteers (Colored) in October 1862, some months before the formation of the better-known 54th Massachusetts. They were recognized for their valor at the Battle of Island Mound, Missouri (October 29, 1862).

conservative surprised every one by offering and advocating a bill to enlist and equip colored soldiers into the United States army, with the understanding that freedom is to be the result. The same surprise was made in the House by a representative hitherto known as conservative; and the fact is that General McClellan's defeat before Richmond has made a great many emancipational converts. And, in this connexion, I would state that General McClellan is severely spoken of in nearly every republican speech delivered in Congress as not the man. While I am opposed to General McClellan, yet I hear him denounced in Congress so severely that it excites my sympathy; and General Halleck is not dealt with any more tenderly. The truth is, every victory the Southerners gain tends to loosen the chains of slavery, and every one the Northerners gain tends only to tighten them, and it will be so till the North is brought to her senses.

And God's plan of teaching her sense is through Southern victories. I have noticed in several instances whenever the Union army is repulsed or the safety of the government is menaced, there is an appeal to negro sympathy, from parties high in position, but so soon as the tide turns, so soon is he discarded. And I now hear it rumored in all quarters that it is probable that negroes will be organized into regiments and armed for the war, and one congressman proposed to arm him and place him in front of the battle. This is very well so far as it goes; but my impression is that they will have a hard time raising negro regiments to place in front of the battle or anywhere else, unless freedom, eternal freedom, is guaranteed to them, their children, and their brethren. To talk about freeing only those who fight and should happen to escape the ball, is all gammon. If our people have not got too much sense for that, they have too much instinct; at all events they will not do it.

General Hunter's answer to the government in relation to arming the colored people of South Carolina, met with hearty applause in all quarters.[17] It is regarded as the noblest piece of gallantry that has yet been set forth. I have been told by some gentlemen, who pronounce themselves rather pro-slavery, that it was the very answer this government needed. The Senate contemplated adjourning on Wednesday next, though several are opposed to it, unless they adjourn to meet again very soon.

The contrabands who come here are dying very fast. It is supposed that some fatal disease is among them. There were some frail sisters got to fighting the other day, and the police arrested them after they had blooded each other's head and broke a few noses, and when the police started off to the work-house with them, they cried out murder several times, and our people, supposing it to be a slave-catcher, started off with rocks, sticks, and every imaginable missile; but, on discovering the truth of the matter, justified the police. Had it been a slave-catcher, sad would have been his condition.

H.M.T.

---

17. Gen. David Hunter (1802–86), a stalwart abolitionist, made repeated attempts to emancipate the slaves and to form black regiments. In late June 1862, when asked by Congress to explain his actions, he declared, "I reply that no regiment of 'Fugitive Slaves' has been, or is being organized in this Department. There is, however, a fine regiment of persons whose late masters are 'Fugitive Rebels'—men who everywhere fly before the appearance of the National Flag, leaving their servants behind them to shift as best they can for themselves. . . . So far, indeed, are the loyal persons composing this regiment from seeking to avoid the presence of their late owners, that they are now, one and all, working with remarkable industry to place themselves in a position to go in full and effective pursuit of their fugacious and traitorous proprietors." He went so far as to declare that he would recruit fifty thousand more soldiers by the end of the fall (Ira Berlin et al., eds., *Free at Last: A Documentary History of Slavery, Freedom, and the Civil War* [New York: New Press, 1992], 56–59).

## "Washington Correspondence"

(*The Christian Recorder*, August 9, 1862)[18]

Mr. Editor:—Through the goodness and mercy of a gracious Benefactor, it is my privilege to address you again, though I have nothing of such great importance to which I can call your attention. But I find since the Bishop question has been smothered up, there is quite a falling off among your contributors.[19] I had not thought of the decrease in that respect, until my attention was called to it the other day by a distinguished gentleman of this city who takes our paper. He remarked to me as follows:—"Mr. ——, I discover, since the Episcopal controversy has stopped in the *Recorder*, the literati of your people are lost for a subject; I wonder if controversy is not a peculiar forte among you?" I won't tell you how I felt, for I can't; but I faced it over as good as I could, and bid good evening.

I had the pleasure of attending the first Quarterly meeting of Rev. H. J. Rhodes, on last Sabbath, in Georgetown. Rev. James A. Handy delivered the eleven o'clock discourse, which was unquestionably one of the finest specimens of pulpit eloquence that we have had the honor of hearing for a long time.

---

18. The "Washington Correspondence" column from August 2, 1862 and the "Letter from Washington" from August 9 have been omitted as they deal solely with church news and church politics.

19. The Bishop Willis Nazrey, a frequent correspondent to the *Recorder*, had recently defected from the A.M.E. Church to become bishop of the British Methodist Episcopal Church, which formed in 1856 in response to fears on the part of ex-slave A.M.E. preachers in Canada following the passage of the Fugitive Slave Act. Nazrey's departure from the American A.M.E. Church sparked a vigorous debate in the African American press starting in the late 1850s and continuing through 1861. For more on this controversy and its effect on the black press, see Eric Gardner, *Unexpected Places: Relocating Nineteenth-Century African American Literature* (Jackson: University of Mississippi Press, 2011), 76–83.

It was announced on the previous Sabbath, that on Monday night last, 27th ult., the Rev. Amos G. Beman would lecture in Israel Church. The time appointed having arrived, Mr. Beman was on the spot; but there were not more than forty persons present. We were, of course, thrown into a great surprise as to where the people had gone, for Mr. Beman declared he could not lecture to so few. While waiting with anxious hearts for more to come in, a messenger arrived and spread the news like wild-fire, that at the Asbury M.E. Colored Church there was a great war meeting of the colored people. The house then adjourned, as no more were expected, and several of us went up to Asbury to see and hear. So on nearing up to the church, we found groups of colored people returning to their homes, and yet about a thousand appeared to be standing before the door. We soon learned that they had convened for the purpose of organizing a regiment of colored soldiers, and tendering them to the President, but that the Trustees had refused to open the church; and so determined were they to carry through their project, that they attempted to hold a mass-meeting on the steps, but the Trustees here seemed to rout them again, and finally the crowd dispersed. A great many of our people in the District think that the nation is freeing them and giving them their word in law equal to any person, white or colored, is a sufficient favor for them to return a corresponding compliment in aiding the government in putting down its rebels. But who was the getter-up of this war meeting, is the great question. Our people certainly did it, but who they were, is the secret. Before leaving this subject, I would say that the stern refusal of the Asbury Trustees to open the church came near resulting in the death of one of them. I was informed that he saved his life by the *logic of fleetness*.

The Hon. J. D. Johnson, Commissioner of Liberia, who has been here some time urging the claims of that young republic, was most inhumanly mobbed on last Tuesday night by the colored people of this city, or, I should have said, by a colored mob. Report says that Mr. Johnson endeavored to get Congress to transport, regardless of consent, all the contrabands who might possibly obtain their freedom, to Liberia within sixty days after the date of their freedom, and hence a committee of colored gentlemen waited upon him to ascertain if the rumor were true, and that he treated the committee contemptuously, which so angered them that they transformed themselves into a mob and let slip vengeance at him. I am informed that nothing saved his life but the intervention of some young ladies. I am sorry that our people acted so rudely in the matter, as I do not think it tends to their honor; and yet if Mr. Johnson thus acted, I am equally sorry that he wished to deprive us of that God-given right of choosing or refusing. I hope our people everywhere will soon begin to look upon mobs as the most contemptible, lowest, rottenest plan in all God's universe of carrying power. Let us come out and expose men's mean principles, but not injure their bodies, remembering that God made the latter, but never made the former; and it indicates an animal predominancy in its perpetrators.

Rev. David Smith has returned from Ohio, and is carrying on an extensive medical practice in Washington and Alexandria.

Rev. M. F. Sluby is in the city. He preached in Israel Church on Thursday night, to a very respectable audience, and a higher state of Christian feeling is seldom seen than attended his discourse; he is peculiarly adapted to the practical ministry.

It is whispered about in Washington that General McClellan sacrificed 100,000 men in the Peninsula, and that his removal is contemplated. Another sensation[al] report says that the rebels will attack Washington before another week. The Republican paper of this city notices a sermon preached by "the Rev. Mr. Turner, colored minister of the African Methodist Episcopal Church," in which it (the Republican), while speaking very complimentary of Rev. Mr. Turner, sets him in a very singular aspect before the people.

It says that Mr. Turner "urged the policy of the colored people taking up arms and sustaining the Government by crimsoning every battle-field with their blood." I was present and heard Mr. Turner's remarks, but did not hear all the Republican says, in a certain direction, though Mr. Turner did say that we should pray for this nation, which is groaning beneath the scathing judgments of a God who never falters his promises nor swerves his threats,—for him to hold indivisibly, unsullied, the integrity and honor of this country; for if she failed in this her hour of trial, farewell, oh, farewell, thou goddess of liberty; hope for the poor, prospect for the oppressed, adieu, adieu, adieu!

Rev. George A. Rue passed through the city on his way to New Bern, N.C. He preached in Israel Church, and stated his mission, and the people voluntarily, without being asked, came up and put $18 in his hands.

H.M.T.

## *"Washington Correspondence"*
(*The Christian Recorder*, August 16, 1862)

Mr. Editor:—Wednesday was a day which will be lastingly remembered by every grade of humanity in this city. It had been previously announced through the papers, there would be a grand war meeting held on the east side of the Capitol, when and where there would be several distinguished orators who would deliver addresses.

At four o'clock, congruently to announcement, the bells of all the principal places in the city began to ring. The drums irregularly arraigned through the streets to beat the war notes; and cannons from surrounding summits, to base with iron lungs and powder tongues so terribly loud, that the atmosphere vibrations numbed the drum of every ear, as we listened to their dreadful roar, imaginarily like awe echoing to awe, or that fear, dread, terror, and alarm had shivered the shaft which dared their wrath, and were contestably dialoguing the plans of their desperation, we could but remember that thus speaking stanza:

> "When shrivelling like a parched scroll,
> The flaming heavens together roll;
> And louder yet, and yet more dread
> Swells the high trump that wakes the dead."[20]

But notwithstanding this threatening din, every imaginable glade of humanity was soon seen wending their way to the east of the Capitol, which, when assembled, constituted such a dense multitude of human beings, that any one interested in the future transpiration of things could hardly hold his lips from uttering:

> "When man to judgment wakes from clay,
> How great will be the throng that day!"

But on the broad portico and steps on the east part of the Capitol building, a large platform had been erected, which was appropriately decorated with the American flag. In view to a display, gas burners had been extended over the arch in front of the platform, and one set of jets consistently taking the form of a star.

The platform was occupied by the President and several of his cabinet, the city council of Washington, invited civil and military guests, speakers and reporters for the press. The ladies occupied the portico, and the great mass stood in front below the platform, and Mr. colored lady and gentleman mingled in the crowd. The speakers were generally very eloquent; but the Hon. G. S. Boutwell was the only one out of all who dared to take a bold stand in favor

---

20. Here, and two paragraphs later, Turner quotes from a Methodist hymn based on Rev. 6.14.

of the colored man. He took the ground that the states of South Carolina, Georgia, and Florida should be dedicated to the black race, and all along the gulf stream, if necessary; and that the mild power of persuasion should be used to get the intelligent colored people from the north to emigrate there and establish a nationality. Shortly after, some man rose up, who apparently worked his upper jaw instead of his lower, and began a raid of intimations upon the abolitionists. . . .[21]

H.M.T.
Washington, August 8th, 1862.

## "Washington Correspondence"

(*The Christian Recorder,* August 30, 1862)[22]

Mr. Editor:—Things in this city have all changed into new activity. Thousands of soldiers are pouring into the city, and thronging the streets,—drums are heard in every direction, and tents are being pitched upon every hill-top and low dale. Seventy-five or a hundred wagons all in a row, can frequently be seen, either loaded with soldiers, tents, or muskets. One would imagine that treason, with all its abominable forms, would necessarily soon have to be crushed out, and that to an eternal non-existence.

But many of us have now concluded, that the judgment of God will never cease its plagues upon this nation, till slavery and oppression shall be foiled, and right, equity, and justice shall be seen in all its grand regalia, leading on in triumphant conquest the victories of humanity.

---

21. Several paragraphs of church business are omitted.
22. It is unknown whether a column was written for the August 23, 1862, issue, as the first sheet of that issue is no longer extant.

This has been one of the most excitable weeks with our people, I suppose, ever known in their history.

The desire of the President of the United States to have an interview with a committee of colored men, and a compliance with that desire on the part of our people, very nearly made some of our citizens frantic with excitement. Many seemed to have thought that it was in the voluntary power of the President to transport at his option all the colored people out of the country. And in this state of excitement every imaginable idea, however absurd to common reason it might be, seemed to have gained a respectable idea of currency in the mind of some class of thinkers.

But the great excitement appears to have grown out of a neglect upon the part of many to sit down and properly read the papers in a spirit of characteristic soberness, and then ascertaining to what extent the President's power goes to enable him to put in force what he has proposed.

There is no need of such wild excitements arising from a mere suggestion, unless the parties have an absolute power to effectuate their repugnant schemes and plans. And that the President of the United States has not, and I don't believe that he would use it if he had.

Somehow a report gained currency, that Rev. H. M. Turner was the prime mover of this whole affair, and that he had waited upon the President, in reference to this Central American project, which brought down in the midst of the upstir a heavy tirade of denunciations upon him in every direction. Though none seemed to vent themselves in his presence, yet many seem to be conscientiously persuaded to credit the report. But Mr. Turner has now corrected the false statement, and gave them to understand that he hated the infamous scheme of compulsory colonization as much as they could. Things took a change immediately, and now the great drift of objections appears to be running in another direction.

Last Thursday was the day on which the committee, sent to wait upon the President, was to make their report to the parties who sent them. At four o'clock, as had been agreed upon, the committee of five, from each of the colored churches in the city, met at Union Bethel Church to hear the report of the five who waited on the President. But through some means, the majority of the committee did not appear, for what reason I cannot tell. However, Mr. John T. Costin, one of the committee being present, offered, I am told by several present, to give a minority report, but it was judged best to adjourn, until they could receive information as to the committee's whereabouts, at which time they will again convene to hear the report of the committee, dismiss them if necessary, and I judge lay the contents of the interview with the President before the colored people of the United States, for their consideration and action. I think there never was a time when a better opportunity offered itself to our people to speak to the civilized world than the present. And I believe so soon as this committee will be able to lay the question before our people in an official manner (as I hope they will take no action before), that the nation will have a chance to hear from the black man in every direction. I suppose no colored man in the nation would have any objection to going any where, if this government pay them for their two hundred and forty years' work.[23]

Rev. Mr. French, formerly of Wilberforce College, Ohio, but now of Hilton Head, S.C., and the distinguished Robert Smalls, the colored man, who came out of Charleston, S.C., with a war ship, guns, cannons, &c., and a large number of other colored people, paid a visit to Israel Church on last Sabbath evening.[24] Af-

---

23. See Kate Masur, "The African American Delegation to Abraham Lincoln: A Reappraisal," *Civil War History* 56, no. 2 (June 2010): 117–44 for an account of this meeting.
24. The Reverend Mansfield French (1810–76) was one of the founders of

ter the sermon, the pastor introduced the Rev. Mr. French, who spoke of his labors South, and gave great satisfaction about that colored regiment which has been so contemptuously spoken of by so many papers, or pro-slavery sheets.[25] After many interesting remarks, Mr. Robert Smalls was introduced, and told the history of his escape, which was mixed with some very sensible details, and created some laughter, and raised any quantity of smiles. It was the first attempt of Mr. Smalls to speak in public, and taking into consideration his unnatural situation, being placed before an intelligent audience of white and colored, numbering twelve hundred, his effort was a great success, notwithstanding his timidity was discernible.

He will accompany Mr. French through the principal cities north, as a living specimen of unquestionable African heroism. This war seems to be destined by Providence to coin out the rare qualities of the depressed humanity of every nation. The German, the Irishman, the Frenchman, and the negro have excited wonder; and though the negro is the last starting out, look out if he does not come out first.

H.M.T.

---

Wilberforce University, the first institution of higher education for blacks in the United States. He also helped establish the National Freedmen's Relief Association and also helped organize teachers for the freedmen's settlement established at Hilton Head, South Carolina, in 1862. On May 13, 1862, Robert Smalls (1839–1915), leading several other enslaved crewmen, commandeered the Confederate ship, the C.S.S. *Planter*, while her white officers were ashore and escaped to Union lines. Accounts of his daring escape filled the newspapers, and Smalls was personally recognized by President Lincoln. Smalls became a Union pilot; he later served in the South Carolina state legislature and in the U.S. House of Representatives.
25. See note 15.

## "Letter from Washington"
(*The Christian Recorder*, Sept. 6, 1862)

*Mr. Editor*:—Our city is full of excitement. A report has gained considerable circulation, that Jackson and his rebel army are within nine miles of Washington, which has thrown the populace upon the heels of excitement.[26] Many are of the opinion that they hear the thunder chattering of war implements conversing most destructively between the defenders of right and the perpetrators of wrong. Every little piece of information coming from across the Potomac is seized by some news-hungry creature, masticated in the jaws of his own opinion, and devoured world without end. Every available vehicle is packed to overflowing with persons in search of the battle-field, while all the boats engaged between here and Alexandria are incompetent to the task of transporting the eager souls who are desirous of going to the scene of the conflict. But the most sad spectacle upon which I have looked is the thousands of wounded soldiers who are being brought into the hospitals of the city. Severed arms and shattered legs are no unfrequent sights, and holes perforated by bullets through hands, ears, shoulders, and calf of the legs, are as common as they are horrible.

From all accounts, the battle is raging most furiously on the other side of the river. About six hundred thousand men are supposed to be engaged—three hundred thousand on each side. Many who have been in the battle pay the highest encomiums to rebel bravery. Contrabands are pouring in from all quarters, and some bring the most enormous burdens on their backs that were certainly ever conveyed by human muscles. One of the contrabands told me that beyond

---

26. Turner is referring to Gen. Thomas "Stonewall" Jackson, whose troops, along with Gen. Robert E. Lee's, came dangerously close to Washington during the Second Battle of Bull Run (August 28–30, 1862). Union forces managed to turn Jackson back on September 1, at the Battle of Chantilly.

Manassas Junction, there was a large body of our people located at a certain place, and that an infamous gang of rebel devils came upon them and shot every one of them, and shortly afterwards two companies of some of the Pennsylvania volunteers surrounded ninety of the secession assassins, and the poor fellows wanted to surrender, but no surrender for such mortal fiends until the Union boys gave death the privilege of a hug at each one. But a synopsis of the inhuman atrocities—the diabolical flagitiousness of the villainous perpetrations done by the snake-hearted squatter-smatters of that hydrophobic dropsy-headed oligarchy—is sufficient to shudder a nervous being, but such vile imps of creation God will judge and reward.

The improvements which have been going on in Israel Church for some three months are now complete except frescoing it. They now have one of the largest and finest lecture rooms that is attached to any church in the city, white or colored, besides a most handsome set of portable class rooms, which they can move at their option. Thus, when occasion requires it, turn the entire hall into one, and then in a few moments convert it into several. . . .[27]

H.M.T.
Washington, Sep. 1, 1862.

## *Untitled*

(*The Christian Recorder*, Sept. 13, 1862)

Mr. Editor:—Somehow the hordes of secesh have made their way so near as to menace this city, and infest Maryland, and the probability is that before this shall have reached you, they may be

---

27. Several paragraphs of church news are omitted, as well as a heated rebuttal to another Washington correspondent, writing under the pseudonym Cerberus, who attacked Turner for the role he played in the presidential conference with church leaders described earlier in the chapter.

in the city of Baltimore. How this can be in the providence of God, I know not, unless, as the Rev. James Lynch once very eloquently, and I now think, appropriately remarked, "That the head of this rebellion was in the South, and its tail in the North, and that God intended to punish the whole as due to its unnumbered crimes," for the contest has been attended with a circumvolution of retreats and re-retreats ever since it commenced.

The whole affair appears to be nothing more nor less than a national scourge. To-day we are gaining great victories, tomorrow we are losing; to-day we are taking prisoners, tomorrow we are being taken prisoners. To-day we are before Richmond, tomorrow the rebels are before Washington. And thus it is so good a man, and so good a boy, all the time, and the war is no nearer to an end now than when it first began; indeed, the South is stronger now than ever; more disciplined, and more cemented together, in the diabolical traffic.

I was noticing yesterday the goddess of Liberty standing at the foot of the Capitol of the United States, with her face directed toward Virginia, as though she were looking at the progress of freedom. Her features appeared to be enlivened with hope, but bearing a physiognomy held by a peculiar anxiety that borders on sadness itself. Once could hardly but feel, when viewing this noble statue, that the great ensign of this and every other nation's pride, was vacillating between the hope of victory and the fear of despair. But when looking at how all great achievements have been wrought for the elevation of mankind, at any period in the world's history, it seems to be the economy of Providence to disenthrall every perverted principle and violated law of nature, slowly, tediously, and at great length.

For in whatever part of this stupendous universe any violation in harmony, or abnormity, exists, the discordancy and conflicting action of its native operations will grate harshly in her onward career until they shall have been resuscitated by the gradual but sure process of those immutable actionary and reactionary forces which are constitutionally warped in its primeval nature, and freedom is one of these grand principles, yea, the chief itself, which shall soon assert its original claims and bid defiance to the hand of oppression.

The people in Washington do not seem to be excited. Almost all believe that the city would be secure though ten hundred thousand rebels harass her suburbs.

Contrabands are coming into the city in great droves, and of all the horrible reports that ever was told, they tell. It appears that many of the contrabands in making their escape (I speak from what they say) threw their little children into the river and drowned them, to facilitate their flight. And there are two intelligent contrabands sitting down now in my house, who tell me that somewhere near Richmond, Virginia, there is a large coal mine, where several hundred colored people are at work, very low under ground, and a quantity of combustible materials are prepared and placed in it, and that a cannon is situated at a respectable distance, so that should the Union forces take Richmond, this cannon is to be fired, which will ignite these combustibles and destroy every one in the coal pit. They further believe that it was God's mercy that prevented General McClellan from taking Richmond, for had he taken it, the lives of thousands of colored people would have been instantly destroyed. But it is needless to try to particularize the horrid, hideous, shocking and inconceivable scenes of suffering which are reported by some of these poor dejected sons of humanity. Oh God, were I not confident that thy mercy endureth forever, I would despair for my people, but still we ask Thee, O thou Prince of Peace, in wrath remember mercy! A few weeks ago, there was a great excitement in this city, which arose from a false apprehension that certain parties were trying to expatriate the contrabands from the country.[28] It is to be hoped that equally as high a feeling

---

28. Lincoln and others did, in fact, support such a scheme. See McPherson, *Negro's Civil War*, 89.

for these homeless human beings will animate them to give of their substance, and divide their comforts, and open their doors, so that these almost friendless souls may find shelter. "Let thy love speak through thy works," was an ancient maxim. . . .[29]

Last Thursday night, a society of ladies and gentlemen gave a festival at the Presbyterian Church, for the benefit of the contrabands, which was presided over by Mrs. Elizabeth Trekly, a lady distinguished both by beauty and intelligence. Those who figured most prominently on the occasion were Mrs. Josephine Steward, Miss Jane Cook, Miss Margaret Cokely, Mr. Jas. Wormly, John T. Johnson, and William Slade. There were others whose names I do not recollect. Though they had the disadvantage of a city somewhat excited in consequence of the army's retreat to contend with, they nevertheless did remarkably well. Such manifestations of our sympathies as this, for the contrabands, are worth a thousand gabblers, in whose sight a quarter looks as big as a wagon-wheel.

H.M.T.
Washington, Sept. 8, 1862.

### *"Affairs in Washington"*

(*The Christian Recorder*, September 27, 1862)

Mr. Editor:—We are in the midst of an anxious suspense still for the *nation's* safety. Fierce and terrible have been the battles fought almost at the door of the Capitol for the last two weeks.[30] Days and

---

29. A tribute to Reverend Henry Taite of the Israel Church and descriptions of activities at Zion Wesley Church and John Wesley Church are omitted.

30. The Second Battle of Bull Run (August 30) and the Battle of Chantilly (September 1) capped off one of Lee's most successful campaigns, in northern Virginia, just thirty miles from the capital. Lee then seized the

nights pass away leisurely even to the most unconcerned, but to those who are to any extent interested in the war affairs, and are hungering for the evening and morning papers, hours appear to creep slower than days formerly.

The streets of Washington, which were thronged with straggling soldiers two weeks ago, now present quite a different state of things. These wandering soldiers have been taken up and properly assigned to a more useful sphere of action, though every public rendezvous is still beleaguered with more captains, lieutenants, and other coat-strapped gentlemen than I have ever seen before. How it is that such fierce battles can be raging on the very suburbs of the United States capital, and so many idle officers promenading the streets, loitering around hotels, and lolling in every kind of saloon at the same time, is a mystery to me. However, it is a very insignificant thing that is of no use at all, and the only use their appearance upon the streets is, that it has a tendency to keep down excitement, for the great mass of the people are led to suppose that as long as the soldiers are so easy and unconcerned, there is but little danger to be feared. And strange to say too; but there is the greatest difference in the world between the last soldiers called for by the President and the first. The first or former soldiers who came to the defence of their country, seemed to have had nothing at heart but their great and glorious mission, and every other consideration appeared to be a matter of contempt, or regarded as undeserving attention; they passed to and fro among the people and treated every one respectfully; such were the manners and becoming courtesy of every northern soldier that the colored people

---

federal arsenal at Harper's Ferry, Virginia (September 12–15) before suffering defeats at South Mountain (September 14) and Antietam (September 17). The Union's success at the Battle of Antietam, the bloodiest single day of the Civil War, was the impetus for Lincoln's issuance of the Preliminary Emancipation Proclamation, referred to in the following letter.

delighted to render every assistance in their power; they would take them to their houses and give them the best to eat the market could afford, and divide the last penny they had to make them comfortable, and it was almost unnatural to hear a harsh word spoken by any of them to a colored person. But these last recruits which are coming into the field, are all the time cursing and abusing the infernal negro, as some say, nigger. In many instances you may see a regiment of soldiers passing along the street, and knowing them to be fresh troops, you may (as it is natural) stop to take a look at them, and instead of them thinking about the orders of their commanders, or Jeff. Davis and his army, with whom they must soon contend, they are gazing about to see if they can find a nigger to spit their venom at. And I believe it is to kill off just such rebels as these that this war is being waged for, one in rebellion to their country, and the other in rebellion to humanity, for that man who refuses to respect an individual because his skin is black, when God himself made him black, is as big a rebel as ever the devil or any of his subalterns were, if James Gordon Bennett is one, he not excepted. . . .[31]

I also visited the office of the *Repository*, and find that our people, like as in nearly every thing else, are growing weary in well doing. When the *Repository* first began to be published monthly, there was a considerable amount of zeal manifested in its behalf, but like the old bell cow, it has now become common, and hence the people are becoming careless. The secret of it is, I do not believe that the ministers manifest any interest in it, with some few exceptions, for I am certain if its claims were held up before the

---

31. Bennett was the founder and editor of the *New York Herald*, a sensational and extremely popular newspaper that broadcast both racist and anti-Semitic views. Turner's description of a trip to Baltimore, sermons given by Reverend S. L. Hammond and Reverend A. W. Wayman, and a visit to the wife of A.M.E. minister James Lynch are omitted.

thousands that compose our congregations, Sabbathly, that we could dispose of at least 5,000 per month, and here we can barely get rid of one thousand. I heard Bishop Quinn say in New York, that the ministers of the A.M.E. Church preached Sabbathly to over 75,000 human beings, and out of that vast number, we can hardly sell one thousand *Repositories,* and it puzzles almost the whole connection to understand how Weaver does to keep the *Recorder* alive, but the ones that are the most puzzled are those who do the least for it. If 75,000 persons, professors and non-professors, who are supposed to compose our congregations through the entire connection, cannot keep up one weekly paper and one monthly periodical (the *Repository*) we ought to go down South and work for old Jeff. No one can find any fault with either the *Repository* or the *Recorder;* their literature is of the best style, indeed, history, art, science, divinity or politics, or any thing else heart could wish, are found in their pages as affluently as any other in this country. No excuse under God's heaven but indifference, or an indisposition to work for our own benefit. God of mercy wake up the people to a knowledge of their *stupidity* and to a sense of their *danger,* for I really believe that it is dangerous to trifle with the means that God has put in our hands to elevate unborn generations, for a man that will oppose literature is no more than any other sinner if he has the means of exerting its blessed power either upon himself or other persons. And the man that will neglect it, commits a sin second only to neglecting his prayers....[32]

The committee who waited upon the President, and to whom he delivered his Central American address, have not yet taken any action. I hear they are preparing a reply, which they contemplate submitting to the people, and if approved of, then submitting it to

---

32. Paragraphs describing the search for a pastor for the 15th Street Presbyterian Church and a visit to Washington by Professor A. M. Green are omitted.

the President. I hope thy will make it speak in power, for if we do not speak now, at a time when the chief magistrate is bound to hear us, I very much doubt another opportunity being offered. May God teach them what to say.

    H.M.T.

    Washington, Sept. 19th, 1862.

## *"Washington Correspondence"*
(*The Christian Recorder*, Oct. 4, 1862)

Mr. Editor:—Much of the harmony that used to pervade the city has returned. The rebel raid in Maryland being at an end, the doubts for the safety of the Capitol are changed into a confidential reliance in the power of Federal protection.

The greatest intelligence we have had about Washington is the President's proclamation which prospectively gives freedom to so vast a quantity of our people.[33] I suppose any thing in the shape of a review from one so humble, would be an intrusion upon your columns, but I must say that I differ with a large portion of our people in not believing that the President wrote his proclamation in good faith.[34] I believe Mr. Lincoln embodied his conscientious promptings when he wrote that proclamation. Nevertheless, I do not doubt but that he has been worked up to it by a series of events which have transpired, but these events have only worked him out of an unnecessary caution, and a useless prudence, and not any love for slavery, because I do not believe he ever had any. And I

---

33. The Preliminary Emancipation Proclamation was issued by Lincoln on September 22.
34. Turner seems to have meant the opposite of what he says here; the sentence should possibly read, "I differ with a large portion of our people *who do not believe* that the President wrote his proclamation in good faith."

will further say, that Mr. Lincoln is not half such a stickler for colored expatriation as he has been pronounced (I am responsible for the assertion), but it was a strategetic move upon his part in contemplation of this emancipatory proclamation just delivered. He knows as well as any one, that it is a thing morally impracticable, ever to rid this country of colored people unless God does it miraculously, but it was a preparatory nucleus around which he intended to cluster the raid of objections while the proclamation went forth in the strength of God and executed its mission. I do not wish to trespass upon the key that unlocks a private door for fear that I might lose it, but all I will say is that the President stood in need of a place to *point to*. But suppose the president did not deliver his proclamation in good faith? What need I care? Or suppose he was driven to it by force of circumstances. What of it? That is nothing to cavil over. Let us thank God for it, for to him be the glory forever and ever. But such suppositions are not founded upon any tangible ground of truthful considerations but are conjured up by some ironical, faulting, evil constructed hearts, for Mr. Lincoln loves freedom as well as any one on earth, and if he carries out the spirit of his proclamation, he need never fear hell. GOD GRANT HIM A HIGH SEAT IN GLORY. . . .[35]

Mr. Joseph E. Williams, of Central America notoriety, is preparing to leave for that place by the 10th of October. He is highly gratified at the prospect, having secured a home for his race, where such a profusion of wealth may be acquired. If Central America ever becomes any thing, Mr. Williams' name will be immortal, for if he has not worked against wind and tide to bring that country to the attention of the people, no one ever did.

    H.M.T.

    Washington, Sept. 28th, 1862.

---

35. Six paragraphs describing activities at Israel Church are omitted.

## "A Call to Action"

(*The Christian Recorder*, October 4, 1862)

Mr. Editor:—The time has arrived in the history of the American African, when grave and solemn responsibilities stare him in the face. The proclamation of President Lincoln, promising in the short space of a hundred days, to liberate thousands, and hundreds of thousands of human beings, born under and held in subjection to the most cruel vassalage that ever stained a nation's garment, has opened up a new series of obligations, consequences, and results, never known to our honored sires, nor actually met with through the long chain of a glorious ancestry. We live in one of the most eventful periods of the world's revolutions—a period, virtually speaking, that "kings and prophets waited for, but never saw."[36]

A generation has passed from among the living since men upon this continent first dared to speak in the defense of human rights. But generations have passed since the God of heaven was first besieged by billions of entreaties, despatched from the earnest hearts of millions of tortured souls, from every vale, hill, and dale, where defrauded humanity felt the grind of oppression's wheel. And amid all the din and dash of legislative and congressional enactments, determined upon the consummate extension of its transitive duration, a circle of darkness shrouded the scheme, and hurled the traffic to the ground, amid a dense rolling fog of dismal confusion, for which a parallel is not to be found.

But now, while many of those warm-hearted philanthropists, prompted by considerations purely divine, are lying in their graves, and while thousands of thousands of prayer-offering saints whose supplications were heard in the skies as a mixture of anxiety,

---

36. From Isaac Watts's hymn, "How Beauteous Are Their Feet," based on Isa. 52:7–10 and Matt. 13:17.

torture, want, and grief have passed from the troublesome scenes of earth to the land of immortal birth, their labors, toils, and efforts combined have, by gradual incursions upon the powers of injustice, through the instrumentality of their continuous and circumfluent lash, pushed on despite the oppositions, the dawn of freedom and the morn of liberty.

And now, we are verging upon a time very unlike the previous days of our American existence. The great quantity of contrabands (so called) who have fled from the oppressor's rod and are now thronging Old Point Comfort, Hilton Head, Washington City, and many other places, and the unnumbered host who shall soon be freed by the President's proclamation, are to materially change their political and social condition. The day of our inactivity, disinterestedness, and irresponsibility, has given place to a day in which our long cherished abilities, and every intellectual fibre of our being, are to be called into a sphere of requisition. The time for boasting of ancestral genius and prowling through the dusty pages of ancient history to find a specimen of negro intellectuality is over. Such useless noise should now be lulled, while we turn our attention to an engagement with those means which must, and alone can, mould out and develop those religious, literary, and pecuniary resources, adapted to the grave expediency now about to be encountered.

Thousands of contrabands, now at the places above designated, are in a condition of the extremest suffering. We see them in droves everyday perambulating the streets of Washington, homeless, shoeless, dressless, and moneyless. And when we think of the cold freezing days of a coming winter, at which time the surface of the earth not unfrequently will be concreted into a solid mass of congelation, our sensibilities of humanity sink under the dreadful apprehensions consequent upon such direful privations.

Every man of us now, who has a speck of grace or bit of sympathy for the race that we are inseparably identified with, is called upon by force of surrounding circumstances, to extend a hand of mercy *to bone of our bone and flesh of our flesh*.[37] And no one can now screen himself behind the nice-natured scrupulosities which have in so many instances redounded to a plausible excuse, to the ever garrulous but never performers, in that, after giving assistance to the contrabands, they would again be returned back to slavery, and thus we would be found as having lavished our charitable expenditures upon a human chattel, destined to a state of perpetual vassalage; the morality of that thing, however, has not only been questionable but grievously condemnable.

But the proclamation of President Lincoln has banished the fog, and silenced the doubt. All can now see that the stern intention of the Presidential policy is to wage the war in favor of freedom, till the last groan of the anguished heart slave shall be hushed in the ears of nature's God. This definition of the policy bids us rise, and for ourselves think, act, and do. We have stood still and seen the salvation of God, while we besought him with teary eyes and bleeding hearts; but the stand-still day bid us adieu Sept. 22, 1862.[38] A new era, a new dispensation of things, is now upon us—*to action, to action*, is the cry. We must now begin to think, to plan, and to legislate for ourselves.

Washington, Sept. 26th, 1862.

## "For the Christian Recorder"

(*The Christian Recorder*, October 18, 1862)

Mr. Editor:—I hope you will not censure me for not writing regularly, as I am both in poor health and very much engaged. I

---

37. Gen. 2:23.
38. Exod. 14:13: "And Moses said unto the people, Fear ye not, stand still, and see the salvation of the Lord, which he will show you today: for the Egyptians whom ye have seen to day, ye shall see them again no more for ever."

merely write these few lines to let you know that I have not forgotten you since the gentle showers of heaven's rain has fallen upon our earth again. The clouds of dust hitherto so annoying to the finely dressed gentlemen and ladies, have condensed themselves into an equal proportion of mud and slop. . . .[39]

We learn that the Central American expedition is deferred till the first of October. This is done in consequence of Senator Pomeroy's delay in Kansas. I hear that over a thousand applications are made to go in the first expedition.

The young men of Israel Church came together on Monday night last and organized a grand Lyceum, to be known as the Israel Lyceum. They elected H. M. Turner President, Thomas H. C. Hinton, Vice-President, J. B. Cross, Secretary, William Tenny, Treasurer, J. T. Castin, McGill Pearce, and Wm. Brown, Managers, &c. The institution bids fair to be one of the very things to wake up the latent powers of the minds of all identified with it. Some twenty-three gave their names immediately, and several more are sending in their applications.

The armies about here are all standing still, as if they were waiting for the first of January, 1863, so as to secure the assistance of millions of colored freemen.

I see that that miserable sheet called the *New York Herald* is caving in on the negro question. Too late now, Bennett; the thing is out, and if you don't repent of your sins, which outnumber the drops of all the oceans in the universe, you will be out, too—but it will be *into outer darkness*.[40] Mr. Editor, I hope you will excuse me for referring to that infamous, rotten scrap of paper and the proprietor of which I regard as an incarnate fiend. But it speaks so

---

39. Descriptions of visits from A. M. Green and the Reverends A. W. Wayman, J. M. Brown, and J. P. Campbell are omitted.
40. Matt. 8:12, 22:13, and 25:30, where those without faith are sent, a place of "weeping and gnashing of teeth."

contemptibly of my race, whether they be the so called contrabands or more intelligent colored men, that it unmans all my Christian gravity to think of it. Nothing less than a hell, where the fire burns forever with brimstone fuel, and where chains are employed to fasten you down to the gridirons of perdition, and where red-hot lead, burning lava, and boiling pewter, is poured down the throat for water, and where the lurid, angry flames, heated ten thousand times redder than imagination can depict or thought conceive, can be adequate to the punishment due one so dreadfully steeped in hatred to his fellow-man.

I still hear nothing of that committee's report from the President. I suppose they are preparing a document to tell with lasting effect. It is looked for with much anxiety.

H.M.T.
Washington, Oct. 13, 1862.

## "The Condition of the Contrabands in Washington"
(*The Christian Recorder*, November 1, 1862)[41]

*Washington, Oct. 6th, 1862.*

Rev. J. P. Campbell and others:—Yours of the 2d inst., requesting me to give a succinct account of the contrabands and all that appertains to their condition, is before me. And in order to better enable me to give a true and proper delineation of their wants and necessities, I procured the assistance of Mr. John T. Castin, who accompanied me to the various camps where the contrabands are now located.

---

41. The "Washington Correspondence" column from October 25, 1862, is omitted as it consists solely of church-related activities.

The first place we visited was the camp of Captain Warner, where I found, I judge, about four hundred of all sorts and sizes. And here we stopped to make observations and propose interrogatories commensurate to the object in view. Captain Warner, being a gentleman of large benevolence, as well as a true philanthropist, invited us into his quarters, and tendered us all the information desired, and then volunteered his services to conduct us to several of their tents, which we found, to our very agreeable disappointment in many instances, much more comfortable than we had anticipated.

They have good military tents, cooking utensils, and the Captain stated plenty of common provisions, but not the kind of delicacies adapted to the wants and disordered systems of the sick, especially that kind of nourishment required for sick children, of which there were a large proportion.

He further informed us that there was a great want of proper clothing; particularly, such as sacks of various sizes, shirts for men, and clothing for children; and as the weather grew colder the exigencies of all kinds of clothing would be considerably enhanced. And I would further state that our communications with the contrabands led us to a still stronger credence in the above statements, from their very many corroborative attestations.

Having made the necessary investigations in this department, we proceeded to the camp of Rev. J. D. Nichols, into which we were admitted without any restrictions, indispensable to the completion of the object of our mission.

Here were nearly seven hundred contrabands, ranging from infants to sires of eighty winters, many of whom were very sick, and most earnestly craving that kind of nourishment suitable to their condition.

We were there informed by the superintendent that they stood in great need of at least a thousand blankets. The matron, a distinguished lady from Boston, also told us that all kinds of clothing were in great demand; that many of the women were merely clothed in rags, and had no changeable apparel even to serve them while they washed what they had on. "But," said she, "any thing and every thing in the shape of clothing would be most gratefully received, for unless Providence opens up some merciful way by which their needs can be supplied, the winter's chilling, blasting wind will carry many of the half-naked contrabands to a premature grave." And she very particularly emphasized upon the needs of the little children, who were not able to help themselves.

We also saw many who were very comfortably clothed, and a very large proportion of others just the contrary. Indeed, some were very finely dressed. But there appeared to be many things over which they had great reason to grieve. The superintendent, however, assured us that the government would provide stoves, tents, wood, cooking utensils, and such like things, plentifully for the winter campaign, but that blankets, bed-ticking, etc., could not be obtained from that source, and all assistance given in that direction would be most gratefully acknowledged. I am happy, also, to state that the greater number of the contrabands who have come to Washington, display an amount of enterprise highly commendable. Hundreds of them never go to the camps provided for them, but seek immediate employment. They say if the government will free them, they ask no other favors. But hundreds are compelled to remain at the camps, because it is impossible to procure a house or room in which to stop. And to the honor of the Washington people, many of them have thrown open their finest parlors, given up their kitchens, garrets, and even closets to shelter these escaping sons of humanity, and every day we are besieged by contrabands hunting houses. I assure you if we had house room and remunerative employment proportionate to the demand, this benevolent appeal would not have to be made. And those who have disseminated it, that the contrabands are all a set of lazy, trifling dupes, are liars to the back bone. But I must congratulate you and your noble-hearted people for that laudable spirit of generosity which has prompted you to engage in such a distinguished enterprise.

I think with what our people in Washington are doing, and with what you are willing to do North, for the relief of the contrabands, we could establish a regular hospital. They suffer mostly in sickness, and it is pretty good dying, out of a camp of seven hundred, for four and five to die nightly, which is really the case among them. I see them often moving along the streets so sick and weak that they can hardly wag. Death seems to be figured in their countenance, and yet no where to go, no where to rest that weary, fevered head, that fainting frame. But it would be needless to try to describe what passes before my actual observation, or to descant the arguments favorable to a colored hospital, for the picture would be too horrible. The fact is, we need a colored hospital, and the next question is, can we have it. I answer, we can if we will try. Let the generous hearts of the great North unite on the subject and Baltimore and Washington do the same, and in a short time we will have a house fitted out, properly officered with intelligent men of our race, with every thing necessary for the sick and afflicted. One cent per week from our people would support as fine a hospital as could be desired. And I believe that many would be willing to give from one to five dollars per month for the sustenance of an institution of that kind. Besides, many of our white friends would greatly aid in the project, and the moral influence which would grow out of it would tell with thrilling effect upon our opposers and calumniators. It would, furthermore, turn the attention of our people to the great subject of their own responsibility, on to the help-yourself doctrine, which must ultimately triumph, if we ever triumph. I hope you and your congregation will give this matter some consideration, and if the plan is approved of, neither myself nor congregation will be found wanting in the sphere which must help to its achievement. Lest I weary you, I forbear. Your brother in Christ,

H. M. Turner.

## "*Our Washington Correspondent*"

(*The Christian Recorder*, November 1, 1862)

Mr. Editor:—The world is still moving onward, not only performing his elliptic revolutions and making one of the sun's grand retinue, which he swings to his side by the power of attraction, while he struts in majestic order the trackless path of boundless space, or whirls by the force of under-laws a thousand things, subjectively menial, but activities are rife in the moral and social world equally proportionate; every observable object bears the insignia of an eternal go on. This necessarily arises from the fact that no law is suspended, nor its claims of obedience neglected; for that homogeneous attraction exhibited in the atomical ingredients of a feather, is as significantly stamped with the force of immutability as that instantaneously transmitted gravitation which binds every thing, from the lowest geological stratum to the minutest particle that floats upon the boundaries of the aerial region, to the centre of its action.

So, when we contemplate the circle of human action, man, by virtue of his own constitutionality, lives in its ever-telling manifestation, despite the efforts to still him; he talks and thinks, he walks and runs, he contends and battles, he lives and dies,—onward he moves regardless of his repugnance to it.

But leaving the sphere of his extraneous mobilities, we come to consider his motive relations. We behold him moving in the confines of will and choice, treading the path of his own selection, or rejecting it with the sternness of defiance, or gliding along its defunct track with a grim countenance of aversion. Oh, what a heaven-granted legacy! but how wretchedly disposed of! Man's inadaptedness to so great a favor is evidenced by thousands of his daily follies. And likely it could not be better depicted than in the slow, tardy move of the American people to come to the place where God would have them. In short, war they have got to fight, blood they have got to shed, the firebrands of devastation they must by force of irresistible circumstances scatter, till they lay waste and desolate every unjustly erected fabrication.

These are the uncontrollable agencies which they neither can thwart, arrest, or subvert; they must, they will, they shall go on.

But, sentimentally, how indisposed they are to look the bull in the eye! Motively, how tardily they creep around the cylinder grooved spiral of God's incompressible plans! for, notwithstanding all their indefatigable resistance, they shall become "willing in the day of his power."[42] The institution of slavery must go into an eternal nonentity, and that by the choice of the American people. Southern sympathizers, under the garb of Northern Democrats, may exultingly elect and send their candidates to Congress, to stay the progress of freedom, but it will prove as vain as did the attempt of Xerxes to stay the waves of the Mediterranean. General McClellan may feed the worms of the Peninsula with the bodies of his stagnant army, or rot them upon the suburbs of Harper's Ferry rather than move upon the enemy—General Buell may hold his great command in the plains of Kentucky as lifeless as death, or permit them to wager for sport, rather than become an element in the great freedom revolution, but, as Galileo said, "It moves, nevertheless."

The weather here is again very dry and dusty. A few mornings ago the wind rose very high for a few moments, and the clouds of dust were so dense that I imagined it resembled the judgment day.

Prof. A. M. Green lectured on the 22d inst., in Zion Wesley

---

42. Ps. 110:3.

Church, to a large audience of white and colored. I am informed he gave Central America fire and brimstone.

The Sabbath School Association gave an exhibition on Monday last, in Israel Church, to one of the most densely crowded houses I ever saw. The children acquitted themselves admirably, and their selections reflected great credit upon the teachers.

A venerable sister, namely, Milly Bell, died on the 22d inst. She was about 60 years of age, and had been a member of the church for 45 years. Her Christian character was unsullied to her death. Her remains were rested in Israel Church, where her funeral sermon was preached by Rev. H. M. Turner. Her high character brought together a very large concourse of people.

Yesterday some 360 new contrabands came into Washington, and went to the quarters provided for them. They are of all sizes, shapes, and colors, and many are in great need. The people of our city are making great efforts to relieve their wants.

Rev. John H. W. Burley, from the New England Conference, is here, and preaching very acceptably to our people. Rev. Mr. Burley is a great friend to literature, and is destined to be one of the great defenders of the Christian faith. I am informed that Mr. Joseph E. Williams, of Central American notoriety, was serenaded a few nights ago, prospectively to becoming the Governor of Lincolnia. I am also informed that some parties who were very recently much opposed to the Central American project, have become its converts, and are going out in the first ship. All I have to say, is, *ecce homo*.

On last Thursday morning a terrible accident occurred at the Alexandria wharf, caused by the explosion of a steamboat boiler. The report was extremely terrific, but providentially the disasters were not so great as was at first supposed. A few colored people, whose names we have not just in mind, were among the killed and wounded.

H.M.T.

Washington, D.C., Oct. 24th, 1862.

## "Washington Correspondent"

(*The Christian Recorder*, November 22, 1862)[43]

Mr. Editor:—Among the most interesting occurrences that have taken place since you last heard from your correspondent, is the removal of General McClellan, that man who was Napoleonized through the papers, and crowned by negro chattel-makers, monarch of America. It was thought by many here, as it was thought of John C. Calhoun in South Carolina, that if McClellan would die the world would end, but he is dead, "and it moves nevertheless."

Though I am informed that a few military epaulet straps became strangulated at the idea, and resigned; but with that exception I believe every body thinks it was done through military necessity.

Abraham Lincoln will yet write his name upon the pages of history so indelibly, that time's indefatigable cycles shall never be able to efface it. Not only has he proved himself above the fledges of partyism by killing General Frémont on the one side, and General McClellan on the other, but that proclamation, over which the triumphant notes of heaven rolled along the confines of bliss, with evidences of higher ecstasies, than customarily reverberated in overpowering rapture, across the boundaries of light and felicity, will tell upon the annals of eternity in character, of such splendor as shall gild the name of Abraham Lincoln forever. Would that Milton's poetic notes could unthread the maze of his virtues, and they were engraven in the rock of ages. But his acts will stand

---

43. The November 8, 1862, "Washington Correspondence" column, which has been omitted, describes a Catholic benefit for the contrabands, an assortment of church news, and a brief reference to the "disgust" inspired by General McClellan's sluggishness. The November 15 "Washington Correspondence" column also is omitted, as it consists almost entirely of church-related news.

emblazoned in colors of glaring glory, amid the retinue of the world honored, till the sun of time shall set no more to rise.

The choir of Israel Church, assisted by some of the celebrated vocalists of Union Bethel and 15th Street Presbyterian churches, gave a grand concert for the benefit of said church, on last Monday and Tuesday nights. The concert was conducted by Prof. J. F. Wilkerson, whose acquaintance with musical science none will question. I deem it inexpedient to deal in personalities in this matter, as so many would be entitled to a panegyrical notice, that adequate remarks might be an intrusion upon your columns. But the pieces were well selected and judiciously executed. The singing, however, was much better the second than it was the first night. This grew out of the fact that they neglected, on the first night, to ventilate the church, and the crowd being so dense, the oxygen of the air was soon exhausted or absorbed, and the house became so impregnated with carbonized matter, that a harsh hoarseness soon followed, which materially disturbed the symphony of the music. But that annoyance was arrested the second night by a more philosophical discretion. And thus nature and art were brought into harmony, with such a glorious success, that the rhapsodical modulations which poured wave after wave through the ravished audience, held them enchantingly till the spell was broken by its *finis*, and then laudatory acclamations burst forth, i.e., shouts, whistles, hand claps and feet stamps, in every part of the house. The concert upon the whole was a grand affair, and not unproductive of a moral lesson.

Several distinguished ladies, belonging to said church, have been holding what they call a festival in the new lecture room for the past week. The names are too numerous to give in detail, but Mrs. Casandra Dent, a lady of unflinching nerve, was the prime mover of it.

The several colored churches in the city were notified last Sabbath to send five delegates on Friday night to Union Bethel Church, as business of importance would demand their attention. In accordance with said notice they met, at which time they temporarily organized themselves into a meeting, by electing Mr. William Slade as chairman and secretary pro. tem., &c. The object of the meeting was then stated, to be for the purpose of organizing upon some systematic basis, a plan by which the contrabands in our city could be cared for, and the commiseration of the various churches could be converged into Union Relief Associations, and stop that too long practised fraud which has been going on by parties assuming to be friends, when their acts prove them inveterate enemies to our people. They, however, adjourned without doing more than laying out the plan of operation. I will give a fuller account in my next.

This afternoon a terrible explosion took place in the hospital lot near Seventh Street bridge. It appears they had some powder condemned by the government, to which they set fire, and the powder proved to be a great deal better than they anticipated. And thus it made the most terrific report ever heard by any in this city. It appeared that the very foundations of the earth gave way, and not only did hands shake and tremble, but the very air vibrations were so dreadfully intensified, that for whole squares it shivered every glass window to atoms. In many places it not only broke the glass, but knocked out the entire sash, split doors and silenced clocks.

I was told that the excitement would likely injure some persons considerably.

The first Baptist church have granted their pastor, Rev. Mr. Leonard, a furlough for six months, for the purpose of visiting Liberia. Rev. Mr. Maddan, recently from the Allegheny Institute, is employed to fill his place till his return.

A venerable sister many years a member of Israel Church, viz.: Sylvia Wilson, died yesterday, Nov. 14th, at six o'clock, P.M., after a week's sickness. She will be remembered by several ministers, as her house was always the receptacle for that class of care-burdened travelers.

President Lincoln has been for several days refusing to see any one, however high their position. He is either preparing his message, or don't intend to be swerved from his principles.

H.M.T.

Washington, Nov. 15th, 1862.


## "Washington Correspondent"

(*The Christian Recorder,* November 29, 1862)

Mr. Editor:— There is nothing of importance that has transpired since you last heard from us. There is some excitement here in regard to a report which has gained currency, relative to Jackson marching upon Washington, though it is thought to be a mere sensation report, got up by some traitorous sympathizer for the purpose of producing an effect.

The friends of humanity are preparing to give a grand dinner to the contrabands, on Thursday, 27th inst., at which time there will be several distinguished persons, who will deliver addresses to them. We hope it will be a grand affair. . . .[44]

H.M.T.

Washington, Nov. 22d, 1862.


## "Washington Correspondence"

(*The Christian Recorder,* December 6, 1862)

Mr. Editor:—Though I am laboring under a fevered head, yet a few words from the capital might be of interest to some.

Our city is verging back to its usual activity, or to that activity

---

44. Turner's description of the election of officers for the Israel Church contraband convention is omitted.

which it usually presents in time of Congress. Senators, Representatives, Clerks, Phonographers, &c., are pouring in continually, preparatory to the opening of one of the most telling sessions which I think will ever convene in Washington.[45] The results of this Congress will touch the nation's heart-strings more than any previous one, not because destinies fraught with more interest should depend upon it (except to the colored), but because that around which the nation's sympathy twirls, will be touched. I may be mistaken, I hope I am; but if any one will closely watch the sentiments of this nation as they are expressed in the papers, speeches, orations, and periodicals throughout the entire country, they will see that many who profess loyalty, had rather see the nation severed to atoms, than that the oppressed should go free. The deep concern now with thousands is, what the President is going to do with the negroes? They will tell you that they ought to be free. But if he is freed, what is he going to do for a livelihood, and where is he going to locate, &c.?

I would like to have the pleasure of whispering into their ears the following words:

1st. That if we are freed, we intend to do as other men and women do:—*Just as we please*. Work when we get ready, eat when we have it, wash when we get dirty, sleep when it is night, get up in the morning, get married when we are suited, fight wars if we can't have peace, serve God or the devil, and die when we can't live. But we never intend to be human chattels again, *World without end,* AMEN.

2d As to where we are going: we have all the world before us. We are going to visit each other; going to play when we get ready; in short, we are going *just where we please*; going to church, going to stay here, going away, going to Africa, Hayti, Central America, England, France, Egypt, and Jerusalem; and then we are going to

---

45. A phonographer is the equivalent of a stenographer.

the jail, gallows, penitentiary, whipping-post, to the grave, heaven, and hell. But we do not intend to be sent to either place unless we choose. But I tell you what we will have to do; if this nation don't mind, we will have to settle this American war. Talk about the mediation of France and England! We will be the mediator, if things don't change.

But you ask what am I grumbling about. Has not the President issued his emancipation proclamation? Yes, he has, but the hearts of the people have not. The President has, but the country has not; and it must be done; else God will blow out the sun, burn up the sea, and thunder his wrath abroad.

Rev. Bishop Payne preached a missionary sermon last Sabbath afternoon in Israel Church.[46] It had been announced on Saturday through the papers, and consequently it brought together a large concourse of both white and colored. His reasoning was masterly, but did not carry upon it that fervid pathos which often distinguishes his able efforts. He also lectured on Monday night before the Israel Lyceum, an organization lately formed. In this effort the Bishop so far surpassed the most sanguine expectations that one could hardly value the lecture for admiring the man.

Those who heard it will never forget it. The papers spoke of him the next day, as being acquainted with the encyclopedia of science, and an oriental and modern linguist; at the conclusion of which, he paid a glowing tribute to the industry of the pastor and congregation of Israel Church, for the improvements lately made thereon.

Professor A. M. Green lectured before the Island Literary Association on Monday night, 26th inst. The subject was, "Things learned in the School Mythology." Permit me to say that he handled

---

46. Reverend Daniel Payne (1811–93), longtime bishop of the A.M.E. Church, guided much of the church discipline during the nineteenth century, advocating for order during church service, educated ministers, and the role of the church in black uplift. He was one of the founders of Wilberforce University.

his subject in a manner, that it appears none but the Professor could have done. He went back in the fields of mythology and brought out symbols browed with an inferential lustre; and canvassed them in such majestic diagrams, portraying them at the same time, in all that archetypal homogeneousness, which were peculiar in their day; so beautifully that those present could not forbear saying, *You are a smart man.*

Thanksgiving day was celebrated in all circles throughout the city. But we will merely notice that part which relates to the contrabands.

Several members of the Freed Men Association resolved, with the assistance of the several colored churches, to give the contrabands a dinner as an expression of our regard, and of their welcome in our midst. However, the different churches last Sabbath collected for that purpose very liberally. The Asbury M.E. Church (colored) collected $51; Union Bethel A.M.E. Church, $30; 15th Street Presbyterian, $27. Israel Church took up no collection, but by the advice of the pastor, each one sent whatever they chose to give to the pastor's study; from whence it was carried to the contraband quarters in a wagon. Consequently on Thursday morning his office was thronged with incomers and outgoers, bringing baked chickens, turkeys, pigs, pies, custards, apples, almonds, candies, &c., to the amount of about $50; some estimated it at about $60, but I think it was worth about $50. I did not hear what the first Baptist Church did, but I am certain it acted nobly. Neither did I hear the sum from the other churches. But every thing was in order by twelve o'clock, at which time they commenced dining. The number of contrabands and citizens present were about two thousand, many of whom (I mean citizens) joined in the jaw-working operation.

Shortly after one o'clock, a stand was erected, and everybody clustered around. The President of the day introduced Rev. Bishop Payne, whose address was much admired. After which, Senator Pomeroy, Rev. Mr. Mitchell, Emigration Agent, the President's private secretary, Professor A. M. Green, Rev. H. M. Turner, and others none less estimable, delivered addresses.

The contrabands evinced through the entire course of the many lectures a great deal of intelligence. The lectures were made up of the best of language, and many points were abstrusely stated, but when any thing suited them, it would be responded to, by glory to God, or Amen, or Hallelujah. It let gainsayers see, that we could understand something else besides *dis, dat,* and *dem*. But the most contemptible thing about the affair was, that some tried to turn it into an emigration meeting; now I am not so tight-brained, as not to want any thing said about emigration. My sentiments are, let it be discussed, and let those go who wish, and those stay who desire; let us have a free expression about it, for all this helps to develop intellect; it sets men to studying the physical and geographical condition of the globe. But to talk about moving the colored people from this country is foolishness. Though Professor Green, in his able speech on the occasion, tore the entrails out of those who broached the subject, I am sorry that any thing was said only what tended to their elevation.

The contraband convention met the same evening at Union Bethel Church, but for want of the constitution, adjourned without doing any thing more than discharging the committee which had been appointed to draft it, and appointing another. Some resolutions were offered and passed. I was very much surprised to see them adopt Jefferson's Manual as a parliamentary guide; a book never designed to govern deliberative bodies, but prepared only for legislative and congressional halls.[47] The President (Mr. William

---

47. The *Manual of Parliamentary Practice for the Use of the Senate of the United States* (1801) was written by then-Vice President Thomas Jefferson and is still used by the U.S. House of Representatives and over a dozen state legislatures. *Robert's Rules of Order* (first edition published in 1876) is more widely used today.

Slade), however, entered his protest to it; yet, on the other hand, the house loomed with intelligence: some enrapturing speeches were made. They meet again on next Thursday evening. I have been requested by a member of the C.S.S. Society to mention the trial of Mr. E. M. Thomas: all I care about it is, *Felix quem faciunt aliena pericula cantum*.[48]

Several marriages came off on the 27th inst., but we will only mention two.

Miss Harriet S. Middleton, to Mr. William P. Rider, by Rev. I. D. Brooks.

And Miss Mary Ann Burke, to Mr. Benjamin C. Bennett, by Rev. H. M. Turner.

There was also a grand supper given in Ebenezer Church, Georgetown, D.C., on the evening of the 27th inst.

H.M.T.

Washington, Nov. 28th, 1862.


## *"Washington Correspondent"*

(*The Christian Recorder*, December 27, 1862)

Mr. Editor:—The most important news in Washington at the time, is the various comments on the retreat of General Burnside.[49] Some supposing he was flogged by the rebels, and others, regarding it as a glorious retreat. From the looks of the morning papers, it

---

48. *A Dictionary of Select and Popular Quotations, Which are in Daily Use* (Philadelphia: Claxton, Remson, & Haffelfinger, 1873) translates this Latin phrase as "Happy are they who can learn prudence from the dangers of others."

49. In the Battle of Fredericksburg (December 11-15, 1862), Burnside, at the hands of forces commanded by General Robert E. Lee, suffered one of the most lopsided Union defeats of the war. Lincoln reportedly wrote in response to this failure, "If there is a worse place than hell, I am in it."

appears that some frail freak has been discovered in the President's cabinet. *God save the nation, is all that I can say,* for the aspect of things never looked more gloomy than they do this morning. When I am so conclusively led to the conviction that this nation is endeavoring to raise us up from thralldom and degradation, and still see the angry cataracts, which pour so violently around the trembling threshold of her safety, falling often like peals of dissolving thunder, from the rugged clouds of an enraged sky, my most hearty commiseration throbs languidly for her. I sometimes hear these hateful politicians speaking so contemptibly of the negro, that all sympathy for the time being leaves me. But when my sober senses begin the work again, I find my affections lingering around the land of my birth, and thus voluntarily, or involuntarily, as the case may be, I find myself saying, *God save the nation.* . . .[50]

H.M.T.

Washington, Dec. 20th, 1862.

## *"Washington Correspondence"*

(*The Christian Recorder,* January 10, 1863)

Mr. Editor:—The time has come in the history of this nation, when the downtrodden and abject black man can assert his rights, and feel his manhood. No longer can the men of our race be legally made to quaff up the scorn and derisions of a misanthropic rabble, many of whom are so inexplicably depauperated from licentious lives and devilish habit, that if they were sent as delegates to form an integral part of a dog's assembly, or sent as ambassadors to the wild cats of the forest, they would be denounced as trying to insinuate themselves into ranks superior.

The proclamation of President Lincoln reaches the most forlorn

---

50. Several paragraphs of church news are omitted.

condition in which our people are placed. When he finished it, and reclined himself back in his chair, the Jubilee commenced in every celestial sphere, where freedom's grand and depictless immunities are realized and enjoyed.[51] The angelic band in helmed array, whose war implements glittered as the watch fires of the sky, and hitherto drawn in martial protection around him who was ordained by God to free the oppressed, burst forth in exclamations of greater ecstasy, than usually enrapture their heavenly environed brow. The first day of January 1863 is destined to form one of the most memorable epochs in the history of the world.

It should form an era in the data of every colored man, and be annually celebrated with as much respect, as the Americans do the fourth of July, or as the English do the day of the discovery of the thirty barrels of powder, which were in 1605 placed under the Parliament in view of utterly demolishing the last vestige of protestant sympathy.[52] That proclamation will constitute the moral basis of all similar exigencies, as long as men press one another beneath the grind of a despotic wheel. The Moors of France, and Serfs of

---

51. According to the Book of Leviticus, slaves and prisoners would be freed and sins pardoned during a Jubilee year, which took place about once every fifty years.

52. In the Gunpowder Plot of 1605, Guy Fawkes, Robert Catesby (the actual mastermind of the plot), and a number of co-conspirators, all Catholics, planned to blow up the House of Lords and the Protestant King James I during the opening session of Parliament on November 5. They hoped that by doing so, they could force the government to take a more tolerant stance toward Catholics. The plot was foiled at the last moment, and Fawkes and several others were executed in January 1606. Guy Fawkes Day is celebrated on November 5 in England, initially to commemorate the triumph of Protestantism in the face of "popish" rebels; beginning in the mid-nineteenth century, however, Fawkes came to be seen as a heroic figure, an individual who stood up against an oppressive regime. Turner, whose anti-Catholic views are apparent throughout his writings, represents the event in the original sense—the triumph of Protestantism over Catholicism.

Russia, though liberated under circumstances not so free from the evidence of a providential interpolation as some have assumed, will only be known among the ordinary things of time, compared to the grand overture which necessarily must mark and signalize the liberty of the bond-oppressed mystic Israelites.[53] The seeds of freedom which are ever rejuvenescent in themselves, have now been scattered where despotism and tyranny ranked and ruled, will be watered by the enlivening dews of God's clemency, till the reapers (abolitionists) shall shout the harvest home.[54]

Through some misunderstanding the people of Washington did not celebrate the new year as many of our cities have done. This was not, however, the result of ingratitude to God or the President, but owing to apprehensions of danger, which I think were more chimerical than real. They meet, however, on Thursday night in mass, at Israel Church, to devise some plan by which an expression of our sentiments can be heard.

The Contraband Relief Association have organized themselves into an *Exhibiting Association,* and are giving concerts for the benefit of the contraband, known as the old folks' concerts. They gave two exhibitions in 15th St. Presbyterian Church, which were so largely patronized, that hundreds had to leave, who could obtain no admission. Indeed the house was so densely crammed that those inside were very disagreeable. The old folks, however,

---

53. During the Revolutions of 1848, slavery was definitively abolished in French colonies, including Senegal (Africans were often referred to as "Moors" during the nineteenth century); Czar Alexander II of Russia issued a decree freeing the serfs in 1861 (although most of the serfs were not truly liberated because they were still expected to pay the nobility for the land they worked). American slaves were frequently compared to the biblical Israelites, who were held in bondage in Egypt until they were freed by Moses.
54. An allusion to the hymn, "This is the field; the world below," which declares, "soon the reaping time will come, / And angels shout the harvest home."

acquitted themselves admirably, and made some $300 for the object of humanity, for which the Secretary of War complimented their efforts in the most applaudatory terms. I am not able in this correspondence to designate the parties who so very pleasurably executed their respective performances on the two evenings, but will endeavor to do it in my next.

The ladies of Israel Church are holding a fair which has been very largely attended by many of our most popular citizens, white and colored.

I received last week, in behalf of the contrabands, a very large box of goods from Bordentown, New Jersey, sent by the liberal flock of Rev. Jeremiah Young. The box contained some three hundred pieces of most valuable materials, which appear to have been forwarded by the special efforts of Rev. Jeremiah Young, President, Gideon Lewis, Secretary, Joseph Green, Treasurer, and a committee, consisting of Mrs. E. Colling, Mrs. R. Wood, Mrs. A. M. Crippin.

Any thing complimentary from me, would be superfluous. The act speaks its merit, and God himself will take cognizance of it, only to bless and reward.

The colored convention met at Zion Wesley Church on Tuesday night last, and resolved upon the erection, as soon as possible, of a hospital for the sick, afflicted, and destitute. They resolved that each delegate should advance ten dollars, as a beginning, to the sum of $5000, which they think will be required to complete the object in contemplation.

The Rev. Caleb Woodyard spoke in Israel Church a few weeks ago and made some very scathing remarks about colored people being refused a seat in the city cars. His tirade was very bitter at the time, but sweetness grew out of it, for several have been since informed that there was no law to keep us out, but if we waited for them to take us up, and set us in, and then ride us too, we would have to wait some time yet.

Honorable J. D. Johnson of Liberia is here again. I am informed he contemplates a heavy lawsuit, with the gentlemen with whom he had an altercation some time ago.[55]

Professor A.M. Green, whose name is so revered in Washington, is looked for here every week.

Several colored men in this city say they are now ready for the battle-field. Abraham Lincoln can get any thing he wants from the colored people here, from a company to a corps. I would not be surprised to see myself carrying a musket before long.

H.M.T.

Washington, Jan. 4th, 1862 [*sic*]

## "*Washington Correspondence*"

(*The Christian Recorder*, January 24, 1863)

Mr. Editor:—We are still surrounded by transforming aspects. The news of the federal reverses which occasionally comes muttering athwart the horizon of our prospects, and for a while beclouds the sky on which we fancied the golden letters of freedom written in matchless splendor, and arched with the bow of irreversible success, becomes not unfrequently a matter of serious meditation. But we must remember that the car of liberty has an enormous burden to carry to the summit of conquest, and we must not feel discouraged when the ascending grade is such as to demand an additional supply of resources. God has made humanity, and placed him upon such a basis, and delegated to him such powers and functions, that his civil, moral, and religious destinies are suspended in the scope of his actions. And all great achievements must materially depend upon the outgivings of his own efforts,

---

55. This altercation is described in the August 9, 1862, "Washington Correspondence" column, which begins on page 53.

while he is often haggardly met by the stern rebukings of disappointments, and checked by the disagreeable luggages of adversity and internal distortions. We need never expect the triumph of civil and religious liberty, unless it is attended with severe trials and perplexities. This, it is true, is the normal condition of man, but he has been in an abnormal condition so long, that his replacement will call for no small degree of patience, accompanied with the mightiest demonstrations of effort. Let us then learn to trust God, rely upon him and the resources of our own actions, and in so doing we shall gain the day.

Mr. Thomas Cross, who was so badly injured by an assault made upon him at the festival, to which I referred some two weeks ago, has very nearly recovered.[56]

The Senate confirmed or ratified the treaty with Liberia a few days ago.

This treaty was drawn up some months ago, but a certain clause which it contained, guaranteeing to every Liberian citizen an equal protection in all parts of the United States, as are given to the most favored nations of the earth, somewhat staggered the Senate, for they could not see how they could grant this, as long as slavery existed in the union as a local institution. But President Benson would agree to no other terms, even if no treaty at all was made; so our Senate finally complied.[57]

This hesitating upon the part of the Senate, did not arise from

---

56. Turner may be referring to a column published in the January 17, 1862, edition of the *Recorder*. This column is no longer extant.

57. A treaty promoting commerce and navigation between the United States and Liberia was signed in London in October 1862, ratified by Congress on January 9, 1863, and proclaimed on March 18. Stephen Allen Benson (1816–65) was the second president of Liberia, serving from 1856 to 1864. Benson was born in Maryland but emigrated with his family to Liberia when he was a young child, in 1822.

a wish of non-compliance on their part, but from a fear it would be violated.

A large representation of the colored people have agreed to celebrate President Lincoln's Proclamation, Thursday, 29th inst. They propose to have orations, speeches, singing, &c.

They held a preliminary meeting in Israel Church, Thursday, 12th inst., when some white rowdies came proposing to break them up; they threw a few stones into the windows, which caused a mighty rush to the door; great droves left the church and ransacked every imaginable place, and had they been found, they never would have disturbed any one else, for the colored people would have laid them down as cool as ice. . . .[58]

H.M.T.

Washington, Jan. 17th, 1863.

## "Washington Correspondence"
(*The Christian Recorder*, January 31, 1863)

Mr. Editor:—Since the hard rains have commenced in our city it has transformed its streets into mud and slop of the most disagreeable kind. Some of the most popular streets look as though a person might swim up and down them much more easily than walk them.[59]

Congress for several days has been considering the financial state of the government; the national expenditures are so large, and such a vast quantity of soldiers and other officers have gone for months without receiving their pay, that it is a desire on the part of several congressmen to remedy the evil.

A bill providing for the equipment of 150,000 colored soldiers was introduced in the House a few days ago, but was laid over for

---

58. Several paragraphs of church business are omitted.
59. Washington streets were not paved until the 1870s.

future consideration; I judge it will come up in a few days, when the policy of the government in that relation will be clearly defined. The various speculations concerning negro regiments, and negro fighting capacity, are too numerous to detail. I was informed yesterday, however, that five cavalry regiments were contemplated to be raised, and experimented upon with the Indians, and if they proved a success, then lead them against the rebels; others wish to dismiss them, and let them return to hewing wood and drawing water. I am very doubtful whether the negro could display his bravery as well against his co-sufferer, as he could against his enemy. Poor Indian, thy suffering and torture could not be portrayed in letters of blood; thou hast been my fellow in miserableness, and would have been a slave if thy ferocious nature had not made thee dreaded. And thou hast cherished no special hatred against my race; thy scalping knife and tomahawk were not shaped nor moulded to injure us, and when thou hast used it against my people, it was because thou didst misunderstand the relation they held to thy inveterate foes. Like us, thou hast been scattered and peeled, and you are fast marching down the road to extinction, and soon, I fear, will no longer be numbered among the races of the earth. Therefore, O Indian, how could I slay thee; how could I cut thy throat, or put the dagger to thy heart? I think this would make up some of the feelings of the colored regiments when led on the battle-field against the Indians.

But turn their faces South and let the Star Spangled Banner flaunt in the breeze, lettered in semi-circular form, LIBERTY TO ALL MEN, AND RIGHT OF FRANCHISE, and if they cannot read it, have it read for them, and I will guarantee without any of their Indian experimentalities, that the negro will engrave his bravery so deep in the rock of history, that the most corroding elements of time will never efface it; let me front my enemy and then demand my courage. I could not fight Weaver as I could Bennet, for Weaver is my co-laborer, but Bennett is my seven-headed and ten-horned *anti*-laborer.[60] Let those who have been crushing our vitals out meet us in battle array, and we will not ask for a Bunker Hill, nor listen to the story of Yorktown: instead, the military glory of Camden shall be eclipsed, and the star of Cambridge shall set forever. Admiral Foot may deny us the lineage of Hannibal, or dispute the color of Scipio, but some Tom, Dick, or Harry will be shot forth from the crater of emergency that shall gild the path and laurel the crown of negro sagacity and bravery.

The ladies of Israel Church, consisting of Mrs. Francis Hughes, President; Fanny Lee, Cassandra Dent, Hannah Patent, Catherine Hutchinson, Mary Thomas, Rebecca Moore, Anna Brown, Eliza Ann Turner, Emeline Hillory, Anna Tunion, Marsalene Woodland, as table holders, and their assistants, too numerous to mention, gave a splendid fair in the basement of said church during the Christmas holidays, and made $500. I do not recollect what each table took in, but as I can remember, it ranged as follows:

| | |
|---|---|
| Thos. Cephas, at the door, | $127 |
| Eliza A. Turner, | $75 |
| Cassandra Dent, | $66 |
| Fanny Lee, | $53 |
| Hannah Patent, | $46 |

This is all I recollect at present, but all did remarkably well, and several ladies who assisted the regular table holders deserve as much credit as those who held tables; for it would be very difficult to tell, in many instances, to whom the most honor is due, for both table holders and assistants worked manfully. This enables the trustees to pay nearly $1,500 on the improvements of said church, in the space of seven months, exclusive of the church's contingent

---

60. Elisha Weaver was the editor of the *Recorder;* John Gordon Bennett, the editor of the *New York Herald*.

expenses and steward's demands, &c., leaving only $100 on the improvements. The pastor of said church, however, is trying to get them under another obligation, by making some additional improvements which he much desires to see before he leaves them, for he believes that with an engineer at their head, they can and will do any thing tending to the good of the church.

Benjamin Newton, an old venerable class leader for many years in said church, is supposed to be near death's door.[61] He has been sick for several months, and does not appear to be recovering.

Andrew B. Finney lost one of his daughters this evening: she died with the small pox. I judge her about sixteen, and she was an amiable young lady.

Rev. H. M. Turner lectured in Alexandria on Friday evening, 23d inst. The audience was large and intelligent, and from all appearances were pleased, as they kept up such a time at laughing and smiling, though the lecturer did not come up to my desires.

The colored people are contemplating a grand demonstration on Thursday next. I hope the report from it will be glorious; let the world see that we are not lost to all sense of appreciation, having our tongues cut loose, that we can speak, and that we will speak, let the consequence be what it may. I find that there are a great many of our people, though freedom has been proclaimed in the district, who are yet afraid to speak above a whisper. That old servile fear still twirls itself around the heart strings and fills with terror the entire soul at a white man's frown. Just let him say stop, and every fibre is palsied, and this will be the case till they all die. True, some

---

61. One of John Wesley's founding principles for the Methodist Church was that members would form small groups, called "classes," of no more than twelve members who would meet regularly to discuss matters of faith. See Clarence E. Walker, *A Rock in a Weary Land: The African Methodist Episcopal Church during the Civil War and Reconstruction* (Baton Rouge and London: Louisiana State University Press, 1982), 6.

possessing a higher degree of bravery may be killed or most horribly mutilated for their intrepidity, but should this be the case, the white man's foot-kissing party will be to blame for it. *As long as negroes will be negroes* (as we are called) *we may be negroes.* But when we unanimously strike for our God-given rights, the power that fetters us will give way. If we had had one half of the Indian spunk, to-day slavery would have been among the things of the past.

    H.M.T.
    Washington, Jan. 24th, 1863.

## *"Washington Correspondence"*
(*The Christian Recorder,* February 14, 1863)

Mr. Editor:—Quietness has gained the day in our city. The newspapers are trying ever and anon to excite the minds of the people, by heading their telegrams with large letters, and falsely coloring the matter therein contained, but it is no use, they cannot succeed in raising an excitement.

The Army of the Potomac is still resting in the mud, or snuffing up the ashes of Virginia pine-knots, and are likely there to sit as long as the weather continues so inclement.

Vicksburg is still the rebel stronghold, and from all appearance will remain so, unless a new order of things occurs. General Banks is still knocking around New Orleans, and from his own indiscretion and hasty decisions in many points, would be as glad to leave there as creditably as he went, &c., &c.[62]

The bill for the enlistment of colored soldiers has passed the House by a large majority; some exceptions are being made at the

---

62. Vicksburg, Mississippi, would not fall until July 4, 1863. Gen. Nathaniel P. Banks (1816–94) was granted his commission due to his political achievements rather than any military experience or schooling.

idea of the colored officers not being privileged to command white soldiers. But I think that is one of the best features in it. I only wish it had been so provided, that no intermingling would have been allowed at all. I still hope that it will be so arranged, that no brigade, corps, or command will be permitted to intermit, unless in a case of special necessity, for unless this is done, there will be a hot time among themselves, for some prejudicial sap-headed soldier will be apt to endeavor to throw some contumelious epithets at the nigger as the Irishman says, and then the nigger will let thunder slip at him. Even if this did not occur, whatever honor we might be entitled to, would be conferred upon some one else, and the negro set down as a coward. No, sir! If we do go in the field, let us have our own soldiers, captains, colonels, and generals, and then an entire separation from soldiers of every other color, and then bid us strike for our liberty, and if we deserve any merit it will stand out beyond contradiction, and if we deserve none, why then brand us with the stigmatic infamy of cowardly dupes as long as there is a skull upon our shoulders. The more I look at the order of Providence in this war, the more admirably does God in mercy appear in all the events of human affairs. How adverse to the conception of man, he helmed the destinies of this nation. If many, yea, if millions could have had their choice, the Bull Run battle never would have been a defeat. General McClellan never would have left the suburbs of Richmond when he was within bell-ring of that traitor-concocting rendezvous, where the forces met in council to defy the armies of the living God, after failing nine times, the space which measures day and night; neither would General Frémont have been removed, nor Hunter recalled; General Butler, instead of sitting at New Orleans with an army much less than a Major General is entitled to, for so many months, would have been plenteously supplied with men, and ordered to take Mobile and sway the nation's scepter wherever he could track a traitor's bloody heel, and so would the hasty rapids of many have borne things along their current; but God in mysterious kindness has held the raging elements with a calmer hand, and with an occasional whisper to the heels over head party, *steady, steady, more slow and sure.* Of him it may truly be said, *omnium, elegantissime, loquitur.* And like the Psalmist, we shall be able to exclaim, "Thou art my Father, my God, and the rock of my salvation...." [63]

I believe Mr. T. E. Green, who is one of the most distinguished members of the Union Bethel Church, has gone on an errand of mercy through the North to solicit aid in behalf of the contrabands. *God grant him success.* I went the other day to their quarters, and the sights which presented themselves before me, would, if it had been possible, have made my skin crawl off my body. If a skinned ox feels as bad as I did, there is no fun in being skinned, I assure

---

63. The First Battle of Bull Run (July 21, 1861) was the first major battle of the Civil War, and was an unexpected rout of the Union by the Confederates. Gen. George B. McClellan became famous for inaction, failing to take Richmond in the Peninsular Campaign of spring 1862 despite superior numbers, training, and position. He was removed from command of the Army of the Potomac in November 1862. Gen. John C. Frémont, an abolitionist, issued an emancipation proclamation in the state of Missouri in September 1861, which was almost immediately rescinded by Lincoln. He was soon recalled from the Western theater and replaced by Gen. David Hunter, who later, as commander of the Department of the South, also issued an emancipation proclamation for the states of South Carolina, Georgia, and Florida in May 1862—which was also rescinded by Lincoln. Hunter was an advocate for arming blacks to fight for the Union, and formed one of the first black regiment, the 1st South Carolina (African Descent), whose members were later incorporated into the 1st South Carolina Volunteer Infantry. Gen. Benjamin Butler became an ardent abolitionist; his role in the Civil War is discussed in the introduction to Chapter Three.

Turner mixes Latin and Italian at the end of the paragraph; "omnium, elegantissime, loquitur" roughly translates to "all things, eloquently, speak for themselves." The biblical reference is to Ps. 89:26.

Discussion of the quarterly meeting of Israel Church is omitted.

you. But you ask, How is this? have not the people white and colored been supplying their wants? Yes, they have, but new contrabands are continually coming in, and old ones leaving; the old ones carry what they have, and the new ones bring nothing, so there is an endless want. Do you see the point?

Charles O. Moore, the newly appointed agent for the *Recorder*, is laboring for its further dissemination with all his manfulness; Mr. Moore is a class leader in the Israel Church, and peculiarly adapted to the extension of religious literature: possessing a wide-spread acquaintanceship among our people, as well as an indefatigableness in the work he is engaged in, makes him one of our best selections. He however regrets the unfortunate unappreciation which our people have for their own literature, which only enables him to sell one hundred copies of the *Recorder* per week, in a city where five hundred ought to be taken with the greatest eagerness.

He also labors equally as invincibly for the *Repository* and *Anglo African*.[64] Excuse the imperfections of this communication, for I have not time to look over it.

H.M.T.
Washington, February 7th, 1863.

## "Washington Correspondence"
(*The Christian Recorder*, February 21, 1863)

Mr. Editor:—I shall be compelled to give you the smallest correspondence this week that I have for some time, as every thing

---

64. The Indiana *Repository* and the *Anglo African* were two other major African American publications. for more on the *Repository*, see Chapter Two of Gardner, *Unexpected Places;* see John Ernest, *Liberation Historiography* (Chapel Hill: University of North Carolina Press 2004), 305–29 for an analysis of the *Anglo-African*.

is so dull in our city, and as stand-still-ness has gained such an ascendancy over the general hurly-burly-ness and activity which have hitherto characterized our thoroughfares and street commotion, that our news is scarce and valueless.

Congress is in session very late every day; the Senate appears to be so exuberantly engaged with the affairs of the nation, that in many instances it is difficult to get an adjournment till late at night. The Missouri question or bill has occupied the Senate longer, I believe, than any matter during the present session.[65]

Mr. Sumner has offered a bill in relation to colored soldiers, as a substitute for Mr. Stevens', which provides that all free-born volunteers of color who may enlist in the army shall receive the same, in every respect, as white soldiers; provided the number does not transcend a hundred thousand, and all freedmen who may enlist to be allowed $7.00 per month, &c. It is presumed the bill will go through like a flash of lightning. I think it will meet with a very favorable reception.[66]

A great many persons prefer Mr. Sumner's bill to the other, because it does not define the colored man's position in relation to

---

65. Because the Emancipation Proclamation only freed states in rebellion (Missouri had remained in the Union), it did not apply to Missouri. The bill Turner mentions would have provided compensation to slaveowners who freed their slaves; it did not pass. Slaves in Missouri would not be emancipated until the ratification of the Thirteenth Amendment in December 1865.

66. Senator Thaddeus Stevens's bill, proposed on January 12, 1863, required the immediate organization of black fighting regiments and was passed on February 2 (Ralph Korngold, *Thaddeus Stevens: A Being Darkly Wise and Rudely Great* [New York: Harcourt, Brace, 1955], 207–10). Sumner's bill for the Employment of Colored Troops, introduced on February 9, 1862, died in committee ("Employment of Colored Troops," in *The Works of Charles Sumner,* Vol. 7 [Boston: Lee and Shepard, 1880], 262–63).

those over whom he is to exercise jurisdiction. I hope none will become enraged at me if I express a different opinion; for I find that in too many instances our people are very little disposed to give idea for idea, word for word, and pen-work for pen-work in the discussion of their idealistic differences, but so soon as a man entertains a view dissimilar to theirs, they are ready to sneak around in every hole and corner, and vent their venom by puffing from their leather tongues such words as these, *He ought to be hung.* You will find them unable to meet an intelligent colored man in argument by giving reason for reason and thought for thought. Yet they will believe nothing he says, nor heed a particle of his advice, but sit with their heads down till he leaves, then to rise up and pour a flood of bitter invective upon him. Now, sir, that same class of our people will go out and meet an Irishman or a Dutchman who can neither read nor write, knows nothing of the country, knows but little more about the colored man's condition than a horse; and he will look up and say, *See here, you negroes better keep quiet,* else you will catch the devil. Down goes every nerve, and they are ready to poke their trembling heads in an auger-hole. Now, it's a pity, but I come in contact with this class of people, to some extent, everywhere I go. And until they take a tramp over Jordan, the uprising and successful distinction of our down-trodden race will be retarded. If Jesus Christ, our blessed all honored Redeemer, whom we are commanded to follow, had partaken of that hateful cowardice, God would have long since shot from the rugged clouds of his most fearful ire and heaven-scathing indignation his sin-treasured wrath, in such terrible volleys and fearful thunderbolts, that the place where the world's ecliptic swings would long since have been blotted from among the glories of the universe, and left a wreck to sink into a state of most disgraceful annihilation.

Now for the point. The reason why I prefer Stevens' bill to Mr. Sumner's is because one, I think, contemplates the colored armies being to themselves, while the other looks to an intermixture. This question, however, I have noticed in my last letter.

Mrs. William. Slade,[67] one of our most distinguished ladies, and one whose circumstances in life might, if she was not a solid-hearted lady, lead to an undue state of elation, informs me that there is quite a large proportion of sickness in the city. No one has a better chance of knowing than Mrs. Slade, as she is constantly among them, and her name will stand gilded in letters of immortality for her invalid sympathy and great-hearted benevolence, when the names of many, far better constituted and physically adapted, will allow their fastidious squeamishness to bury them in the lake of oblivion.

The S. S. C. Society[68] has appointed two agents for each ward, to hunt up the colored children, ascertain their condition, whether they go to day or Sabbath schools, whether freed or born free, the amount of taxable property, &c., and report to the body at a specific time. This is a judicious move, and highly commendable. I am sorry to inform you that the convention for the erection of a hospital has come to no decisive point. I was informed that a residentiary question had staggered its contemplated measures. But I think the indifference of the members to the call of the President, Mr. William Slade, has done it more harm than the question of residence, though I regard the entire residential question as foolishness, unless they are going to build the hospital, and generally such agitators give the least.

Rev. Mr. Turner desires me to state that he has seen his name in several papers in connection with Mr. Joseph E. Williams, as being one of a party who contemplated opening a recruiting office in this city for the enlistment of colored soldiers, and that he had contradicted the report through the same channel from whence it

---

67. This is possibly a reference to Katherine Slade, wife of William Slade, a member of the White House staff during Lincoln's presidency.
68. This is possibly the Sabbath-School Collection Society.

emanated. He wishes his friends to know, through the *Recorder* (if any have seen the report), that the idea of him leaving the ministry and engaging in the recruiting business had not yet entered his mind; but he is not opposed to the measure, and don't know what events may evolve.

There has been a protracted meeting going on at Israel Church for the last week. Much good has been done.

I believe the Rev. J. D. Brooks, pastor of the Zion Wesley Church, has had a protracted meeting going on at his church ever since last August—over six months. That's pushing the gospel car, indeed.

A marriage took place on Thursday evening, 13th inst., between Mr. John Lucas and Miss Adelaide D. Wallace. The nuptial party were among our most popular residents. The young Miss appeared on the floor so very attractive, that the preacher could not look in his book while reading the ceremony for viewing her.

I was walking down the Avenue a few days ago, and to my great surprise I saw several horses pulling a machine through the street, that appeared to be cutting up a dash. Such a winding and twisting I never saw before. After making some inquiries as to its business, I found it to be a street-sweeping machine. The longer we live the more we see. I told you in the commencement that I would be unusually short. So I must stop, if I would keep my promise.

Just as I had closed my letter, Mr. Joseph E. Williams came into my office, and informed me that he had just been told by one of the generals, high in command, that the recruiting offices for colored soldiers will be opened on and after the 4th of March, and if rumor is to be accredited, I am fearful that colored men this side of Mason and Dixon's line will stand but a poor chance in refusing to fight, whether they desire it or not, though I presume that's a hoax.

H.M.T.

Washington, Feb. 14, 1863.

## "Washington Correspondence"

(*The Christian Recorder*, March 7, 1863)[69]

Mr. Editor:—Washington is again the theater of life and stir—activity prevails, and every thing is operative. The streets are thronged with every species of mankind, from Indian women dressed in men's clothes, to any other color, shape, or size you may call for. Strangers are coming in from all quarters and flooding every hotel and restaurant that can be found.

Congress is in session night and day, and every gallery, lobby, and vestibule is unintermittingly crowded with spectators of every sex, hue, and caste. The Republican party, in view of the secession tincture that they fear will be so largely embodied in the next Congress, is pushing bill after bill through in rapid succession. They are fortifying the administration with money, men, and means sufficient to meet whatever exigency may occur in the unfolding emergencies of the future. This they are doing notwithstanding the incessant goat-bleats of such hydra-headed, blear-eyed copper-bellies as Voorhees of Indiana, and Cox and Vallandigham of Ohio, who do nothing but oppose the administration, and sing psalms to General McClellan.[70] It is well for them that death will hold them motionless: for if they were to torment their graves as they do Congress, they would have to vomit them up before Gabriel blows his horn. However, the old problem is, "give the devil his due," and I

---

69. The second "Washington Correspondence" column published in the February 21, 1863, issue is omitted as it mostly regards church business. Turner's column from the February 28, issue is also omitted, as the first half of the column is on the first sheet of the paper, which is no longer extant, and the rest has to do primarily with church business.

70. Daniel W. Voorhees (1827–97), Samuel Sullivan "Sunset" Cox (1824–99), and Clement Vallandigham (1820–71) were all Democratic congressmen from Union states affiliated with the anti-war Copperhead faction.

must say for Vallandigham that he is a good speaker, and if he had not perverted his moral nature so as to render himself a stench in the nostrils of mankind, his name might have stood emblazoned on the pages of history to the latest generation as a man for whom God and nature had done well. But as it is, his name will go down to posterity under the curse of a traitor, and the denunciations of all civilized nations. He will be known only to be hated.

I went to Congress on Wednesday to see the Conscript Bill pass, and every conceivable strategy was resorted to in order to have inserted *white male citizens,* instead of simply male citizens. The copperheads were so fearful that a negro would get a crack at a secesh, that it appeared they would have been willing to have voted their wives and daughters into the battle rather than allow a negro to take a part. But it was no use, the bill passed in its original form by over a two-third majority; and twelve border state members voted for it. I was glad, not so much from the fact that I considered the fighting trait the highest development in a man's constitution, but simply because our enemies desired to deprive us of what they conceived to be an honor. It is no honor to be fighting and quarrelling—it only shows how low down in the scale of moral depravity we are. It sets forth the brutality of our natures, the minimum of our Christianity, and how far the people are from God and that which is right. Christ said, "there shall be wars, and rumors of wars," &c., but its actualization does not result from a divine injunction. It is no predeterminate arrangement in the counsels of Heaven. The pugnacity of a man does not establish his greatness. But Christ foresaw that feuds would breed and fester, and that men's growing virulence would lead them on to dreadful collisions, out of which they should purgatorially emerge from their own throttled and ruptured combats, with lessons experimentally learned, which should gradually advance them to a higher degree of conception of their rights and wrongs.

Colonel Dart, a very brave officer, who has fought through every battle in which the Army of the Potomac has been engaged, has been authorized by the Secretary of War to enlist colored men (he says). He showed me one of his muster rolls yesterday, which reads as follows:

COL. DART'S MUSTER ROLL.

We, the undersigned, do volunteer our services and enlist into the service of the United States as soldiers, to be governed by the rules and regulations to govern colored soldiers, to be commanded by Col. Alfred Dart.

February 23d, 1863.

| NAME. | RESIDENCE. |
|---|---|

I also saw a recommendation given by Hon. Simon Cameron, ex-Secretary of War, to Governor Joseph E. Williams, of Central American notoriety, to Mr. Stanton, present Secretary of War, which stated that he (Cameron) had known Mr. Williams from boyhood, and that he (Williams) was a trustworthy man, and in every way fitted to commence the work of enlistment with the colored people, &c., &c. I suppose that Mr. Williams has before this gone to see the Secretary of War, but I don't know with what success he has met.

Rev. W. A. Hughes, a minister of the A.M.E. Church, who could not easily be too highly panegyrized, and John Crew, Esq., of Baltimore City, are to debate a heavy question before the Israel Lyceum, on next Monday evening. Rev. Mr. Hughes, though 56 years of age, is as expert upon his feet, and as sanguine for knowledge, as a man at twenty. If some of our bull heads, claiming to be young ministers, were half as anxious for information as Rev. Hughes, who is old enough to be the father of many of them, they would find something to talk about, instead of blabbing out such consummate foolishness.

And this leads me to notice an article in the *Recorder*, issued February 21st, under the head of *An Educated Ministry*, by Rev. George T. Watkins, of Baltimore—or I might have said, Article No. 3. I need not comment upon the merits of the article, or refer to the finished calibre of its author. Suffice it to say that it is a deep-thoughted, well-digested, and properly-timed contribution to the aspiring ministry. And though it has been published in the *Recorder*, I wish to extract one paragraph for republication in this correspondence:

"He must possess, as a basic qualification, the ability to 'search the Scriptures,' to give attendance to reading. In order to fulfill this apostolic injunction, a man must certainly *know how to read*, and read, too, understandingly. I believe that God calls no man to expound the Scriptures who cannot read them. He may be moved by the Holy Ghost to *prepare himself* for the work, but not to perform it. Too many mistake the call to prepare for the call to preach. The time has come to speak plainly and boldly on this subject. I repeat what I have already remarked, that a man should be able to read the Scriptures correctly and understandingly, or he is no more than a ministerial caricature, and his so called preaching a ridiculous comedy. He may say many very excellent things while in the pulpit, so can a parrot. The one is as much called to instruct as the other."

This does not embody the half nor the quarter of what is of invaluable worth in the article of Rev. Mr. Watkins, but it may be inexpedient to intrude further.

Your very accomplished Brooklyn correspondent, who is, by the way, no ordinary writer, is receiving great applause in this city from the religious and benevolent part of our people, from the bold and intrepid manner that he attacks the useless expenditures of money and means in New York, to *demonstrate*, when there are so many contrabands in our city, dying at the rate of ten and fifteen per day, with the small-pox and other diseases, from the bare facts that their wants and necessities are unprovided for. Would to God that some of those eloquent gentlemen whose speeches, as reported in the *Anglo-African*, tower sky high, would lend a few of their glowing orations to the cause of suffering humanity....[71]

I saw a gentleman (colored) from New Orleans to-day, who says that our churches are open. Rev. Brother Doughty is presiding over the church so long under the pastoral charge of Rev. John M. Brown and Dr. Revels. Reverends Miles, Vance, and Campbell are all well, and still claim to be African Methodists; and though the grass had grown up around our church doors (they were shut up in 1858), it now exhibited a very different aspect. The colored people were holding great union meetings, and were really ruling the city. I presume that some of our Conferences will send a minister down there as soon as they meet. The present ministers there are non-itinerant by virtue of their long inactivity. That is my decision. I don't know how Bishop Payne would accept it.

H.M.T.

Washington, D.C., Feb. 28th, 1863.

## *"Washington Correspondence"*

(*The Christian Recorder*, April 18, 1863)[72]

---

71. A synopsis of an article written by Reverend James A. Handy for the *Repository*, and several paragraphs of church news, are omitted.
72. The "Washington Correspondence" columns for March 14, 1863; March 21, 1863; March 28, 1863; and April 11, 1863, are all omitted. The column from April 11 describes a debate staged at the Israel Lyceum,

Mr. Editor:—A skeptic once in reply to an interrogatory relative to what numerically constituted the Godhead, said: "There are in the Godhead and Godbody, *i.e.* in the imperishable mansions of Father-God and mother-nature, all the persons that were ever developed on the earth, or any star in the firmament. All men, all spirits, all angels, all archangels, cherubs and seraphs, which people the immeasurable spheres of life and animation, for we live and move and have our being in the divine existence whose body nature is, and God the soul."

It requires no mental effort to see that the above is an attempted refutation of the fundamental doctrine of God's tripersonality, which we as protestant believers regard as being so lucidly set forth in the guide book of inspiration. But we will not cavil over or make a higgledypiggledy of all that is objectionable in its different clauses, for a vein of glaring heterodoxy, and attestations backed up by no scriptural responses, miserably contaminates every sentence, yet if considered abstractly, some philosophical truths might be gleaned in its declarative assumptions, but because it is the product of one who disputes the triuneness of God, and would dare to nullify his essential attributes, that part which is worthy is resolved into a caricature of such abominable absurdities, that whatever part may bear the semblance of truth, is embezzled of its reality by virtue of its bad company.

The way that the order of things is in this world, a little corruption, however minute it may be, out-magnifies purity a hundred per centum, wherever there is an effort to combine them. A man may seemingly possess the highest Christian attainments, even to a large share of the seven graces, which is the most lofty point he can reach in this life, and yet the discovery of one moral taint will blur all of his other excellencies. A minister may declaim the truths of

---

which may be of interest to those studying the development of African American oratory.

the Bible, and hang them out before the eyes of his audience in such glowing colors, or paint them by the gift of oratory so picturesquely, that none could offer a conscientious objection to the subject thus delineated; but if he should, through some mental or moral freak, endeavor to theologize a point which is presumed not to have divine sanction, the crown which his anxious admirers built in their enraptured estimation, falls from his brow, and his masterly labors are left a wreck to float and sink in their inexorable disgust. Says a certain medical writer, "In most instances, a particle of small pox, too small to be detected by the most improved microscopes, inflames and prostrates the strongest constitutions that can be found." One thing is certain, truth and error have no connection, good and bad no unity, friendship and hatred no alliance. No man can love and hate you at the same time. "Ye cannot serve God and mammon."[73]

Now there are certain big men (as we sometimes say) who would run down our throats great regard for the negro race, at the same time are known by all who want to know it, to be an open enemy of our people. If a man tries to hang me, and God in his mercy thwarts his plans, and I should by chance meet him in the street next day, and he should say, "Well, my friend, how are you to-day? I am glad to see you! I have always been a friend to you, and hold you close to my heart now. Why have you not been round to call on my family? My wife thinks you are the finest gentleman that ever lived," &c. Would any sane man listen to him, unless he had shown some grounds of repentance, or confessed that he was mistaken in the person? I think not. If he did, however, the next attempt he made for his life ought to be a success.

This class of big men to which I have referred are men whose pro-slavery principles are notorious, whose moral natures are corrupted, whose love for the colored man corresponds to the love that the colored man has for his dog, horse, or hog, whose principles, if

---

73. Matt. 6:24.

established as politically advocated, would have resulted in converting North America into a theater of the most abject and deplorable vampirism, so far as the interest of the negro was concerned, of any place that God ever frowned upon. And now as they have seen that all their efforts have been abortive, that slavery is doomed, that the proclamation is in force, and that they are so dead politically, and soon were to be dead so naturally, that it is questionable whether a thousand toots from Gabriel's trumpet would toot up a resurrection or not, they are beginning to turn with anxious concern and tearful eyes to the *poor colored friends*.

And I am sorry to learn that in some cases their miserable sophistry has been effectual; that the poor colored friends (God knows they are so in a certain sense of the word) have concluded that Mr. Lincoln is laying a plan to kill them off. The bandy shank copperheads wrote, spoke, and voted against the negroes being armed, as long as there was a place found to vote in, and as they could not succeed, they are going about preying upon the weak minds of our people, telling them, "Don't you go to war; if you do, you are dead men; for I know the plan of old Abe and his Generals, that it is to get the poor colored men into the war, place them in the front of the battle, so as to kill them all off." But I cannot at this time enumerate their endless quantity of different shaped and colored lies.

But the point I wish to get at is this: if a man would make you a slave, which is really making you a brute, he is entitled to no hearing or confidence from you. He may say something like the skeptic, philosophically true, but what is his reason for saying it? The devil sometimes tries the truth, but he always tells it to make you believe a lie. These pro-slavery advocates may point out the prejudice that exists against the colored man, and comment upon it very truthfully, but with what view? Only to keep you down. But I have been too long on this subject. I must notice it again. . . .[74]

---

74. Several paragraphs of church news are omitted.

A great Mass Meeting is to be held in Israel Church next Thursday evening to endorse the action of Bishop Payne in securing the Wilberforce University. Similar meetings will be held in all the churches. The 15th Street Presbyterian Church has tendered their suffrages, for which God Almighty bless them. A Washingtonian waxed so enthusiastic on the subject in conversation about it that he exclaimed, *supernumerate* every Bishop, and *locate* every preacher who will not support the measure.

 H.M.T.
 Washington, April 14th, 1863.

Chapter Two

# Petersburg

(June 25, 1864–December 17, 1864)

TURNER WAS APPOINTED CHAPLAIN of the 1st U.S.C.T. in the fall of 1863, and joined his regiment on November 15. However, he was soon sidelined by several serious illnesses, including smallpox, which prevented him from accompanying them to the Virginia front until the spring of 1864. He was clearly missed by the soldiers: in the April 9, 1864, issue of the *Recorder*, correspondent Thomas Hinton wrote, "We hear that Rev. H. M. Turner is coming soon. I hope it is true. The chaplain lives in the hearts of his countrymen here, I can tell you. Some one is asking about him every day."

Turner resumed his chaplaincy—and almost immediately after, his correspondence with the *Recorder*—in late May 1864. He witnessed his first battle at Wilson's Landing, Virginia, on the twenty-fourth of that month. The 1st U.S.C.T did Turner proud on this occasion, defying predictions made by both Northern and Southern whites that black troops would quail in the face of battle. "The coolness and cheerfulness of the men, the precision with which they shot, and the vast number of rebels they unmercifully slaughtered, won for them the highest regard of both the General and his staff, and every white soldier that was on the field," he wrote. From Wilson's Landing, the 1st U.S.C.T proceeded to Petersburg, where they faced Confederate troops at the Second Battle of Petersburg (June 15–18) and settled into a protracted siege. Turner clearly found it difficult to describe the scenes of battle. On a practical level, it was extremely difficult to collect one's thoughts—or even find pencil and paper—on the battlefield. In his July 9, 1864 column describing the 1st U.S.C.T.'s assault on Petersburg, he commented wryly, "A man thinks very little about the niceties of literature when bombs and balls are flying around his head." But he also had difficulty describing the magnitude of the carnage he witnessed. In the same column, he wrote, "Nothing less than the pen of horror could begin to describe the terrific roar and dying yells of that awful yet masterly charge and daring feat."

Turner, perhaps fortuitously, was sent to Washington during the summer of 1864 and missed the momentous Battle of the Crater (July 30, 1864). In this battle, Union forces successfully blew a hole through Confederate defenses by detonating nearly 4,000 tons of explosives under the front lines, creating a large crater over 30 feet deep and 100 feet around. However, after this successful maneuver, miscommunication and a lack of training resulted in white troops being sent into the crater, at which point they were fired upon by will by the Confederate troops who surrounded it. Black troops were sent in afterwards. A humiliating number of casualties were suffered by the Union, and heated reprisals were subsequently issued by members of both white and black regiments. Black Quarter-master Sergeant James H. Payne, of the 27th U.S.C.T., wrote that the black troops "drove the enemy from their breastworks, and took possession of the blown-up fort; but while they did all, the white soldiers lay in their pits, and did nothing to support our men in the struggle: they lay as though there was nothing for them to do. . . .

How easily Petersburg could have been taken . . . had the white soldiers and their commanders done their duty! But prejudices against colored troops prevented them."[1] Despite the heavy losses suffered in the catastrophe, however, black soldiers throughout the Petersburg campaign had demonstrated their courage and their willingness to die for their country. Sgt. John Hance, for example, wrote that black soldiers' actions in these battles "have proved to the world that we are men. Soldiers, not slaves!"[2]

*The Recorder* during this period, it should be noted, exists only in tatters: the front pages of both the July 2, 1864 issue (following the Second Battle of Petersburg on June 15) and the August 13, 1864, issue (following the July 30 Battle of the Crater) are no longer extant. These issues were likely "read to pieces" by subscribers; the absence of these pages from the historical record, while frustrating, can also be read as a marker of the *Recorder*'s historical importance in the African American community, especially in the North.

The Siege of Petersburg would continue for another eight months. Gen. Robert E. Lee finally ceded Petersburg and nearby Richmond, the capital of the Confederacy, immediately before he surrendered at Appomattox Courthouse on April 9, 1865. As for Turner, once the siege began, he turned his attention to less martial concerns—in particular, cultivating literacy among the black troops, instilling Christian values and practices in the community, mediating between black and white soldiers on both sides, and instructing the *Recorder*'s readership on how they could best help in the war effort. Turner's account of these nonmilitary activities

---

1. James H. Payne, "Army Correspondence," *The Christian Recorder*, August 20, 1864.
2. "Letter from Sergeant Hance, 4th U.S.C.T.," *The Christian Recorder*, August 20, 1864.

provides a window onto the Civil War often passed over by Civil War historians: the fact that battles occupied only a small portion of the wartime experience.

* * *

## "*From Chaplain Turner*"
(*The Christian Recorder*, June 25, 1864)

Headquarters 1st United States Colored Troops
City Point, James River, Va.,
June 13th, 1864.

Mr. Editor:—Having a few spare moments, I embrace this opportunity of communicating to you a few events connected with my work since I last saw you. Having been absent from my regiment for nearly three months, by reason of a severe attack of the small pox, I left your city (Philadelphia) on the evening of the 10th of May. Stopping but a short time at home (in Washington) and taking leave of my family, the 12th of May found me in my department at Fort Monroe, Va., where I recorded my name as present for duty from a leave of thirty days. Here being informed that my regiment was at Wilson's Landing, some eighty miles up the James river, I went to Portsmouth, Va., remained there a few days, and then left for my regiment. My arrival, among both the officers and privates, seemed to be a source of much joy. Indeed, so flattering was my reception, in some instances, that I could hardly recognize its sincerity, until the assurances were so implicitly evidenced that the indulgence of further incredulity would have partaken of the meanest ingratitude. Things, however, moved on very quickly until the 24th ult., on which occasion I was retiring from dinner, feeling very jolly over the idea of having eaten quite heartily once more of a fat chicken, &c., which is generally something special in

Fig. 2. Black soldiers, Ordnance Wharf, City Point, Virginia, 1864. United States Army Military History Institute.

camp, when my attention was called to the front of our works by a mighty rushing to arms, and shouts that the rebels were coming. I immediately joined the proclaiming host and bellowed out (I reckon in fearful tones), "The rebels! the rebels! the rebels are coming!" At this period the long roll began to tell that doleful tale that she never tells unless the enemy is about to invade our quarters. Then commenced another rush to arms, fearful in its aspect. Notwithstanding many were at dinner, down fell the plates, knives, forks, and cups, and a few moments were only required to find every man, sick or well, drawn into line of battle to dispute the advance of twice, if not thrice, their number of rebels. Captains Borden and Rich, of the 1st U.S. Colored Troops, with their gallant companies, were at some distance in front, skirmishing with the advance guard of the rebels. And here permit me to say, that this skirmish was the grandest sight I ever beheld. I acknowledge my incapacity to describe it, and thus pass on. By the time our pickets had been driven in, a flag of truce was seen waving in the distance, when General Wild gave orders to cease firing. Lieutenant-Colonel Wright was immediately dispatched to meet it, and found it to be a peremptory demand from General Fitzhugh Lee, for the unconditional surrender of the place, with the promise that we should, upon such compliance, be treated as prisoners of war; but upon a refusal, we would have to abide by the consequences, assuring us, at the same time, that he intended to take us for he could and would do it.[3] General Wild told him to try it. In fifteen minutes rebel balls were flying like hail all around our heads; but gallantly was the compliment returned. It would be contraband to tell you our force on that occasion. But this much I must tell you, that the 1st Regiment of the United States Colored Troops, with a very small exception, did all the fighting. I am also sorry that it is inexpedient to give you a full description of that terrific battle, which

---

3. Edward Augustus Wild (1825–91) served in the Crimean War as a medical officer before enlisting in the Union Army at the outbreak of the Civil War. An ardent abolitionist, Wild actively recruited African Americans for the Union and commanded the brigade that came to be known as "Wild's African Brigade" (55th Massachusetts Infantry and 2nd and 3rd North Carolina Colored Volunteers).

Elias Wright (1830–1901) was commissioned as a second lieutenant in Company G, 4th New Jersey Volunteer Infantry, in 1861, and rose to the rank of brigadier general in January 1865.

Fitzhugh Lee (1835–1905) was the nephew of Robert E. Lee; while he achieved the rank of brigadier general during the Civil War, he would attain greater prominence after the war, first as governor of the state of Virginia (1885–90) and then, as a diplomat and military governor in Cuba during and after the Spanish-American War (1898–1900). Fitzhugh's offer to treat the black soldiers as prisoners of war implies that the soldiers would not be executed or returned to slavery, fates common to black troops taken by the Confederacy during the war.

lasted several hours; but the coolness and cheerfulness of the men, the precision with which they shot, and the vast number of rebels they unmercifully slaughtered, won for them the highest regard of both the General and his staff, and every white soldier that was on the field. And the universal expression among the white soldiers was, *That it is a burning shame for the government to keep those men out of their full pay.*[4] Indeed, many of the white soldiers of the battery actually cursed and swore about the government not paying the colored troops their full pay. And I would here remark, and I do not care if Congress and the entire administration see the remark, *that unless the colored troops get their full pay very soon, I tremble with fear for the issue of things.* The tardiness of Congress in this matter has been watched by the colored soldiers with an undying eagerness, and every paper is ransacked with a view to their pay. But God grant that the evil may be speedily remedied, is all I will now say.

Resuming the battle question, allow me to say that the rebels were handsomely whipped. They fled before our men, carrying away a large number of their dead, and leaving a great many on the field for us to bury. They declared our regiment were sharpshooters. Our loss, considering the terribleness of the conflict, was almost incredibly small.

From that place, we went to Fort Powhatton, a few days after which we came here, and will remain here till we receive marching orders. A few days ago, we went in front of Petersburg, [and] our regiment even went under the guns of the rebels and laid down

---

4. The colored troops were paid only seven dollars per month, in contrast to white Union soldiers, who were paid thirteen. As a result, many black soldiers refused to accept any pay at all out of protest—boycotting their salaries until they received "full pay" (Edwin S. Redkey, A *Grand Army of Black Men: Letters from African-American Soldiers in the U.S. Army 1861-1865* [Cambridge: Cambridge University Press, 1992], 3).

while their bombs were flying over our heads. We would have gone in the city had we been permitted; but we accomplished all we were sent to do, and then we returned.

There are many things which I would like to speak of, but as I will have to defer some to another time, I will close by informing you that I have had the pleasure of becoming once more associated with my old friend and brother, Rev. William. H. Hunter,[5] chaplain of the 4th Regiment U. S. Colored Troops. And I do it the more freely, because when at the Baltimore Conference, which met in Washington D.C., and the General Conference which met in Philadelphia, I was almost hourly interrogated as to his whereabouts and literary silence. Chaplain Hunter has been with his regiment until the army arrived at this point, then he was detailed for the purpose of superintending contrabands, and is now the superintendent of all the contrabands in this department. I take pleasure in saying that the A.M.E. Church has, in the person of Chaplain Hunter, given a model chaplain to the army, and a noble representative. The same characteristic energy and administrative ability which always so eminently fitted him for his pastoral responsibility, now equally fits him for his present work. No better selection could have been made to see after the contrabands, than he. He can take a man from the very rubbish of slavery, and in a few hours infuse into him all the manhood and energy necessary for any purpose of life. His regiment, to a man, admire him. He goes into a hospital where every thing wears the drapery of gloom and sadness, and in a few minutes life sparkles upon every countenance. And he never falters to tell men their duty, from general officers down to privates. I predict for the chaplain a future reefed with laurels.

---

5. William H. Hunter (1831–1908), an A.M.E. minister from Baltimore, was appointed chaplain of the 4th U.S.C.T. and, according to some sources, was mustered into the army a month before Turner (Angell, *Bishop Henry McNeal Turner*, 53).

Before this shall have reached you, the probability is that we may have met the enemy in battle. Should it be the case, you need not fear the consequences, for our entire division has been under fire more than once.

General Hinks,[6] our noble division commander, has the utmost confidence in the valor of our troops, and will lead them on to victory as soon as he shall be permitted.

I have the honor to be, very respectfully,
    H. M. Turner
    Chaplain 1st U.S.C.T.

## *"A Very Important Letter from Chaplain Turner"*
(*The Christian Recorder*, July 9, 1864)

*Front of Petersburg, Va., June 30th, 1864.*

Mr. Editor:—As I promised in my last letter to give you a further account of our doings, I embrace this opportunity of complying with said promise. You will not look for any thing like rhetorical flourishes, I trust, nor even excellence in composition, as you will perceive by the heading of my letter that I am actually on the field of battle; and allow me to inform you, if you are not already aware, that a man thinks very little about the niceties of literature when bombs and balls are flying around his head, for if such a shower of iron hail as was falling an hour ago over and around our camp was in hearing distance of your editorial chair, I think your leaders would be few. I need not refer to this evening particularly, yet it was rather more severe than usual, but might, with incredulous

---

6. Edward Winslow Hinks (1830–94) commanded the 19th Regiment Massachusetts Volunteer Infantry before being assigned to command the 3rd Division of the 18th Corps of the U.S.C.T.

propriety, refer to every day in the week, and Sunday, too, for the last two weeks.

On the morning of the 15th inst., I awoke from sleep at a later hour than usual. We were then at City Point, Va., nine miles in our rear now. The sun was up, and everything seemed quiet and still, with the exception of awful cannonading and musketry which appeared to be about three or four miles distant towards Petersburg. This did not raise my curiosity, as it was a very ordinary thing; but, on looking out, I was much surprised to see our camp-tents, but no men in them. This natural query, however, was soon settled by being informed by Quartermaster-Sergeant Pollard that the regiment had moved that morning at three o'clock, and it was thought unnecessary to interrupt me at that hour. I soon learned that not only had my regiment moved but that the Fifth Massachusetts Colored Cavalry, which were encamped next to us, and all the batteries had done the same.

Shortly after the reception of this intelligence, I started in pursuit of my regiment. Several of the boys, who had for various reasons stayed behind, fell in and left with me, so that I soon found myself surrounded by a pretty strong guard. Thus traveling for about four miles, I found a house, to which several of the Fourth, Fifth, and Sixth United States Colored Troops were quartered, having been wounded; a few had also been killed. But seeing so few of the men of my regiment there, I went on to overtake them. A few paces, however, brought me to another house, which had been converted into an hospital. Chaplain Hunter found several of his men wounded (I omitted saying that Chaplain Hunter left camp with me, and accompanied me all the way); yet I still found but few of my men. Here I returned thanks to Heaven that so few in my regiment had suffered, and went on again. The cause was, that our men were on the left wing at the time the charge was made, and happily escaped the rebel grape and canister. The prosecution of my journey soon led me to where the first conflict had taken place. The rebels had a line of rifle-pits and embrasures thrown up across the road which led to Petersburg and intended to stop our headway if we attempted to pass; but the colored troops told the rebels that it was too early in the morning for such fun as that. Consequently, they charged upon the rebel works, took all their cannon (four pieces) and flayed the scoundrels as they would a set of mad dogs. Those of them who escaped the death-pills of our boys played a most successful game of skedaddling, many of whom won their life by it. My regiment then led the advance, and drove the rebels some five or six miles, keeping up a continual skirmish all the time.

Our gallant and official Colonel, John H. Holman,[7] having been placed in command of a brigade by General Hinks, the division commander, the duty of leading our regiment devolved upon Lieutenant-Colonel Elias Wright, whose military genius and strategic skill in maneuvering his regiment to save his men, and at the same time evincing the most surprising bravery himself, and inspiring his command with the same spirit, purchased for him a place in the affections of the regiment that I doubt whether time, circumstances, or events will ever obliterate. With this noble officer in front, our regiment followed the rebels in hot pursuit till they came in front of the five forts on the heights around Petersburg. These forts and fortifications were regarded impregnable by the rebels. Here my regiment, in the advance, and the rest of the colored troops, lay under the galling fire of the rebel forts and

---

7.  John H. Holman (1824–83) was commissioned as a second lieutenant in the Missouri Reserve Corps, and became one of the first white officers to be placed in charge of the U.S.C.T. He was promoted to brigadier general by President Johnson in 1865. Holman played a significant role in the settling of Roanoke Island, North Carolina, with newly freed slaves following the end of the Civil War, as related in Chapter Five.

sharp-shooters for nearly eight hours, part of which time I was with the advance skirmishers, and the only chance a man had for his life was to lie as flat on the ground as a leech upon his prey.

A shell would often burst in the midst of the ranks and sever arms and legs from the bodies of our brave soldiers with as much ease, apparently, as if they had dropped off themselves. Sometimes the rebel forts would be playing on us and over us in the front; and our artillery playing on us (not knowingly) in the rear. Several of our men were killed by our own shells that day. In this precarious predicament we had to gain foot by foot and inch by inch towards the rebel forts, till late in the afternoon, when Colonel Holman resolved that he would keep his men under fire no longer, unless it was to accomplish some end more than had been achieved for several hours. So he rode down the line of his brigade and told the men to get ready to take the forts, which was glorious news to the boys. A few moments only intervened before the bayonets were fixed, and away went Uncle Sam's sable sons across an old field nearly three-quarters of a mile wide, in the face of rebel grape and canister and the unbroken clatter of thousands of muskets. Nothing less than the pen of horror could begin to describe the terrific roar and dying yells of that awful yet masterly charge and daring feat.

The rebel balls would tear up the ground at times and create such a heavy dust in front of our charging army that they could scarcely see the forts for which they were making. But onward they went, through dust and every impediment, while they and the rebels were both crying out—"Fort Pillow."[8] This seems to be the battle-cry on both sides. But onward they went, waxing stronger

---

8. At the Battle of Fort Pillow (April 12, 1864), several hundred members of the U.S.C.T. were massacred in cold blood. The battle subsequently became a rallying cry for black troops.

and mightier ever time Fort Pillow was mentioned. Soon the boys were at the base of the Fort, climbing over abatis,[9] and jumping the deep ditches, ravines, &c. The last load fired by the rebel battery was a cartridge of powder, not having time to put the ball in, which flashed and did no injury.

The next place we saw the rebels was going out the rear of the forts with their coattails sticking straight out behind. Some few held up their hands and pleaded for mercy, but our boys thought that over Jordan would be the best place for them, and sent them there, with a very few exceptions.

Thus ended the great battle for that day, after driving the rebels six miles, taking their fortifications, killing many, and capturing five forts that were considered impregnable, all their cannons, wagons, ammunition, &c., &c.

It is my intention to send you a list of the killed and wounded as soon as I get time to prepare it, which I have not time to prepare now, as there is not a minute, from one week's end to the other, but what a gun is firing. Whether it be night or day, all you hear is bang! bang! either with muskets, cannons, mortars, or shells. I would remark, however, that the loss in our regiment amounts to one hundred and fifty-six killed and wounded, one hundred and forty-six soldiers and ten officers. I am sorry to mention that Orderly-Sergeant George W. Hatton[10] was shot through the leg near the knee. Sergeant Hatton was widely known for his usefulness

---

9. Abatis were defenses formed by felling trees and piling them on top of each other, with the branches facing toward the enemy.

10. Hatton was also a correspondent for the *Christian Recorder*. In a letter written from the hospital after he was wounded, he related his father's inability to attain a furlough for him that would allow him to return home to recover, even as a white man who had accompanied his father for the same purpose was successful in his request. Of this blatant act of discrimination, Hatton wrote,

in the Israel Lyceum in Washington, D.C. When he was shot, he fell and exclaimed to Brother Hunter, who was nearby, "Chaplain, I am shot, and am dying for my rights." But, thank God, he was not dying, though he thought so then. I wish I had time to mention dying expressions made by those who did die and those who thought they were dying. Some of the sentences were too sublime for earthly being to utter, and every one patriotic.

I must refer, however, to one man whose arm was blown off by a shell near his shoulder. In his helpless condition he begged another soldier to load his gun while he fired, and was only got off the field by persistent measures.

There is one thing, though, which is highly endorsed by an immense number of both white and colored people, which I am sternly opposed to, and that is the killing of all the rebel prisoners taken by our soldiers. True, the rebels have set the example, particularly in killing the colored soldiers; but it is a cruel one, and two cruel acts never make one humane act. Such a course of warfare is an outrage upon civilization and nominal Christianity. And inasmuch as it was presumed that we would carry out a brutal warfare, let us disappoint our malicious anticipators by showing the world that the higher sentiments not only prevail, but actually predominate.

---

> Such deception as that I thought was crucified at the battle of Fort Wagner; buried at Milliken's Bend; rose the third day, and descended into everlasting forgetfulness in the Appomattox River at the battle of Petersburg. Mr. Editor, when, oh! when can one of my color, and in my position, at this time, find a comforter? When will my people be a nation? I fear, never on the American soil; though we may crush this cursed rebellion." *The Christian Recorder,* July 16, 1864; republished in *Grand Army of Black Men,* 256–57.

After the war, Hatton led the St. Paul M.E. (Methodist Episcopal) Church in Paris, Kentucky.

Before closing I would say that the brilliant achievements of our boys in front of Petersburg was more than timed, and did more to conquer the prejudice of the Army of the Potomac than a thousand newspaper puffs. Providentially, the most of that immense army had to pass right by the forts taken by the colored soldiers. Every soldier with whom I came in contact had but little to say except to pay the most flattering compliments to the brave colored men of our division. After that the white and colored soldiers talked, laughed, and ate together with a friendly regard, not surpassing by any previous occasion. Let the Forts of Petersburg hereafter add new stars to the glorious constellation, which are glittering with untarnished brilliancy above the horizon. Let them stand a monument to his bravery, heroism, and daring. But I must now close this letter, it being entirely too long.

Mr. Editor, before closing, permit me to say that I have received a copy of the General Conference Minutes; and if I understand it, I have learned that no bishop is assigned to the work in California. I hope I am mistaken. But it appears that Brother Ward is to act as superintendent over that field. Please inform me if such is the case; for if it is, I shall certainly write out my opinion, regardless of friend or foe.

I have also read with pleasure that the General Conference proposed to present our regiment (1st U.S. Colored Troops) with one thousand Hymn Books. I must have the boys tune up their vocal organs preparatory to the presentation.

You will hear from us again very soon.

I have the honor to be, very respectfully,

    H. M. Turner

    Chaplain 1st U.S. Col'd Troops

## "Everybody Read This"
(*The Christian Recorder,* July 16, 1864)

*Headquarters, 1st U.S. Colored Troops,*
*In the field, front of Petersburg, Va.*
*July 4th, 1864.*

Mr. Editor:—I wish to inform the relatives and friends of the soldiers of this regiment, that they will confer a favor upon us by directing their letters to this regiment according to its established name; which name is, 1st Regiment, U.S. Colored Troops, or they may say, 1st U.S. Col. Troops, and not as some directs them, —U.S. Col. Troops, and several other directions which nobody can understand but themselves. And I will also embrace this opportunity of remarking that the friends and relations will confer another favor upon the regiment in answering all letters as speedily as possible, which are sent to them from the regiment. No one knows, in civil life, how much a soldier appreciates a letter from those whom he regards as near and dear to him. In many instances our soldiers will beg paper and ink enough to write some dearly beloved wife, brother, sister or friend who would apparently shake their hand off at home, and after receiving their letter, they are too contemptibly lazy to answer it. I know this from experience; for often when I am traveling, persons will say to me, Chaplain, tell such a one I received his two or three letters, and he must write again. They don't know that some of the letters sent to them cost a very big price, for many of the soldiers who can't write themselves have to pay others to do it for them. And sometimes, it is almost impossible for a soldier either to get paper, ink, pen, or pencil. Any wife that is a wife, or a friend that is a friend, or a relative that is a relative, should never think it is too much to write a soldier two, three, or four times, before getting an answer from him. For that very soldier probably can't get means to write with, as he may be on picket duty for forty-eight hours, where every moment demands the greatest vigilance to keep himself out of the way of sharp-shooters, or being detected by his own men, for sleeping on post is certain death. And by the time the soldier gets back to where he might possibly write a few words, he is so exhausted that without even eating, probably, he falls to sleep, and when he wakes, some thief, likely, has stolen his paper, ink and pens, or it has rained and destroyed all his paper, and thus he can't write after all; but I can not now enumerate half the obstacles labored under by a soldier. But this I do say—that all persons receiving letters from soldiers should answer them immediately, and if they care anything about the brave defenders of justice, right, and equality, they should write to their husbands, brothers, and sons without being written to first. I have seen soldiers go from day to day asking for letters, and on a continual answer in the negative, they would look so down-hearted, that I would feel sorry for them in my heart. I have seen others, after a long suspense, get a letter, and it seemed to have illuminated their very souls with joy. Let the friends of the soldier write to him, and if you know of those whereabouts of the regiment, write to him first, and then write again. And cheer him up, while lying from day to day under the ball and shell of your and his enemy, and do away with that lazy timber-headed sluggishness.

 A certain friend wrote to me a few days ago and sent me some envelopes, pens, and postage-stamps. I thought highly of the favor; if the example were adopted by the soldiers' friends generally, it would be a great blessing to both parties. I have the honor to be,

  H.M. Turner,
  Chaplain, 1st U.S. Colored Troops

## "Letter from Chaplain Turner"

(*The Christian Recorder*, August 27, 1864)

*Headquarters 1st U.S.C. Troops,*
*In the field near Point of Rocks, Aug. 14th 1864.*

Mr. Editor:—It has been some time since I have written any thing from this part of the country. This has been mainly owing to my absence from the army on extra duty. Having, however, returned for a few days, I was glad to see every thing have so cheerful and hopeful an aspect as were exhibited upon the countenances and seen in the general outgoings (whether spoken or acted) of the thousands here assembled for the defense of the nation.

Quietness, as a general thing, prevails throughout the army, with the exception of an occasional shell, which may be seen or heard spitting its venom through the air, or hurling its vengeance in shattered missiles over or in some camp, startling for the time the one nearest its approach, and making laughter for those who saw others dodge or squat behind some supposed breast-work or defense.

The most disagreeable feeling that we now experience is that which grows out of the protracted dryness of the weather, the intensity of the heat, the clouds of dust, which neither respect eyes nor clothes, and the swarms of flies, some of which, I learn, can draw their ration of vital wine through a fellow's coat, waistcoat, and shirt without any apparent encumbrance. If rebel flies are specimens of themselves, they are pretty rocky Johnnies.[11]

Nothing of much importance has taken place lately in our noble 3d Division 18th Army Corps, more than that we have another division commander. Colonel John H. Holman, who has been in

---

11. Johnnies, i.e., "Johnny Rebs."

command since the retirement of General Hinks, having taken sick and gone home, was soon succeeded by General Payne, who is, to all appearance, the man for the place.

I had the pleasure of conversing with him for some time, and found him to be very approachable, affable, and mannerly; perfectly unassuming and seemingly awake to every motion and gesture that a man might make.

He presents no great physiognomical wonders to the ordinary spectator, nor assumes a dictatorial majesty upon an introduction, but with eyes that sparkle with evidence of a superiority over mankind in common, you can see in him a mind highly intensified with the elements of an intellectuality, measuring credibility, if not completely with his arduous responsibilities.

I cannot speak of his philanthropy, and the principles of his humanitarianism; for hereafter I do not intend to call any man even a gentleman, in public print, until I have proved that fact sufficiently. I have been so often deceived on that point, that I think it is now time to think twice and speak once. I only grant that God may bless our commander, and grant him great success in all his efforts.

Last Tuesday, City Point was made the theatre of an awful carnage, by the tragic display of opposing elements. A boat loaded with ammunition, lying in the wharf through some stealthy artifice, took fire and exploded. My attention was first called to it some fifteen miles below the Point, on the James River, by a dense column of smoke, the base of which, in exciting grandeur, seemed to rest upon the bosom of the river—and in length stretching across both the river and its adjacent plains.

No one on the boat at the time appears to have known the cause, but speculations are rife. What interpretation to give it no one knows, so we comforted ourselves with supposition till we arrived near the point, where we saw thousands on the wharf and upon the hill, as well as the effects of some desolating sweep which seemed to have completely demolished the grandeur and effaced the beauty of this former site.

Many then supposed that General Grant was about to retreat and was destroying the place. In this state of heated curiosity we soon ran up to the wharf, and learned that an ordnance boat[12] had been blown up. To attempt a description of the frightful scene would be assuming to do what our ability would be inadequate for. But the long line of storehouses—many of which were blown to distant quarters—the immense quantity of guns, saddles, harness, wagons, tents, express and mail matter, and the terrible effects produced throughout the neighboring vicinity by the awful atmospheric concussion, is not to be compared with the loss of life which followed the august battle which matter had with nature.

A pile of dead men had been collected and placed on the hill, some of whom looked frightfully mangled, while pieces of human bodies lay in terrific profusion in every direction.

Some dear wife will anxiously await her husband's arrival; some father his son; some sister her brother, and so on, but they will never come. The place was crowded with people as is always the case, therefore they suffered irrespectively.

Before closing this letter, I must remark, in honor to certain friends, that it has been my privilege to visit Washington recently in connection with certain duties, which I was ordered to perform. It was my privilege to get several important articles for the benefit of our soldiers, besides bringing with me a large quantity of personal packages for several different regiments.

Without intentional disrespect to any person, however small and inconsiderable they may be, I will mention the name of Mrs. Henry Cover, who presented me on behalf of the Colored Ladies' Soldiers' Relief Association in Georgetown, D.C., $20 in money

---

12. An ordnance boat, i.e., a boat filled with ordnance, or artillery.

and several articles to be given or administered as the case may be, to such cases of necessity as might come under my personal observation. To say this was noble, would not be to use an epithet entirely inadequate. Let the act then speak for itself.

I take pleasure also in mentioning the name of Miss Laura Simms, who is better known as the agent for the *Recorder*, in Washington, D.C. She is a lady of splendid literary attainments, and an indefatigable advocate of educational development. She also presented me with eight or ten dollars' worth of literary matter, sundry in its nature.

There is another I would like to mention: he is a large, fat gentleman, but his name is beyond my recollection. Should his name come to my memory, I will mention it at some future time. He visits Israel Church. My thanks, however, to all parties on behalf of those who shall be benefited by them.

I have the honor to be,
Very respectfully,
H. M. Turner,
Chaplain 1st U.S.C. Troops

## *"Army Correspondence"*
(*The Christian Recorder*, September 3, 1864)

*Headquarters 1st U.S.C. Troops*
*Near Point of Rocks, Va.,*
*August 24th 1864.*

Mr. Editor:— There is not much of interest going on in our immediate portion of the army, but as I promised you to correspond for the RECORDER, I wish to keep good my word, or as much as I can, practically, in connection with my other duties; and yet it is not without some diffidence that I correspond at all, especially when I see from the articles recently published, that they are nearly all the productions of soldiers.

The ministers of the A.M.E. Church must either be asleep or absorbed in some deep mathematical problem, which has so engaged all their intellectual forces, that a few leisure moments can't be spared to write an occasional article for the benefit of your patrons.

The RECORDER has an extensive circulation amongst the colored troops in this department. Its approach is watched with the utmost vigilance, and when it makes its appearance, it is seized and read with eager avidity.

That portion of our divines who stay at home, could do incalculable amount of good by sending us through the open columns of the RECORDER a short sermon, occasionally. Unless our ministers come to the RECORDER's assistance, it will go down in the estimation of the better-informed class of readers. But they say the editor this, and the editor that.

But I say the editor has now more to do than any two men ought to do. He is the General Book Steward for the entire connection, having all the Conferences to visit,—more than any one of our bishops,—Minutes, Hymn-books, Disciplines, &c, to publish, revise and correct. Money or no money, this must be done, or else there is a whine and a growl through the whole church. The RECORDER must be published every week, and some able leader of editorial is looked for, and valuable productions abounding with the chasteness of grammar, rhetoric and logic—ever and anon darkened and lightened as the case may be with interspersed phrases of Latin, Greek, French and German.

I now ask. Is there a man in the connection who could do it without help? No, sir! He is not yet born.

Allowing this to be an established fact, let every minister in the

A.M.E. Church who has the ability, write something for the RE-CORDER, while the rest work pecuniarily.

If we had fifty young men in the ministry like R. H. Cain, B. T. Tanner and Henry J. Rhodes, the RECORDER would shine like the morning star.[13] Yes, its balmy dews would emit a flavor in this very army that would tell in the salvation of as many precious souls as any for whom Christ shed his blood. But there is a natural characteristic about our people, the issues of which are deplorably regretful. That is, unless there is some bone of contention at stake, it is next to impossible to arouse them. Since the days of the Bishop Nazrey controversy, there have been but few contributors, and now the bishop is gone.

The Canadian affairs are settled, Bishop Green's party having failed to be recognized and Clarke's mould having been filled with two additional bishops, I presume we need look for nothing of much consequence for some time, unless it be an occasional criticism, fault-finding, or a big-worded challenge from an awful empty stomach. But I hope this evil will be remedied by a plentiful supply of rich articles, coming flush from the pens of our ministers, on all subjects calculated to enlighten the mind, and Christianize the hearts, of our soldiers especially.

Nothing would be read more pleasantly and to more profit in this department, than a good, plain, yet practical gospel sermon.

---

13. Richard Harvey Cain (1825–87) was ordained an A.M.E. Church elder in 1862, and after the war, organized numerous churches in South Carolina, rose to bishop, was elected to Congress, and served as president of Paul Quinn College in Waco, Texas. Benjamin Tucker Tanner (1835–1923) was named Secretary of the A.M.E. General Conference and editor of the *Christian Recorder* in 1868, and became bishop of the A.M.E. Church in 1888. He was the father of the painter Henry Ossawa Tanner (1859–37). Henry J. Rhodes (d. 1873) served congregations in Pennsylvania but died before attaining the prominence achieved by Cain and Tanner.

Our regiment is once more favored with quarters where we can have some leisure hours from duty to spend in mutual benefit, such as drill practice, preaching, prayer meetings, choir-singing, reading, spelling, writing, &c.

Our inestimable Lieutenant Colonel Wright, having been promoted and taken from us to command the 10th U.S. Colored Troops, leaves with the warmest regards of all in this regiment. Men who are brave and noble-hearted never fail to climb the ladder of distinction and fame with rapidity.

This naturally involves the command of the regiment upon Major Perkins, as the colonel is absent, caused by sickness.

Major Perkins is a tall, spare-formed gentleman, with features quite prepossessing. He has neither constitutionally nor assumptionally any of those austere, haughty, tyrannizing qualities which are too often exhibited by men who are his inferiors. He has a voice mellowed by a sense of his high position. No effect is necessary to discover that he is kind, affable, easily approached and tender in his restrictions, though as a disciplinarian he never varies, but is positive, pointed, and ever to the purpose; possessing none of that sneaking treachery that would smile in your face one moment, and the next in some surreptitious manner tear your vitals out. May his life long be spared to command the brave troops of color.

We are surrounded here with a retinue of brave regiments. 1st, 4th, 6th, 10th and 22nd Regiments U.S. Colored Troops.

The Johnnies take good care not to come into these quarters, and it is well they do not, for they would certainly find very inclement times in this part of Old Virginia.

Most of the regiments, however, look much smaller, particularly my own. It often makes me feel sad when I remember how large and stalwart it once appeared, and how thin its ranks now appear to former days.

The canal—which is known as Butler's Canal, and which has

been in process of excavation for some weeks—is progressing finely; the rebels, though, harass the working parties occasionally by complimentarily saluting them with a few shot and shell, at such intervals as they may propose.[14]

The general in person visits the party almost daily, which is a source of great encouragement to those who are all the time perilling their lives.

We will close this communication, as the pickets are gone to fire in another direction; we have not heard them lately. It possibly may be the prelude to a great contest. Should it be, they will have a sweet job of it.

I have the honor to be,
Yours very respectfully,
H.M.T.

## *"Army Correspondence"*

(*The Christian Recorder*, September 17, 1864)

*Headquarters 1st U.S.C.T.,*
*Harrison Landing, Va.,*
*Sept. 10, 1864.*

Mr. Editor:—The news that continually pours in here from various quarters is commingled with every impassioned element in a human being.

---

14. General Butler's troops, with the assistance of African American laborers from the Roanoke Island Freedmen's Colony and members of the U.S.C.T, were building a canal at Dutch Gap, on the James River, that would allow Union boats to circumvent several Confederate fortifications. The canal was not completed until after the end of the war. Turner relates his visit to the canal under construction in his correspondence of Sept. 18, 1864.

The news of Farragut's triumphs at Mobile and Sherman at Atlanta[15] creates no small amount of fighting energy in this department. We can all realize the hopefulness of finally achieving the end for which we are battling, amid the privations and ills which we are necessarily subjected to in an army life. Every victory, like a new sunbeam, sheds its radiance in brighter aspects over the dark vortex of this raging strife.

The infamous catalogue of principles embodied in that infernal instrument called the Chicago platform,[16] the framers of which ought to every one be hung till dead by the neck, or shot till riddled like Napoleon's lion, has not affected the determined conclusion to strike down the last foe to the American flag, and her free institutions. Who would have thought that an American heart could have been so perverted at this stage of events, as to publicly endorse such audacious resolutions as those incarnate devils at Chicago formed as the basis of a Presidential campaign? They are enough to revolt human modesty, and turn our most pridish promptings into confusion and burning shame. Never let the American people, in all coming time, stand aghast at any thing again.

England's false neutrality, and the manifest treachery of France in making a cat's paw of the Austrian Prince, culminates at third-rate compared to the diabolical tories before whom Mr. Lincoln has bowed and honored with the highest positions. Had the President from the beginning administered the stern mandates of moral and political justice to the enemies of the country, who came as goats in sheep's clothing, until they were fostered and nourished

---

15. Rear Adm. David G. Farragut commanded federal forces in the Battle of Mobile Bay (August 5, 1864). Atlanta fell to Sherman on August 2, 1864.
16. The "Chicago platform" proposed by the Democratic Party and endorsed by its candidate, Gen. George McClellan, in 1864, established reunification as the "indispensable condition" of the war's outcome—implying that other conditions, such as the abolition of slavery, were negotiable.

into strength, the evil they are now perpetrating, and the injury they are doing the government in its efforts to crush the rebellion, would have been entirely obviated. But like the man who warmed and animated the frozen serpent, to only sting his children to death, and forever demolish the comforts of his household, had half the encouragement been tendered to the negro, which has been given to the Copperheads, the nation might have rallied to-day over two hundred thousand colored soldiers, who would have struck terror to the heart of the rebellion, and swept the seceded states with a tornado of desolation, such as would have silenced the clang of war, and hushed the rage of battle. But instead of this, the country's most inveterate enemies have been permitted to lounge upon the most comfortable seats, and plot and plan its ruin, only to leave a wreck where the eternal bastions of a free and happy Government should have stood, forever founded upon the rock of grandeur, glory, and honor.

True, the nation is passing through a terrible revolution: such a one as she doubtless needs to purge her from the dross of base corruption, and this seeming progression and retrogression to which she is, by force of circumstances, compelled to succumb, may all, in God's providence, be working for her good, but there is no law in nature, physical or intellectual, which may not require, as a means, some repulse to properly secure good results. Reverses, political and moral, may sometimes be commuted for glorious ends, but to conclude these channels of indispensable necessity, is to acknowledge the existence of the devil as important as the existence of God, in the scale of physical and moral elevation.

Some people have a kind of placid logic, that accounts in a very easy manner for every thing that transpires, and they work every thing up to be a part of the machinery infinitely designed to the accomplishment of some great good. But never will I believe, this side of eternity, that any thing reversive, or any thing contrary, ever was or ever will be used by infinite Wisdom, as an indispensable requisite for political or moral good.

The argument that Mr. Lincoln was obliged to court the affections of the Democratic parties, to secure the co-operation of the North, is nothing more than a farce. The principles which should have governed him were those of eternal justice; they were clearly laid down in the Bible, and engraved upon the tablets of nature; they were throbbed in every pulsation of the human heart, and preached by the proclamation of John C. Frémont, in the opening of the war.[17] And had these principles been his *modus operandi*, or his compass, to run the national ship by, amid the stormy winds and lurid siege of war, this opposition party would have sat in profound dumbness until the last foe had bitten the dust at his lordly feet. But instead thereof, they rise with indignant majesty before him, contemning, insulting, and trying to defame that name which should have been as dear to the American heart, as Washington to America, or Cromwell to England.

We will, in some future time, treat this subject more largely.

I presume your readers will be much surprised to hear of the intimacy which has recently taken place between the rebels and the colored soldiers.

Having for some time heard that the colored and rebel pickets were exchanging words, and that the venom to each other had somewhat ameliorated, I was led to doubt its truthfulness from a previous knowledge of the uncompromising hostility they had hitherto cherished toward each other. But a short time since, my regiment was ordered to the trenches, where their proximity to

---

17. John C. Frémont, made a general of the Union forces by Lincoln early in the war, issued a provocative proclamation August 1861 that declared martial law in Missouri and emancipated all slaves in that state. Lincoln, fearing that the proclamation would alienate conservatives in Washington, revoked the proclamation and removed him from command.

the rebels was not more than a hundred yards. Here, to my great surprise, I saw the rebels and the soldiers of my regiment, talking, laughing, exchanging papers, tin cups, tobacco, etc.

Some of the rebels deserted and came into our lines, and cursed the rebellion, and thus they had a jolly time with our boys.

I learn they are now acknowledging our soldiers as prisoners of war.

This sudden transition, though, should be carefully watched: there is evidently some deep-laid treachery at the bottom of so singular a move.

Colonel John H. Holman, of our regiment, who has been absent on sick leave to Boston, returned a short time ago, and such a shout never was heard, as the boys gave him: one unanimous ring reverberated through the adjacent woods and over the hills, which, I suppose, woke up the rebels; for next morning they made three charges upon our works, but were driven away without any trouble.

We are now at the famous Harrison's Landing, made so by General McClellan's inglorious retreat in 1862.[18]

There is nothing very significant about the place, more than some very fine houses, which are all deserted, and marks of its former greatness in the days when slavery was rampant in this vicinity, and men with immortal souls were chained, whipped, and driven like brutes before the prowess of Southern chivalry.

I have the honor to be,
    Very truly,
    H.M.T.

---

18. In the Seven Days Battles (June 25–July 1, 1862), Robert E. Lee drove Union forces, commanded by McClellan, to Harrison's Landing, on the James River, effectively ending the Peninsula Campaign.

## "Army Correspondence"

(*The Christian Recorder,* September 24, 1864)

Headquarters 1st U.S.C.T.,
Harrison's Landing, Va.,
Sept. 18, 1864.

Mr. Editor:—Harrison's Landing has been the theatre of wonderful transitions. Many are the relics yet extant, which give evidence to this fact.

The neighboring houses, though rid of all their furniture, bear an internal splendor of unexceptionable interest. Some of them are said to be two hundred years old, and were built of brick transported from England in the days of William IV, if my recollection of history be not at fault.[19] Some of them also bear marks of architectural grandeur which, though now considered ancient, will vie strongly in skillful genius with the most refined style of modern date.

The Goddess of Opulence seems to have lavished her most profane blessings upon the heads of the old slaveholding inhabitants of this place, until she was succeeded by the present god of the Democrats (General George B. McClellan), whose army, in 1862, greatly defamed its natural beauty and artificial attractions. But this great god of Democratic economy and frugal thriftiness endeavored, on his departure, to make due reparation for all the inadvertent defacements wrought by his comrades. To do so properly, he left government property to the supposed amount of $200,000, vast quantities of which were carried off by the rebel army, and the rest gathered by the neighboring inhabitants.

But, as I may refer to this subject again, we pass to notice a recent

---

19. King William IV was the third son of George III, serving as the king of England from 1830 to 1837. Turner is probably remembering King William III of Orange, who ascended to the throne during the "Glorious Revolution" of 1688 and reigned over England until his death in 1702.

visit made to Dutch Gap. Having a detachment from my regiment up there, I left this place a few days ago to visit them, and very singularly, just before I arrived at that place, the rebels, who are almost incessantly shelling the working party, ceased firing, which rendered the opportunity exceedingly favorable to inspect things in general.

The river, at this point, takes a bend southward, which continues four miles, then, curling around a high mound of earth, runs in the precise direction it did before it takes the first bend, thus forming a peninsula, the neck of which is not more than a hundred yards wide. Across this neck General Butler is trying to cut a canal sufficient to admit gunboats and monitors.

This canal has been in process of excavation for nearly seven weeks, and, taken from the water-line, is about eight-tenths complete. But there yet remains a depth of eighteen or twenty feet below the water-line to be excavated. That portion is, I learn, to be cut by mud-machines. Some time will yet be required to complete the work.

The workmen are constantly harassed by the explosion of rebel shells in their midst, which sometimes occasions fearful destruction among them. But a calmer and more jovial set of men cannot be found. Laughing, talking, singing, praying, clapping hands and dancing go on as though no foul foe were within a hundred miles. Five rebel batteries are visible on the right. Our pickets and the rebels' are within talking distance.

I neglected to say, that the entire working party is comprised of colored men. The rebels call them black Yankees, and they call the rebels gray-backs, rebs. Papers as well as words are exchanged.

Gunboats and monitors lie around the working party, looking as though they were charged with fearful vengeance. After remaining there twenty-four hours, I left for Deep Bottom, but had not more than got out of the place, than I heard the whiz of a shell, and looking behind me, saw the earth being terribly ploughed up by the dreadful explosion of a monster shell. Then commenced an awful duel between our forces and the rebels.

Arriving at Deep Bottom in the afternoon, the night was very agreeably spent with Chaplain Stevens and Tho[ma]s Chester, the very efficient colored correspondent of the *Philadelphia Press*.[20] I took a survey of the works, after visiting another detachment of my soldiers. I was informed that several colored soldiers of the Thirty-sixth United States Colored Troops had deserted from that post, only a few moments previous to my arrival, and had gone over to the rebels. Another soldier of the same regiment, in attempting to do the same thing, was caught and placed in custody. He was awaiting his doom, which I presume will be death. I can neither hear nor imagine the reason why these men desert to the rebels. Perhaps it is a mere wife-love, some of them having wives South to whom they feel much endeared, and not knowing any thing concerning their condition, it seems to prey upon their minds, until all fear, dread and manhood is lost. And thus they desert.

But the government is determined to shoot them as fast as detected in the attempt. This leads me to speak of three soldiers, with whom I conversed freely. They were laboring under much mental anguish on account of receiving intelligence that their wives at home had married or taken up with other men—the wives of two of them had remarried, and a third had absconded. My advice in the premises was asked, and I know of no answer which suited any feeling of indignation more than this, which I freely gave: *"Let them go to the devil!"*

Any cowardly civilian who would take advantage of a brave soldier's wife, on account of her poverty, owing to her husband receiving only seven dollars per month and the failure of the Government to pay him regularly, ought to have his rotten tongue pulled out by

---

20. The Reverend David Stevens was the chaplain of the 36th U.S.C.T. Thomas Chester's columns for the white-owned *Philadelphia Press* have been collected and published in *Thomas Morris Chester, Black Civil War Correspondent: His Dispatches from the Front*, ed. R. J. Blackett (Baton Rouge: Louisiana State University Press, 1989).

the roots, his throat cut, his heart burned, and his infamous carcass devoured by snakes.

I am very happy to inform you that there is quite a religious element in our regiment. Last Sabbath we had church three times, and nearly every night in the week we either have preaching or prayer meeting. We have partially organized a church, and our membership is rapidly increasing. I am often reminded of old Methodist churches when I hear the loud and hearty "Amens" coming up from scores of voices.

I have licensed one preacher in my regiment who is proving himself very useful. Besides, I have another very efficient local preacher from Washington City, who was formerly a member of my charge in that city. I have reference to Rev. John Hames. His usefulness is incalculable. Some of my brave soldiers wish baptism by immersion. Their wish shall be granted, God being my helper. I wish I could baptize the whole regiment, Colonel and all.

Having just received a letter from my wife, informing me of the death of one of my dear children, I will now close.

  Very truly,
  H.M.T.

## "A Letter to the Bishops of the A.M.E. Church and Superintendents of the Z.A.M.E. Churches"
(*The Christian Recorder*, October 1, 1864)

*Headquarters 1st U.S.C.T.,*
*Harrison's Landing, Va.,*
*September 21, 1864.*

*Bishops and Superintendents of the A.M.E. and Z.A.M.E. Churches:*
 I hope it will not be considered presumptive nor sacrilegious for a poor soldier upon the field of battle to solicit your grave attention a few moments.

I can form some theoretical idea, at least, of the multiplicity of your engagements. The heavy cares of the Church, the charge of the ministers, the weight of thousands of immortal souls, your individual and influential responsibilities to an infinite and just God, and the short time allotted for so much of its performance as will enable you to render a strict and rigid accountability to your Bishop of Bishops, are sufficiently expressive to inform me that your time is precious.

Should you think strange of my addressing the Bishops of both connections, when I only hold a very humble identity to one, I can offer no apology other than that I very happily learned that in the Convention held in the city of Philadelphia, which contemplated the consolidation of the two connections, very promising overtures were made by both sides, looking quite favorably to its effectual issue, and that the result of this Convention elicited such fraternal negotiations as formed the basis of a practical reciprocity of action, *restricted, of course, to Diocesan non-interference.*

I also learned that such action, *ex necessitate rei,* met the hearty cooperation of the Bishops; that all are looking for such a consolidation at the meeting of the next General Conferences, and that they pledged themselves not to wrangle nor preach a feudal gospel, south of Mason's and Dixon's Line, during the next four years, regardless of their imaginary technicalities. I say, with these things admitted, I claim the unquestionable right of addressing you all.

I presume you have heard of the recent victories of the Federal army and fleet before Atlanta, Georgia, and Mobile, Alabama; and in all probability, unless some checking disaster overtakes the Union arms, success will soon perch upon their banners, to the capturing of Mobile, Selma, and Montgomery, Ala., and Macon, Athens, and Augusta, Ga.

Should this be the case, in all these cities, there are flourishing colored churches of the Methodist Episcopal and Methodist Protestant faith, in all of which I have often tried to preach; and thus prompted by a knowledge of the aforesaid churches and many of their members and local preachers, I have felt it my duty to pen this epistle.

The point to which I wish particularly to call your attention is this: Several of the ministers of the Methodist Episcopal Church are chaplains in the army, and being very zealous for their Church, they lay hold of these colored churches with an eager impetuosity immediately upon their entrance into the captured city, and, I am informed, they have actually ordained elders and deacons out of some of the colored preachers found in said churches, for the purpose of securing their allegiances to the Methodist Episcopal Church, regardless of the qualification of such preachers to receive such orders, even admitting its loyalty.

This usurpation of power and church monopoly South, I think, should be most vigilantly watched by us, so far as the colored churches are concerned. I, for one, would be willing to concede to the Methodist Episcopal Church all the white Methodist Episcopal churches South, but not the colored; for colored soldiers too are fighting the battles of this country, and many of them are members of the churches over which you preside, and I think are justly entitled to some of the spoils. Besides, the Methodist Episcopal Church can advance no higher claims on the Methodist Episcopal Church South than you can; for it is a distinct organization, separated by a much wider territory in sentiment than we ever were. Throughout the state of Georgia you will find colored ministers of the Presbyterian, Baptist and Methodist Protestant faith, regularly ordained and installed pastors of churches (with some restrictions, of course), but not of the Methodist Episcopal Church South.

To suffer unauthorized parties to take possession of these churches and ordain any body, through an imaginary emergency, for the purpose of securing allegiance to their espoused faith, is, I think, an assumption which, I think, demands your attention, especially so when we have such a supply of able Bishops and active ministers.

I would not dare to outrage your superior judgment by questioning it so much as to suggest my idea of a remedy; for I am fully aware that the extent of power and the strength of your instrumentalities will be wisely considered and judiciously applied, if you take the same view of the matter as I have.

Having done what I intended, viz.: called your attention to my notion of an evil that might be nipped in the bud, I take pleasure in acknowledging myself

Your obedient servant,
HENRY M. TURNER
Chaplain 1st U.S.C.T.

## "Army Correspondence"

(*The Christian Recorder,* October 8, 1864)

*Headquarters U.S.C. Troops,*
*Harrison's Landing, Va.,*
*Sept. 25, 1864*

Mr. Editor:—The change of events which are so singularly and significantly revolutionizing other localities are not wanting in the place we now occupy. Two years ago, a torn, shattered, and demoralized army under General McClellan fled to this place for refuge, where the wrecks of his scattered and peeled forces are still visible to the spectator. But now the scene has changed; our regiment is here, with some other companies, holding this as a post well garrisoned by a brave set of Uncle Sam's sable sons, who have passed through the fiery ordeal more than once, and are found to be free from dross or gross materials, with a formidable fort, through whose embrasures several angry-looking howitzers and rifled cannons seem to be madly peeping for a reb; besides, a ten-gun man of war lies out upon the bosom of the James, ready at a moment's notice to spit her lurid vengeance into the flanks of any invading foe—accompanied by a small war tug, which pickets around and makes itself quite a busy body, especially by trying to pry into whatever rebel matters indicates an interference with us. It reminds me of what we frequently term a little fice dog, barking around at every thing it hears, until it gets the old, shaggy-headed bull-dog aroused, and there is a great fuss.

But this does not constitute one-half of our defenses. We are regularly fortifying ourselves as securely against the devil and his subalterns, or angels, as we are against the rebels. A glorious revival is going on in our regiments, and stronger appeals for mercy were never heard from human lips. We have preaching three times on every Sabbath, and most of the remaining intervals are consumed in prayer meetings, besides preaching or prayer meeting every night in the week. While I am now writing, brothers John Hames and Stephenson are pouring the words of eternal life into the ranks of the regiment, regardless of whom it may riddle asunder. During the entire night, mourners can be heard groaning and praying in every direction for God's pardoning grace; and, thank God, several have not mourned in vain, having found the pearl of great price.[21]

I must tell you a circumstance which lately occurred, which tried my faith to its very bottom: it is this. A short distance from our camp there is a graveyard, where the Harrison family is buried, as were several of McClellan's soldiers two years ago. It being a very beautiful grove, where there are several trees and green

---

21. Matt.13:45-46.

verdure, I pitched my quarters there, for the purpose of securing retirement and the shade, and also to have a good view of the passing boats,—concluding that the dead were very quiet company and not as apt to talk or interrupt one as the living. So every thing moved on very nicely, for I was lord of all I surveyed throughout the graveyard, night and day. A few nights ago, about 11 o'clock, while reading the *New York Independent*, I heard a conversation going on right among the graves. I stopped and listened, but still things seemed to talk on. As a natural consequence my curiosity was aroused, because I knew that no one had any right there but I and the dead, and it was not customary for the dead to talk in my part of the country. I got up, however, and went out to look around; and, in spite of all I could do, I thought my hair would turn to hog bristles, for it rose up, and pushed off my hat, as though every hair had eyes, and was trying to see what was the matter. But I asked God for faith, for I never felt more need of it, because the talking party, as I imagined, seemed to get more and more conversational. Lifting up my feet to see if I could walk, I found my legs exceedingly nimble, and judged I could have given a locomotive quite a race from that graveyard, and all others, if that were the way the dead were going to talk. But determined to see what was the matter, I set out to find my loquacious guest; and after blundering around some ten minutes, I found one of my soldiers near the iron railing of some graves, lying upon his face, pleading with God on behalf of his sinful soul. After feeling his head, body, feet, and pulse, to be certain it was a living person, I rose on my feet, and said (I do not know how it came out), but I know I said "AH THANK GOD," for it was a great relief, and I returned to my tent, cherishing my former conclusion that the dead don't talk.

Today I received a new order from the War Department, designating the Chaplain's uniform, which I will give verbatim:—

"General Orders, No. 217.
War Department,
Adjutant-General's Office,
Washington, D.C., August 25, 1864.

"The uniform for Chaplains in the army, prescribed in General Orders, No. 102, of November 25, 1861, is hereby re-published, with modifications, as follows:—

"Plain black frock coat, with standing collar, one row of nine black buttons on the breast, with 'herring bone,' with black braid, around the buttons and button holes.

"Plain black pantaloons.

"Black felt hat, or army forage cap, with a gold unbraided wreath in front, on black velvet ground, encircling the letters U.S. in silver, old English characters.

"On occasion of ceremony, a *chapeau de bras* may be worn.

"By order of the Secretary of War.

"E.D. TOWNSEND,

"Assistant Adjutant-General,

"(Official.)

"Chaplain 1st U.S. Col. Troops."

This uniform, prescribed by the Secretary of War, is fine enough for any man; indeed, it is too fine. Black cloth is the worst in the world for field service; a few rains and dusty rides will soil it more than five times the same amount of exposure will blue cloth—nor can one buy this suit (ready made) in any store, but must always have it made to order;—nor can he get such a suit, with the rest of the necessary attire, for less than one hundred and twenty-five dollars. If he have much marching to do, he will require four suits a year (or be an ashy-looking chaplain), which will cost annually five hundred dollars. That is pretty expensive dressing. Mr. Chaplain, though you will be very fine, the Secretary of War has ordered it, and you must be silent. Chaplains have now, I think, every thing they deserve. They have a special rank assigned them between a major and captain, two horses allowed them, and a fine uniform. Well done, good and faithful chaplain, enter thou into the labors of thy work!

I have often spoken concerning the white officers of my regiment, commending them when I thought they deserved it, but my soldiers have been referred to aggregately. I intend hereafter to call attention to some of my colored officers too, whose soldierly deportment and brave deeds of daring merit the widest circulation.

Probably there never was such an anxiety to learn to read and write as there is now in the colored regiments. I am called upon so much for spelling-books, and have to refuse because unable to comply, that it mortifies me exceedingly, especially when I know many second-hand spelling-books are lying about through the country, for which there is no use. I occasionally run off a few days and ransack all the benevolent institutions that can spare a book or primer, besides the thousands of papers, tracts, and periodicals which I weekly procure for those who can read, and the weekly packages of *Recorders* and *Anglo-Africans*. As soon as my return is known, my quarters are invaded by hundreds of soldiers, shouting over each other's heads, "Chaplain, for pity's sake, if you have a spelling-book, let me have one." "No," says another, "I am ahead of you." And thus rages the spelling-book clamor, until one or two hundred are eagerly grabbed and carried off. Then comes the cry from one or two hundred more, "When are you going to get more? When you do, save me one." "Yes, save me one, too." And a hundred or more cried out the same thing. Then follows the rush of those who can read—"A hymn book, a Testament, a Bible, if you please." *Christian Advocate, New York Independent, Boston Herald, Anti-Slavery Standard*, &c., come in a general cry from every direction, until several hundred are gone. But what we mostly need are spelling-books; as for reading matter, we can get the best the country affords very easily, and in great abundance.

I have the honor to be yours very truly,
H.M.T.

## "Army Correspondence"
(*The Christian Recorder,* December 17, 1864)

*Headquarters, 1st U.S.C.T., near Richmond, Nov. 28th, 1864.*

Mr. Editor:— It has been some time since I last penned any thing for your ever interesting columns. This failure is either attributable to indolence, or business. You may act as umpire in the case. It would be a contradiction of truth to say there were nothing here interesting to persons in civil life, yet there is nothing of that character which is generally pleasing to those who are always in anxious suspense to hear of great battles, but are never willing to take part in fighting them. It is a very easy thing to say, "Well done, brave soldier, bravely did you contest that ground, gallantly did you make that charge, and nobly did you die."

But when the clamorous parties are invited to shoulder a musket, and assist the noble enterprise, they shrink back horror-struck and stand appalled at the very idea. And should the uncompromising hand of stern draft seize him by the collar, which is generally relentless amid sighs and groans, a wailing cry is soon substituted for "Hurrah, hurrah, brave boys hurrah."

The *Recorder* is looked for weekly, as a precious visitor in this part of our noble army. It is dearly prized by many of our gallant soldiers, who, I am happy to say, are trying to prepare for whatever position the future may offer them: likely nothing could have inspired a more eager ambition into the men of my regiment, for literary attainments, than the vast number of *Recorder* and *Anglos* which weekly find their way into our different companies.

One very ordinary-looking fellow takes up the paper, and begins to lay open its columns and to throw a glare of interest, where, to the uneducated, all seems to be darkness and gloom, and a more stalwart and finer-looking fellow listens awhile, and becoming jealous at the idea, starts off in search of a spelling-book, saying to himself (as he fancies his superior abilities), "I won't listen to him. I am going to do my own reading," and away he wends himself from tent to tent, and from one place to another, until a spelling book is procured, regardless of price. All that is then necessary, is to watch him a few months, and you will see him blundering through a newspaper like a child learning to walk. You had as well loose him, and let him go then, for you may be sure he is gone.

But the most pleasing feature about the *Recorder* is its rapid progress, editorially and in all other respects calculated to enhance its value, and raise it to the standard of a first-rate paper. When it was first resurrected from its long entombed silence, it continued for some time to be the organ of pic-nics, fine suppers, Sabbath-school demonstrations, and other such trashy matter, as no well-informed person could be induced to appreciate. But the day of small things was not to be despised: with good reason and effort on its side, it ploughed through every seeming impossibility and has begun to demand a respect that none dare gainsay. I have lately read several articles with pleasure that the faulty ones could not mar. Theology, philosophy, science and all other questions connected with religious literature, are now treated or discussed with a surpassing masterliness.

I neglected to inform your many patrons of our narrow escape on the 28th ult., when our regiment charged upon the works before Richmond, and nearly 200 were either killed, wounded or captured, when our colonel and several other brave officers suffered by wounds, death and capture, when I rode among the rebel pickets, and made a narrow, but merciful escape, &c.[22] But, as it is too late to refer to it now in detail, I wish to say that the remaining portion are as eager for the fray again, as though no devastating hand had swept among their ranks.

Thousands of colored soldiers are here, standing, as it were, upon the very threshold of Richmond. In the distance several fine mansions can be seen towering high in the atmosphere, while broad acres of land lay silently to our front and rear, on which many of our armed colored heroes once labored, purchasing the most bitter execrations by the sweat of their brow, and were rewarded by the infamous lash, whose marks they are now carrying and will carry to the grave. They are anxious to winter in Richmond, and I have heard hundreds say, if General Butler will let them winter there, they would do it, or shake the doomed city to its very foundation. But as Dutch Gap is nearly finished, you may look out for startling news before long.

Having received a letter inquiring after Quartermaster Sergeant George H. Pollard, I avail myself of this opportunity of saying that this very efficient officer is here, and quite well. I take great pleasure in speaking of him, from the fact that his quietness amid the possession of such rare attainments is very remarkable. It is needless for me to say that he is a gentleman; all who know him can bear testimony to that fact. But his intellectual sagacity, and ready wit, blended with a fine English education, which fits him for any

---

22. Turner is referring to the Battle of Fair Oaks and Darbytown Road, October 27–28, 1864, where Maj. Gen. Benjamin Butler's forces were soundly repulsed by Confederate troops protecting Richmond. Over six hundred Union soldiers were taken prisoner.

suitable position that fortune may ever offer him, is a subject paramount in consideration to all others. There is not a man from the colonel down, but what places the highest importance upon his judgment, touching any point in the sphere of his duties, and many things disconnected with it.

I am looking forward to the day when he shall fill some office of trust with honor and distinction.

It would be rather difficult to say too much in favor of Orderly-Sergeant Henry Green, who is also both a gentleman and well-versed in military science: all that disqualifies him to command a company is the want of a commission. Its requirements are thoroughly understood, and his ability is unquestionably adequate to the task, yet both of these gentlemen hail from a hard part of the country: the former from Mobile, Ala., and the latter from New Orleans, La. Pardon the defects of this letter, as it was written at intervals.

    Very truly,
    H.M.T.

*Chapter Three*

# Fort Fisher

*(January 7, 1865–February 18, 1865)*

THIS GROUP OF ENTRIES, dating from January 7, 1865, to February 18, 1865, includes Turner's accounts of the First and Second Battles of Fort Fisher (December 23–27, 1864 and January 13–15, 1865, respectively), which the historian Rod Gragg describes as "an expedition riddled with controversy."[1] Fort Fisher, sometimes referred to as the "Gibraltar of the South" due to its formidable position at the mouth of the Cape Fear River in North Carolina, was a key Confederate stronghold protecting ships from the Union blockade. By taking the fort, the Union would effectively cut off one of the Confederacy's last remaining supply lines. Gen. Benjamin Butler proposed an unusual strategy for taking the fort: loading a barge with explosives that would then be detonated close to the fort offshore. Butler's naval counterpart, Rear Adm. David D. Porter, was skeptical of this plan; indeed, his skepticism was fueled by an active animus against Butler. As a result, some historians

---

1.  Rod Gragg, *Confederate Goliath: The Battle of Fort Fisher* (Baton Rouge: Louisiana State University Press, 1994), 97.

speculate that Porter ensured the failure of Butler's strategem by detonating the barge too far from Fort Fisher to do any damage.

On the night before Christmas Eve, witnesses as far away as Wilmington, fifteen miles north, and even Beaufort, some seventy miles up the coast, heard the explosion. The fort itself, however, was left unscathed.[2] Turner did not even note the explosion in his dispatches to the *Recorder*. The next day, under heavy naval bombardment, Butler sent his troops ashore to take the fort. Of this maneuver, Turner wrote, "This is the grandest day I ever witnessed; and, I think, this day's bombardment was never equalled upon an American shore. . . . I regard the sight as far transcending any I ever witnessed, or probably ever will, this side of eternity."

However, after hours of battle Butler inexplicably commanded a retreat. He later testified to a congressional committee tasked with investigating the failure of the expedition that Fort Fisher was impregnable, and that he decided to withdraw in order to prevent unnecessary casualties. The press, already convinced of Butler's ineffectual leadership after the catastrophic failure of the powder-boat gambit, ridiculed Butler's logic, and Grant took the opportunity to ask Lincoln to relieve Butler of command.[3] White troops cheered this decision. "We all believe Butler to be a rank traitor and a coward and everything but a gentleman," wrote one soldier.[4] Turner, however, echoed the sentiments of the black regiments who defended Butler: "Will the government see its wrong, and replace General Butler, and beg his pardon?" he wrote. "If they don't do it, some

---

2. See Gragg's description in *Confederate Goliath*, 52–53.
3. Shelby Foote argues that General Ulysses S. Grant, dissatisfied for some time with Butler's ineffectual leadership, took the opportunity of Butler's failure at Fort Fisher to request that Butler be relieved (Foote, *The Civil War: A Narrative, vol. 3, Red River to Appomattox* [New York: Random House, 1958], 739).
4. Qtd. in Gragg, *Confederate Goliath*, 104.

Fig. 3. The 1st Regiment U.S.C.T. at Petersburg. United States Army Military History Institute.

judgment will surely follow." The black troops' loyalty to Butler may have resulted more from his stalwart abolitionism and progressive racial attitudes than it did his military strategy; on his departure, he told them, "With the bayonet you have unlocked the iron-barred gates of prejudice, opening new fields of freedom, liberty and equality of right to yourselves and your race forever."[5]

Over the course of the two battles, Turner experienced firsthand the dangers of naval warfare. His fear of drowning at sea is expressed in nearly comical terms, though the seas surrounding Cape Hatteras, not far from the Bermuda Triangle, were admittedly treacherous. On December 20, a few days before the first Battle of Fisher took place, a ferocious storm blew in; Turner wrote, "many

---

5. Qtd. in Gragg, *Confederate Goliath*, 104.

of us gave up all hope. I lay down, and bade my mother, wife and children farewell . . . I begged the Lord to put me to sleep, and that if it was His will that the ship should be dashed to pieces, I should remain asleep and be spared the heartrending spectacle of nearly fifteen hundred men launched into eternity in one moment."[6] In these battles, even more than in the Battle of Wilson's Landing, he witnessed incredible bloodshed. After surveying the battlefield, he recalled that "dead bodies were lying, in desperate confusion, in every direction. In some places they were lying in piles and heaps." During and after the battles, he was put to work caring for wounded soldiers and burying the slain. In this work, he provided succor to both Union and Confederate wounded, and was surprised, he wrote, when "I found twice the number of rebels calling upon God for mercy to what I found among our own wounded soldiers."

The Union victory at the Second Battle of Fort Fisher led to the successful taking of Wilmington, North Carolina, the Confederacy's last open seaport, which was abandoned by Gen. Braxton Bragg on February 22, 1865.

\* \* \*

## *"Notes by the Way to Wilmington, N.C."*
(*The Christian Recorder*, January 7, 1865)

*Thursday, Dec. 8th, 1864.*
After marching hither and thither for several days and passing through the ordeal of the reorganization of the 10th and 18th Corps,

---

6. Turner harbored a hearty respect for the sea for the rest of his life; some twenty-five years later, he expressed similar sentiments about sea travel in his "Letters from Africa," an epistolary account of a visit to Liberia (Turner, *Respect Black*, 83–134).

into the 24th and 25th Corps,[7] we received, on yesterday evening, orders to prepare to move at a moment's notice. Tents were instantly struck, and every thing movable packed up for the contemplated journey. Shortly afterwards, we were informed that nothing besides one suit of clothing and five days' rations could be carried.

About 8 o'clock, we broke camp and moved off, in light marching order, amid a thousand speculations as to our destination. Thus marching for about three miles, we halted near General Butler's signal station, or Point of Rocks. Here we bivouacked for the night, but were occasionally interrupted (very pleasurably so) by the arrival of different regiments, which continued to cluster around us until nearly day this morning.

During the night the weather changed cooler, the water froze, the winds blew, and we shivered and clustered around campfires. Once in awhile the smoke got disagreeable, by rushing up our olfactories and making our eyes smart, which caused considerable sneezing, and moving from one side of the fire to the other, and cracking jokes over the smoke following the one who was the prettiest.

At the dawn of day the drums beat, and off we started. But instead of one regiment, there was a whole division on the move. Troops, for miles in length, were seen performing the war tramp, and moving in majestic procession. Whilst generals, colonels, and their respective staff were dashing in different directions to regulate their various commands, onward, however, the seried line proceeded, until we halted at Bermuda Hundred, where the James River teemed with transports of every size, dimension, and

---

7. On December 3, 1864, the 10th and 18th Corps were reorganized into the 24th, made up of white soldiers from the 10th and 18th, and the 25th, made up of black soldiers, placed under the command of Maj.-Gen. Godfrey Weitzel. Turner's 1st Regiment, U.S.C.T. was made part of the Third Brigade, commanded by Col. Elias Wright, of the Third Division of the 25th Corps, commanded by Brig. Gen. Charles J. Paine.

description. Our division stopped for some hours, in an old field fronting the wharf (1st Division, 25th Corps, but formerly 3d Division, 18th Corps), to give time for the embarkation of a white division which arrived before us. There we remained till late in the afternoon, when our turn for embarking on the transports arrived. The 4th U.S.C.T. then moved up to the wharf and commenced to go aboard, and other colored regiments in turn, and thus they continued to embark, until our whole division were stored away on the boats, to completely effect which required a very late hour. My regiment and the 37th U.S.C.T., having taken quarters on the *Hermon Livingston*, General Payne's headquarter's boat, we moved out in the center of the James River to rest for the night. Every one being very tired, we took our blankets and laid down any where to rest. Soon, silence prevailed, and all were asleep. But about 1 o'clock at night, this recuperating slumber was terribly broken by the cold bracing winds of the north, and such shivering and rattling of teeth I never heard. Fire was sought for in vain. Blankets sufficient to repel the cold were also sought in vain. But the night had to be disposed of in the best manner possible, which, I assure you, was very badly to all above either of the decks. The troops in the steerage fared much better, in consequence of the great number, which tended to keep each other warm.

*Friday, Dec. 9th.*

This morning we left Bermuda Hundred, came down the James River, and anchored off Fortress Monroe, in the Hampton Roads. The weather is exceedingly cold. The ship has no heating facilities. Everybody complains. Some of the soldiers frostbitten. We have all suffered severely to-day. I thought strongly of my comfortable home; but I am willing to suffer with my regiment, knowing that they have no more at stake than myself.

*Saturday, Dec. 10th.*

This morning found us still at anchor. General Payne goes ashore. The weather still very cold. The transport is disagreeably crowded, and we can hardly find room to turn around.

The only thing I have truly enjoyed, since I came aboard this boat, is the sumptuous meals which are cooked and served up so finely. This provision is only made for the officers, and none bears off more table incumbents than this dear brother. The soldiers have to prepare their own grub.

I must be careful and not let Rev. James Lynch know I am writing about grub, or he will send a gale of objugatory eloquence over here, and sweep ship and me all away. Brother Lynch cannot bear any one to write about good victuals. I know it is annoying to read about such things, when we are hungry and cannot get any, and I suspect it is rather dry times about Hilton Head, S.C.

This afternoon I asked permission and went ashore, and there saw Chaplain Asher of the 6th U.S.C.T. He says they have comfortable quarters on his boat, and I also learn from others on shore that all have better quarters than we. I returned to my ship late at night on a steam tug, in company with General Payne and several other officers. I had to hunt several hours to find it, in consequence of the dense fog. It is still cold, and the soldiers talk more about home than I ever heard them before.

*Sunday, Dec. 11th.*

Still at anchor; large fleet collected in Hampton Roads; boats of all sizes moving in every direction; weather still cold; wind very high; several soldiers complain of frost bites; I never felt more like resigning.

The curiosity to know of our destination has given rise to many speculations. Some say we are going to Savannah, Charleston, Hilton Head, Mobile, &c.; others say to the Shenandoah Valley, East

Tennessee, Harper's Ferry, &c. But no one knows, therefore we solace ourselves by the old adage, that "soldiers have no right to think, much less to know."

I went ashore again, and there saw Samuel Nichols, of Washington, D.C., by whom I sent a message to my wife.

Also, by permission of General Payne, I proceeded to visit Norfolk, where I arrived about dark, and spent the night with Rev. J. M. Brown. I found him enjoying good health and in fine spirits.

*Monday, Dec. 12th.*

This morning, I returned from Norfolk to Fortress Monroe. The wind being very severe, and the waves rolling very high, and our steamboat being very light, she was tossed about so recklessly that considerable apprehension was felt in behalf of our safety. The captain informed me that the boat was perfectly safe, and immediately turned to one of his crew and ordered him to prepare the lifeboats, which was a contradiction of the statement just made to me. We arrived safe at Fortress Monroe, and saw General Butler moving around in some haste, preparing the expedition for what may be a perilous adventure. Here I spent the day in chatting with different persons about the Fort, until near night, when I went aboard my boat in a yawl. Our boat is still lying at anchor at this place.

*Tuesday, Dec. 13th.*

This morning, when I awoke, I found our boat was in motion, and the whole fleet moving. But to our great surprise, instead of going South, we were running up the bay towards Washington. All day we continued to run up the Bay and Potomac River, so late in the afternoon, that the boys of the gallant 1st U.S.C.T. began to look cheerful and smile at each other, as they seemed to get in sight of Washington, D.C. Indeed, we came so near to the city, that I knew of no stopping place that high up, except Alexandria or Washington. I was so confident that I was to be at home in an hour or so, that I commenced to fit up and prepare for it.

Just as the regiment had got on the heel of excitement, and began to sing, "We are Going Home," the steamer *Baltic*, which was leading the fleet, turned square around in the middle of the Potomac and started right back from where she came; and the whole fleet followed her, and back we went.

This threw the privates and several officers into a hubbub. We were all disappointed except the generals, who understood the program, for such boat-whirling is seldom seen. As a revenge for not carrying us to Washington, officers and men all rushed to their respective quarters, determined, if possible, to dream into reality the pleasure which we expected on our arrival in the city.

The design of carrying the fleet up the Potomac River was, I suppose, a strategical feint. Next time they take me so near my wife and children, I hope they will take me a little farther.

*Wednesday, Dec. 14th.*

This morning, we halted and anchored somewhere in the mouth of the Chesapeake Bay; all in great suspense yet; no one knows our destination; twenty transports, loaded with troops, stand huddled together, far away from bottom or shore; bands are played; drums are beaten; songs are sung; cheers are given. About two hours before sundown, signals were given and off we started, bound around Cape Hatteras, the place so many dread.[8] The winds were calm, and we promised a safe trip.

---

8. The severe weather, strong currents, and the dangerous Diamond Shoals around Cape Hatteras led seamen to dub the area the "Graveyard of the Atlantic." The famous ironclad USS *Monitor* fell victim to these waters, sinking on December 31, 1862.

*Thursday, Dec. 15th.*

Those who were asleep awoke this morning and found our fleet about midway Cape Hatteras. Our boat was rocking delightfully. The sun rose in unclouded grandeur, and darted his luminous rays over the agitated Hatteras, while a host of ships, each looking like sea monsters walking in fabulous strength, ploughing their way through the trackless waters, while thousands of protruding heads were visible in the bosom of each.

About 2 o'clock to-day, a suspicious looking vessel was seen at a great distance, moving along with her sails flying to the winds. The captain said it looked like the rebel pirate *Tallahassee*.[9] Every spyglass was brought into requisition, and some considerable excitement prevailed. After some time, she disappeared to the joy of every one; for if she had got among our fleet, with our naval fleet ahead, she would have made terrible havoc with us.

*Friday, December 16th.*

Last night, the fleet all stopped off Wilmington, some twenty miles from land. We have had fine weather for two days. The ocean is perfectly smooth. Not being able to find anchorage, the vessels were compelled to float about.

The weather is very warm here. We have to pull off our surplus clothes. Water is getting scarce, and our fine tables are getting more common. There, I am writing about victuals again. Brother Lynch will not find me out. If he does, I am gone.

---

9. The Confederate cruiser C.S.S. *Tallahassee* captured and destroyed twenty-six vessels off the New England Coast in August 1864, and six more in November 1864. According to the historian Kevin Foster, the raids "thoroughly panicked Northern shipowners and coastal residents" (Foster, "Where They Lie: C.S.S. Tallahassee," *Confederate Naval Historical Society Newsletter*, no. 6 [February 1991]: 5).

*Saturday, December 17th.*

This morning found us in the same place. A large naval force appears near us, and stops. The weather is fine, but every body wants to land. We kill time by fishing, laughing, talking, &c.

*Sunday, December 18th.*

We still float in the same place. Every body wonders why we lie here; but no one, with the exception of General Butler and Admiral Porter, knows.

I counted more than thirty ships lying around us. To-day being Sabbath, I propose to preach for my regiment; but the officers request me to preach to them first. At the time appointed, I proceeded to do so; but disliking some misconduct exhibited by men whose character should be exemplary, I stopped immediately, without pronouncing the benediction, and left the place to hold service with my regiment. We had a glorious meeting. The cause of my stopping the services which I was conducting with the officers was not that I felt myself to be personally insulted, but because I considered their conduct very ungrateful to God.

I was amused this morning at a colored boy, who came to wait on the table. He was so much surprised at seeing me, a colored man, eating with white officers, that he did nothing but stand and look at me. I suppose that he never saw such a sight before.

At night the wind blew very hard. It was so warm, that we were unable to sleep. We sat on deck and killed time by telling long yarns.

*Monday, December 19th.*

This morning we were still at the old place, some twenty miles off Wilmington. The weather was smooth and calm. About ten o'clock, the wind commenced to blow, and increased in violence until late at night. The waters rolled in great torrents, and the ship was tossed as a mere bubble over the seemingly frightened billows of the great deep.

Last night being Sabbath evening, the officers of our regiment set a noble example to the others, by spurning to indulge in an exercise upon which God would frown in terrible vengeance.

I am proud of our officers in two respects—they will reverence the Sabbath, and honor divine service. Every body wanted to disembark. We were all tired of the ship, and wanted to see land once more.

I counted forty-two ships, to-day, lying around us. Our numbers seem to increase. I fear for the monitors to-night. The waters are very rough.

*Tuesday, December 20th.*
Still lying off Wilmington. Last night a heavy gale blew nearly all night. This morning the wind was quite moderate, but the waters were rough. A great many were seasick. The universal cry all day was, "We want to land." About ten o'clock to-day, I counted sixty-three vessels, some of which were monitors. To-day, I raised some excitement about my horse. I declare, he is ruined forever. The officers laughed at me, and one reproved me from the Bible, and told me, that I should be more composed, even if I had lost my life, much less my horse.

This afternoon a heavy northerly wind set in. About five o'clock, we received orders to put into Beaufort, N.C., for the purpose of getting coal and water. We are now, while I am writing, on our way there. The gale is terrible, and the ship seems to ride mountain high. I can only say, "Save, Lord, or we perish!"

*Wednesday, December 21st.*
This morning we came up to Beaufort, having had a considerable gale all night. Before the pilot-boat could convey us over the

bar and bring us into the harbor, the wind began to blow more terribly, until the waters became too rough for us to attempt to cross the bar, and so we were compelled to make for the sea, with our water and coal nearly exhausted, and not knowing how long the storm would last. We all felt very solemn and anxious in regard to our safety, besides the dreadful thought that if the vessel did not founder, perhaps we would have to endure the pangs of hunger, and be left, without steam-fuel, far out on the ocean's bosom. However, we then had only time to think of the ship, which was new, and had never before been in such a gale.

About twelve o'clock, the ocean was covered with white foam and rolling waves; but still the wind increased, and higher did the billows roll, until great mountains, towering, apparently, up to heaven, came dashing along, in sublime vengeance.

Our ship, to all appearance, would sink down to the very bottom, and then her bow would rise, pointing upwards to the sky, with her stern away down in the waters. She would then pitch, with a frightfulness that baffles all description.

Many, for awhile, tried to laugh and shake off their fears; but about eight o'clock, we all ceased laughing. I had been praying all the time, and I believe many others were. Now all began to feel serious and solemn. Even the crew looked and spoke apprehensively. Finally, an awful sea came, and broke in our wheelhouse. Still the raging waters and howling winds grew worse.

At last many of us gave up all hope. I lay down, and bade my mother, wife and children farewell, and, after asking God to protect them, and bring us together in heaven, to be separated no more, I begged the Lord to put me to sleep, and that if it was His will that the ship should be dashed to pieces, I should remain asleep and be spared the heartrending spectacle of nearly fifteen hundred men launched into eternity in one moment.

God answered my prayer. I went quietly to sleep; and when

I awoke, I found that the storm had subsided, and the ship was again on her way to Beaufort, where we are this morning (December 22d).

The whole fleet was in the storm. We have not yet heard of the casualties.

### "Notes by the Way to Wilmington, N.C. (continued)"
(*The Christian Recorder,* January 14, 1865)

*Thursday, December 22d.*

After passing through one of the most terrific storms yesterday ever witnessed by mortals, we this morning came into Beaufort, N.C., after casting anchor in the ship-harbor. I disembarked and went ashore, hoping to find Mr. Galloway, not knowing any one else, but he being in New Bern, N.C., and it being too late to get back aboard the ship, and it being very cold, I was taken by a gentleman to one Mr. Washington, where I was introduced as a stranger, desiring a place to stay all night. And after I was denied, upon the ground that they had no accommodations, I asked permission to sit by the fire during the night, as I did not want to lie in the street; but this privilege was denied me also. The gentleman then conducted me to an old sister's house, viz., Clara Fisher, who offered me all the comforts of her house, and soon prepared me a fine supper. After learning I was very dirty, and how long I had been deprived of clean clothing, she soon got me a clean suit, and washed and ironed mine, and next morning turned me out clean, for she had me to wash too. God bless Clara Fisher!

*Friday, December 23d.*

To-day has been spent by myself in looking about Beaufort and Moorehead City, and at the transports taking in coal and water. At night, I visited a school in Beaufort, where I found several young colored ladies and gentlemen, taught by the Rev. Mr. Lyman and several white ladies of the North. I was much pleased.

*Saturday, December 24th.*

To-day, about 2 o'clock, we put to sea, having replenished our coal, water and eatables. The soldiers all seem cheerful, and sing, and many hold prayer-meetings, and all things move off very pleasantly; they, almost to a man, express quite a desire to do something, as they say they are tired of doing nothing.

*Sunday, December 25th.*

This morning (Christmas), we found ourselves off Wilmington, N.C. The light of day made visible a large collection of vessels, both of the navy and transports, amounting, in all, to near a hundred. About 8 o'clock, General Butler came in the steamship *Bendeford*, by the fleet of transports, and gave orders to follow him. During this time, the immense naval fleet, with monitors, whose turrets were barely visible above the water, ironclads, which wore an impregnable aspect to every missile in rebel possession, and a large number of regular man-of-war and gun boats, began to move toward the shore and wind serpentinely around Fort Fisher, which protects the entrance to Wilmington, on the Cape Fear River. About 10 o'clock, the firing commenced from a procession of naval boats fully six miles long, including those which were shelling the water-batteries along the sea beach, to effect a landing for the infantry, when broad-side after broad-side was fired, until the reports became so continuous, that, in many instances, it was one unbroken roar, which seemed to be awful enough to shake the world. At times, shells would fall and burst in the rebel fort, as fast as one could wink his eye; and though the fort seemed to be lined with guns of the largest caliber, yet they could only shoot at intervals, in consequence of our incessant hail of iron and fire; and from that time till night did the lurid flame flash, and the grim roar mutter, while every thing trembled as if it were rocked in the cradle of consternation.

About 2 o'clock, the gunboats had effected a landing for the infantry about four miles above the Fort, and all the yawl boats were employed to land the troops, as the ships could not get within two hundred yards of the shore. These small boats were therefore sent ashore filled with soldiers, and on landing, salutes were given by broadsides from several ships, while the band played, "Hail, Columbia."[10] A few moments after their arrival on shore, a white flag was seen waving from a little mound, behind which was a rebel water-battery; at this sight, the two Divisions raised a shout of triumph, which was only excelled by the terrific roar of cannon. Our landed troops, seeing them, went to the place, where some thirty came out and surrendered. At this stage of events, our troops raised a more vociferous shout than ever. In about an hour from then, the rebels came in heavy force to stop the landing of our troops, but they were soon driven back. About dusk, General Butler gave orders for the troops to re-embark, for what reason I know not.

This is the grandest day I ever witnessed; and, I think, this day's bombardment was never equalled upon an American shore. To hear about six or seven hundred guns of immense caliber spitting forth their lurid thunder in an unbroken succession, while the frightful clamor was conveyed by water to distant shores, is an occurrence seldom and far between. I regard the sight as far transcending any I ever witnessed, or probably ever will, this side of eternity.

*Monday, December 26th.*
This morning exhibited several of our troops still on shore, having several prisoners captured last night. The atmosphere has been

---

10. "Hail, Columbia" was popular during the nineteenth century as an unofficial national anthem. It was composed in 1789 for the first inauguration of George Washington, with lyrics written in 1798.

very foggy all day—the attack has not been renewed on the Fort—so we spend the day in drifting about and looking at each other. At 10 o'clock, this morning, General Butler put to sea, and disappeared in the distance: we all wondered where he was going, but no one knew. The troops expressed great fear that he intended giving up the siege; as they were all eager to land and charge the fort, believing they could take it. They say they do not want to return without doing something.

*Tuesday, December 27th.*

This morning, we were still lying near the rebel Fort Fisher. Several gunboats had left during the night, leaving us, naturally, to infer that the expedition contemplated no further aggression. Shortly afterwards, our troops on shore began to re-embark, and all necessary preparation is being made to leave. Several soldiers and a few officers expressed considerable regret, as they do not wish to return without landing the infantry and charging the Fort; others seem delighted at the prospect of returning; while others say, they are here to obey orders, and do not care what they do, that they only have their time to put in, any how.

Shortly after 12 o'clock, we all put to sea, leaving for Fortress Monroe. During the day, one of the soldiers died, belonging to the 37th U.S.C.T. I was called upon to inter the body; which was done by sewing it in a large cloth, and tying a bag of stone-coal to his feet, and laying it on a plank, which, after the ceremony was ended, was slid overboard. The sight produced a solemn sensation in all. All due respect was paid to the occasion by every officer on board the ship, from the General to the humblest private. Many had never seen such an instance before, nor had the Chaplain ever attended on such an occasion.

*Wednesday, December 28th.*

After traveling all night, we found ourselves this morning off Cape Hatteras light-house. The weather was ordinarily warm, the wind was blowing severely, causing the ship to rock a little more than usual; but shortly after sunrise, however, it cleared off most beautifully, and the blue ocean presented all of those ravishing charms, which are so natural to an admirer of physical grandeur. In the afternoon, the weather changed, and a dense black cloud lowered over us, having the appearance of a harbinger of awful consequence; but it resulted only in darkening the sky, and passed away. Finally, Cape Henry light-house appeared in view, at which sight several rejoiced. Passing on, we soon anchored again in the harbor at Fortress Monroe. Here, the boys spent the entire night in singing, laughing, cheering, &c.

*Thursday, December 28th.*

Having anchored all night off Fortress Monroe, we received orders this morning, at daybreak, to proceed up James River to our old quarters, which we did more than willingly, the weather being much colder than any we had felt since we left this place. So up James River we came, passing several points made memorable in by-gone days, viz., Wilson's Landing, Fort Powhattan, Harrison's Landing, City Point, Bermuda Hundred, and stopped at Jones' Landing, where we disembarked, and several bid the ship adieu with a hope never to see it again. So after some difficulty with my horse in getting him ashore, I took passage on his back, and here I am.

## "Army Correspondence"

(*The Christian Recorder,* February 4, 1865)

*Headquarters 1st U.S.C.T.,*
*Between the sea beach and Cape Fear River, N.C.*

Mr. Editor:—The details of the capture of Fort Fisher I presume you have read long before this will reach you, for our mail facilities are so poor here, that my letter has been unnecessarily detained. On Sabbath afternoon, of the 13th inst. about 3 o'clock, we had so fortified ourselves in this place, that the General concluded he could venture to attack Fort Fisher, consequently two brigades of the white troops were marched down from before our works, which were thrown up to protect our rear, in case the rebels should come down the river side, and attempt to capture or bother us while we made a land attack upon the fort. I might here say that our naval fleet had been bombarding the fort nearly three days before the infantry had got in such a position as to carry the fort with safety. Notwithstanding my regiment was not engaged on the fort, yet it fell to my lot to accompany the attacking party, as I had been chosen by Surgeon Barnes (medical director) to act as his aide for the occasion, which was no easy job, considering the land was sandy, and no horses were to be had. Shortly after our forces were drawn up in front of the fort, I was ordered to the rear with a despatch, which prevented me from seeing the strategetical maneuvering of our commanders in preparing for the desperate contest. By the time I had returned, however, they had approached near enough to commence the attack, and with an awful yell and dauntless courage, they could be seen running over an open space, in all apparent fearlessness, intent upon capturing the strong works which then lay in full view to every soldier. But the rebels replied to the charge and yells of our boys with the most awful volleys of musketry, grape and canister, which mowed down our troops in fearful numbers. Yet our boys cut them down in heavy proportions.

And thus the contest raged from that time until about 10 o'clock at night, on our left, near the seashore. Finally, the marines and sailors came off the gunboats and war-ships and helped to charge the fort. They were cut down in frightful numbers. They fell so thick and with such destruction, that the marines at one time broke and fled; but the sailors stood their ground. Thus the sailors actually evinced more courage and bravery than the marines. The land forces on the left, however, in no instance, broke nor exhibited any cowardice, yet they were terribly slaughtered. Never had I seen grape and canister used so effectually as the rebels used it on our troops on this occasion. At one time I thought they could never stand it; neither do I believed they would have stood, but for the fact that they knew the black troops were in the rear, and if they (the white troops) failed, the colored troops would take the fort and claim the honor. Indeed, the white troops told the rebels that if they did not surrender they would let the negroes loose on them. But it was a noble sight to see our troops hanging on to the sides of the fort like so many leeches sticking to an afflicted man. Each embrasure was formed by high mounds of earth being thrown up on each side of the guns; and after our troops gained a foothold on the fort, each party would stick to those mounds, and fight around them. You would constantly see them, by twos and threes, fall off and roll to the bottom, and there lay weltering in their blood and gore, manifesting the greatest agony amid the death heaves which, too often, lasted but a few moments. One of the most singular things that ever occurred with me, was while I was going up to where they were fighting to help a wounded man, three balls in rapid succession came right by my left ear, which I thought was a warning to go back, and I turned immediately and ran to the rear, but not too soon to escape a load of grape, which would have swept me, in a moment's time, into eternity.

 I was not surprised to hear balls fly past my head, nor to hear bombs burst over me, but the three in succession, to pass my ear, somewhat startled me. This I regarded as a warning to move, and sure enough I just moved in time. However, the battle raged amid the terrific fire of deadly missiles until after dark, when I was so exhausted that I could no longer stand up, for I had been seeing after our killed and wounded up to that time. About this time I retired some distance from the scene of conflict, and lay down till about ten o'clock, when the news spread that Fort Fisher had surrendered. The guns then ceased firing, and a great shout rang through every camp, and every vessel sent up sky rockets, and illuminating lights were seen decorating every ship, while others were waved to and fro. The cry of victory! victory! was bellowed from thousands of lips. At this news I jumped up and went to survey the fort, and behold the results of our conquest.

And great was the scene. The fort had been ploughed by our shells until every thing looked like a heap of destruction. All the barracks had been burned to the ground, and dead bodies were lying, in desperate confusion, in every direction. In some places they were lying in piles and heaps. Several rebels had been utterly buried by our shells. Guns of the largest caliber had been broken to pieces, and their carriages swept from under them. The wounded were groaning and begging for assistance. The soldiers were ransacking every nook and corner in search of trophies and other memorials, such as tobacco, segars, clothes, pistols, &c. The surrendered rebels were standing in the center of the fort and speaking in audible tones of the bravery of the Yankee soldiers. Many seemed glad they were in our hands, while others seemed anxious to know if we were going to kill them. Yet we all talked and laughed so freely with the rebels, that they soon came to the conclusion that we would not kill them, and seemed quite well pleased after a short time.

After walking around in the fort for some time, viewing it by the light of the moon, I found myself shot at twice from some unknown corner. This led me to believe there were rebels still secreted in some undiscovered spot, whom we had not found. Others were similarly fired upon, but could not tell who had done it. So I left for camp, and told several to stay away, otherwise they would be blown up. Nothing disastrous, however, occurred that night. But at an early hour the next morning, my attention was attracted by an awful explosion, which I perceived had taken place toward the fort. The said earth was seen flying in great banks towards the very heavens, and the debris were spreading like monster wings, and the shafts of vengeance seemed to be flying from the mouth of an awful crater to the summit of the angry elements. The flames shot upwards with lurid tongues, forked prongs, and the clamor of an awful concussion. These were echoed by the surrounding water—which soon told every one that something was wrong. This threw every body in anxious suspense, and many speculations were indulged in. But a few minutes only intervened before the intelligence spread every where that one of the magazines had blown up. This circumstance cast a more serious gloom over our army than all the casualties which had happened on the previous day, and caused more oaths to be uttered than I ever before heard in the same length of time. Many were for killing all the rebel prisoners, while others were for blowing them up too, &c. I immediately started for the fort, to see for myself the dreadful scene of carnage. I found the news true. A magazine had exploded, and hundreds of our men were apparently the deadly victims of the misfortune. The whole fort was covered with the effects of the explosion, and parties were employed in excavating the vast numbers who had been blown up, and covered in the dirt.

I stood there till a row of dead men were dug up, and laid out side by side, each one bearing such frightful marks of the disaster, that I could no longer endure the sight. But the disasters of the previous days' battle, together with the explosion, caused dead men to lie around in all directions.

It fell to my lot to bury, with religious ceremony, many of our noble dead, which I did with a sensation not felt in any previous instance since I have been connected with the army. It would be impossible to describe what I witnessed among the wounded. But one thing I must mention as a fact. I found twice the number of rebels calling upon God for mercy to what I found among our own wounded soldiers. One rebel particularly, whom I passed, was saying in a most pathetic tone, "O, Lord God, have mercy on me! Please have tender compassion on one who is a sinner, and comfort me in this my hour of trial! O, Lord, have mercy on me this one time more." When I commenced talking with him, and he discovered I was a chaplain, his countenance seemed to be illuminated with joy. But the prayers that went up from the rebel wounded completely bought off my prejudice, and I rendered them every comfort in my power. Their doctors, who were permitted to attend to their own men, assured me, if I ever fell in their hands, I should have the best treatment possible.

On the south side of the fort, where the most of our shells had exploded, the earth was literally covered with iron, and every house within two squares of the fort that had not been consumed in the flames, was torn to pieces and entirely demolished, while the ground had been ploughed as with the shaft of destruction. Had the rebels not been protected by the strongest bomb proofs in the world, our shells would have torn them to atoms long before we reached the fort with infantry. But being protected as they were, we might shell for a month without injuring them; for the earth over them was fully twenty feet thick.

The rebels had some of the finest guns ever made; but our guns from the navy were so numerous, that they could never work them while we were shelling.

I asked several rebel officers if they killed the colored prisoners they took. They told me they did not. They also told me if they were free men from the North, or even from any slave state in our lines, they were treated as other Yankee prisoners are; but if they were slaves, whose owners were in the Confederate States, and such colored men could be identified, they were treated as house-burners and robbers.[11] And as for you, said they, you would get the same treatment as other Yankee officers.

---

11. Arson and burglary were capital offenses in many states until after the Civil War.

I learn General Butler has been removed, because he failed to land his troops and attack Fort Fisher on Christmas Day. The wisdom of General Butler, in that case, was admirable, because I have been told by quite a number of rebels, as well as by a large number of colored persons, that twelve or fifteen thousand rebels were here that day, and waiting for the Union troops to land, so as to capture the whole expedition. They all say if the Union forces had landed that day, not a man would have escaped. Besides that, when we landed and went back in the woods, we found tents enough—made of boards and brush—to hold at least ten thousand troops. A colored woman told me that the rebel soldiers were so thick that day, that they nearly smothered her waiting for our troops to land, but that they were not expecting us at this time. Will the Government see its wrong, and replace General Butler, and beg his pardon? If they don't do it, some judgment will surely follow. I believe the removal of General Butler is a harbinger of some national calamity, as firmly as I believe I am alive to-day. I would be afraid to publish the indignant expressions I have heard uttered by the colored troops about the removal of General Butler; but some are willing to lay down their arms.

H.M.T.

Jan. 18th, 1865.

## *"Army Correspondence"*

(*The Christian Recorder,* February 18, 1865)

*Headquarters 1st U.S.C.T.,
near Ft. Fisher, N.C.,
Jan. 29, '65.*

Mr. Editor:—I am happy to say we still occupy the same ground we captured from the rebels a few weeks since, and which was so sternly and stubbornly held by them. I presume most of the Northern papers have mapped and described the topography of Fort Fisher in such glowing delineations that it would be useless for me to attempt a further description of it. Our present position, however, is all that one could desire. Fort Buchanan, being on the extreme point between the sea-beach and the Cape Fear River, was protected by Fort Fisher, which stands a little further up on the beach at the mouth of the channel leading into the Cape Fear River. Fort Buchanan is simply a high mound thrown up, on which there are only three guns, but of immense caliber, while four or five more mounds stand along the channel side, between Forts Buchanan and Fisher, each of which mounted two guns. When I say mound, I mean earth thrown up, and prepared with all the necessary arrangements for mounting the desired number of guns.

On the most of these mounds were the finest and most effective cannons, doubtless, in the Southern Confederacy, not any of which had been materially injured by our terrible bombardment. The above named forts or mounds did not by any means suffer as did Fort Fisher.

But as I started to speak of our present position, I will now proceed to do so. Supposing Fort Fisher to be the centre of the sea and river (but which is not really the case), we have a battle-line drawn, and ourselves intrenched about two miles in the rear, with our left resting on the river, and our right resting on the sea. This line is about a mile long, being the distance from shore to shore, along which are several formidable works protected by batteries and cannons. At a proper space in the front are posted a strong picket-line. This is also well supported by works, which would puzzle the rebels considerably to drive us from our position. And then, in the space of about three hundred yards, in the rear of our main line, we have another line of flanking works, which would, by the aid of the gunboats, enable us to withstand any force the rebels may bring against us; for we not only have a triple line of the most formidable works, but our gunboats are prepared for a crossfire, from both the sea and the river.

Thus you may see, placed as we are in this formidable position, and surrounded by such works as I have just described, we are presenting an ugly front to any rebel force which may, perchance, pay us a visit. And here we are, waiting for the rebels to fortify Wilmington with insurpassable obstructions before we move. We waited four years for the rebels to fortify Fort Fisher and the entrance to Cape Fear River, and now, after taking it at a great sacrifice of life, to push forward for Wilmington would not be characteristic of American gallantry. Such "war fanatics" as Sherman might affect to take advantage of his opportunities, but we, who have been trained by the army tactics of the Potomac, have a higher conception of military science than to take advantage of an enemy. We find it best to take a place after giving the enemy as much time as possible to fortify and strengthen their position, so that they may be able to make a bold and strong resistance. Then sit down and dilly-dally for several months, wait to see what the newspapers have to say about it, ask for several promotions, discharge somebody, call for more troops, idle out weeks of good weather, and as soon as a rainstorm commences, the wind to blow in frightful gales, and when every congealable liquid freezes, then look out for marching orders about twelve or one o'clock at night.

But to criticize our General's tardiness is useless. They were founded on the strategetical maneuverings of McClellanistic genius, when this war began to exhibit its gigantic proportions; and its seeds are destined to run coeval with its existence.

Parallel to our picket-line, but somewhat in advance of our line of fortifications, on the opposite side of the river, the rebels have a fort which pretends to guard the river or channel. How formidable these works are, none of us know; but to suppose them a match for our naval fleet is folly, unless, indeed, by torpedoes. Notwithstanding, our navy would not find the same convenience in operating upon it as they did Fort Fisher, because they would not have the sea room.

As to the number of rebel troops who are in our front, prepared to dispute our advance, I have no reliable knowledge; but judging from the light of their campfires, they must be in some force. Deserters, however, say there are one or two brigades there, but they are much discouraged, and could easily be driven or completely demoralized.

Several free colored men, who are now employed by us, were captured with the rebels in Fort Fisher, and have informed us that during our bombardment of the fort, they were not allowed to enter a bomb-proof for shelter, and yet not a man was struck. And while the rebels had free access to all the bomb-proofs, yet they were slaughtered without mercy, while the poor colored men, who were denied every shelter except the mere privilege of dodging behind the sides of the fort, all escaped. And yet I cannot imagine how they did escape, for every spot was covered with fragments of shells, while every nook and corner in and around the fort appeared to be ploughed from centre to circumference. How manifold are thy mercies, O, Lord! They are stupendously deep, and transcendingly high.

This being the Sabbath day, we had a regimental meeting this afternoon which was well attended. But the most interesting part of our services consisted in a few hours spent in my quarters by some of the young men, who told over several incidents connected with their early Christian experience. I find, in rehearsing my former religious experience, that it has quite a tendency to strengthen my faith (and I have no doubt it has the same effect upon other men), which is calculated to become languid in an army life; but it is no easy matter to stand flinted and steeled to all the demoralizing influences which are brought to bear upon a man in the field. From morning till night one's ears are continually contaminated with the most vulgar oaths and obscene language ever uttered by mortal beings.

 Yours truly,
  H.M.T.

Chapter Four

. . . . . . . . . . .

# *Freeing Slaves, Meeting Sherman*

(February 25, 1865–June 10, 1865)

IN FEBRUARY 1865, TURNER was sent to North Carolina to help recruit newly freed slaves for the Union Army. While there, he also took the opportunity to recruit new members of the A.M.E. Church from these "great Southern fields." On both fronts, Turner reveals the complex interplay between white and black, Northerner and Southerner, civilian and soldier. He shared the experiences of newly emancipated slaves, and also witnessed the dismay of defeated Southern whites.

One highlight of this section is his account of the meeting between his regiment and General Sherman's troops, who had plundered Georgia and the Carolinas in the March to the Sea and the March through the Carolinas. The two wings met up on March 24: of the encounter, Turner wrote, "This was a sight equally novel to both. We all desired to see Sherman's men, and they were anxious to see colored soldiers, particularly the colored heroes of Petersburg, as they called us." The meeting was a shocking disappointment to Turner. Sherman's storied conquest of the South led Turner to expect a well equipped, highly disciplined force: a glistening

Fig. 4. Colored troops liberating slaves in North Carolina, 1864. *Harper's Weekly*, January 23, 1864, 52. North Carolina Collection, University of North Carolina Library at Chapel Hill.

war-making machine. Instead, the troops were disorganized, disorderly, and sloppily dressed—many were not even in uniform. "It was hard to tell if some were white," Turner wrote. Another black chaplain, William Waring, of the 102nd U.S. Colored Infantry, confirmed Turner's observations, writing to the *Weekly Anglo-African*, "Taken altogether, Sherman's army certainly does not come up to the common idea of a well-appointed body of troops."[1]

Turner was disappointed by the lackadaisical appearance of Sherman's army, but he was even more dismayed by their actions. Critical of his own troops for engaging in the practice of

---

1. Letter dated February 15, 1865, printed in the March 4, 1865, *Weekly Anglo-African;* reprinted in Edwin S. Redkey, *A Grand Army of Black Men: Letters from African-American Soldiers in the U.S. Army 1861–1865* (Cambridge: Cambridge University Press, 1992), 76.

"foraging"—a term that became a euphemism for outright pillaging—he was utterly appalled by the destruction Sherman's men had left in their wake. As he traveled deeper into North Carolina, Turner wrote, "And here we just began to learn what destruction was. We thought our men had been doing outrageously, but now we were convinced that we were all good fellows." Turner concluded, "I do not regard it as *the* army of America. That is all I will now say.... So much for Sherman's army."

Seeing the 1st U.S.C.T. side by side with Sherman's men left him even more proud of black soldiers. He praised their valor in the skirmish at Moccasin Creek on March 24, and also noted their humane treatment of the Confederate prisoners of war, saying that "they manifested more feeling for the rebels than did the white soldiers." The treatment of captured soldiers was a vexed issue throughout the war, and exacerbated when the Union began enlisting black troops. Early on, prisoners of war were either exchanged (the two sides returning prisoners to each other, ready for combat once again) or paroled (released with the understanding that they would not take up arms until notified that they had been exchanged). However, the Confederacy refused to return black prisoners of war, claiming that ex-slaves serving as Union soldiers were, in effect, in a state of insurrection and should be dealt with under state laws—which is to say, they would either be returned to slavery or summarily executed. Lincoln, in turn, declared that if Jefferson Davis carried out his threat, he would command his soldiers to execute Confederate prisoners-of-war in retaliation. When Davis refused to capitulate on this point, Lincoln suspended all prisoner exchanges, resulting in the creation (or expansion) of large, crowded prison camps in both the North and the South, where reports of inhumane treatment of prisoners in the periodical press outraged the nation and resulted in retaliatory treatment by soldiers on both sides. Turner's comment demonstrates the black soldiers' forbearance despite the fact that they knew they would not be treated humanely should the situation be reversed, even knowing that their white compatriots would not protest if they were to flout standard procedures.

According to Turner's account, black soldiers also demonstrated self-possession with respect to the "secesh" civilians they encountered in North Carolina, though they, including Turner himself, also asserted themselves as citizens and even conquerors. Turner describes a group of black soldiers as "magic lords" when they encounter a group of Confederate soldiers, at which point their "black faces seem to glisten in the rays of the sun, their caps whirled over on one side of their heads, burning the rebels' own narcotic, under the appellation of segars [cigars] ... with heads thrown back and eyes elevated so high that they seem to say, I wouldn't look down if I knew I were wading through greenbacks." In another instance, Turner asserted his right to walk on the sidewalk rather than the street, refusing to give way to a group of white women until "we had effected a collision, when we both stopped and looked at each other, until they gave me the pavement." Ironically, of course, within decades blacks would be forced off the sidewalks again due to the entrenchment of Jim Crow laws that segregated public spaces and facilities throughout the country.

As a commissioned officer of the occupying forces, Turner mediated disputes between civilians. In one interesting case, he discovered that a white woman had secreted away the child of a woman who had once been her slave, and claimed her right to do so because the child was her property. Turner then acted as a kind of modern Solomon, declaring he would hold one of the white woman's children hostage until the black woman's child was returned. "The words had hardly left my mouth, before such a running, crying, and squealing took place among the children that my indignation melted down into laughter," Turner relates; more soberly, he continued, "But look at the inconsistency: they could not feel the colored woman's grief; yet when the same pill was offered to them, they were frightened into fits."

Ministering to the needs of both his regiment and liberated slaves, he witnessed the rapid changes affecting both. Initially, upon seeing the liberated slaves, he was dismayed by the extent to which "the foul curse of slavery has blighted the natural greatness of my race!" Soon, however, he was gratified by the immediate changes wrought by his presence as an authority figure among the Southern whites. After he commandeered the Smithville, North Carolina, courthouse for a church, he noted smugly that the sight of him at the platform "was as much gospel as they [whites] could swallow in one week ... any more would be murder." Ultimately, he concluded, "the colored people are giving evidence of commendable manhood"; when he saw white women ogling black soldiers fording the river at Smithfield, rather than evincing embarrassment (this was the Victorian era, after all!) he noted that the soldiers carried themselves as though they were saying to their admirers, "Yes, though naked, we are your masters."

However, Turner also witnessed harbingers of what was to come after the end of the war—specifically, the exploitative arrangement between former slaveowners and former slaves that would come to be known as sharecropping, where blacks would be permitted to farm land they did not own in return for a share of the crop. Turner recognized this new financial arrangement as a new form of slavery that would "perpetuate the institution now broken up by the Yankee influx."

We only have brief comments from Turner concerning two key events marking the end of the war: the surrender of Gen. Robert E. Lee at Appomattox Court House on April 9, 1865, and the assassination of President Lincoln on April 15. When the troops heard of the surrender, Turner describes the reaction in characteristically vivid terms: "all day long, from that time, would regiments and brigades cheer, shout, whoop, shoot guns, while companies join and whistle Yankee Doodle and Hail Columbia, until I wished every mouth was crammed full of mush to stop the noise." Yet he devotes only a single paragraph to this momentous event. Lincoln, of course, was assassinated less than a week later. Given Turner's devotion to the President, one must assume that he deeply mourned his death. However, although he indicates that he will address the assassination at greater length at the end of his May 6 column, unfortunately, the May 13, 1865, issue of the *Recorder* has been lost. Clearly, it is in this issue that he expressed his thoughts regarding the President's death. By the time his column appears again, weeks later on May 27, he admits that he has become "somewhat delinquent" in his correspondence, due to the fact that "acuter minds and abler pens can be substituted for mine."[2]

It was true that the April and May issues of the *Recorder* suffered no shortage of commentary on either the end of the war or the death of the President. Of Lee's surrender, the *Recorder*'s editor, Elisha Weaver, described the "grand carnival" atmosphere in Philadelphia; letters from soldiers throughout the country related the triumphant occupation of Richmond, Virginia, as well as the ending of the war in other theaters. Poems mourned the President's death; letters expressed fears and concerns about the fate of the country. Turner, clearly, decided to give way to this flood of correspondence; certainly, he had no shortage of other duties and obligations to fulfill in a time so "pregnant with events and pending with immortal issues."

* * *

---

2. The *Recorder* did publish a letter from Turner in the April 29, 1865, issue, promoting entrepreneurial activities in Wilmington, North Carolina. This letter, which is clearly intended as promotional activity, is not included in this volume.

## "Army Correspondence"

(*The Christian Recorder*, February 25, 1865)

Smithville, N.C.,
February 4, 1865.

Mr. Editor:—Having by the assignment of Major General Terry, at the request of Brigadier General Paine, come to this place to assist 1st Lieutenant Holmes to recruit men for our army, it was my privilege to pack up early on the morning of the 30th ult., and start for a new sphere of labor for awhile.[3]

Smithville, I judge, is about ten miles from Fort Fisher, nearly at the mouth of a sound that runs to the right of Cape Fear River, and forms one of the inlets leading into said river. It formerly was the residence, I should judge, of about seven thousand inhabitants, and had become quite famous, of late, for blockade running. The entrance to this town from sea was protected by Fort Caswell, and Fort Johnston was designed to protect it from any invading force that might attempt to cross over the island, directly in its front. Fort Johnston, built on the wharf, in the centre of the town, was an exhibition of one of the most ingenious blunders ever displayed by the Southern chivalrists.[4] Having arrived here late in the evening,

---

3   Gen. Alfred H. Terry (1827-90) replaced Gen. Benjamin Butler after he was relieved of command after the failed First Battle of Fort Fisher, and succeeded in taking the fort as related in Chapter Three. Gen. Charles Jackson Paine (1833-1916) served in both battles of Fort Fisher and after the war was appointed district commander at New Bern, NC.

4.   Turner is most likely referring to the fact that after locals stormed the fort in January 1861 and commandeered the keys from the fort's lone caretaker, Ordnance Sergeant James Reilly, they returned the keys—to Reilly—after North Carolina's governor ordered them to do so, thus returning the fort to Union hands. In April, after the fall of Fort Sumter, the Confederates took possession of the fort, and Reilly, having joined the

I failed to be an observer till the following day, when, after taking quarters in a splendid rebel mansion, I commenced a street perambulation, to see and be seen. I found several magazines had been blown up, several boats fired and burned, and considerable destruction otherwise, for after we took Fort Fisher, the rebels at this place became dispirited, destroyed a great deal, and retreated. Consequently, we had the pleasure of taking this place without firing a gun. Our forces had been here about two weeks prior to my arrival. Many of the inhabitants were still here, though the most wealthy had generally left, carrying off many of their slaves. Notwithstanding there were enough left to show quite a population. The white people, nearly without an exception, showed a bitter and chagrined countenance, while the blacks appeared timid and doubtful. Small squads of rebels could be seen standing on the corners, conversing, I presumed, over the dubious records of blighted prospects, while the women would bend over and poke some of the ugliest faces out of the windows I ever saw. When some would see you coming, they would look up the street until you got parallel to them, then they would whirl their noddles around, and look down street.

In one instance I made quite a narrow escape. As it happened, I turned off just in time to let a woman whirl her long nose around, which, if it had struck me, I don't know where I would have been now. Whether she hangs her nose out in the street to blockade its passage, or to knock people over with it, or to smell the senses out of folks, or to snuff the dirt from her pavement instead of sweeping it off, I have not yet learned.

The second morning of my stay here, I was sent for by an old lady to breakfast with her, to which I willingly complied and

---

Confederate Army, became custodian of the fort again. He would eventually surrender Fort Fisher—and Fort Johnston—to the Union in 1865.

went; having determined to see that no distinction was made in the serving up of it, and taking a few of my soldiers as a guard in case of necessity. All things went off in nice style. The old lady expressed much joy at our being here, though she had always been free. By request, I went back again about dark, and walking in, sat down. In a few moments several white women came into the yard and commenced a jabber about some wood, which the colored lady was appropriating to her use. She told them it was Yankee wood, and not theirs, and the tongue battle raged most furiously for some minutes, when one of the white women called her a liar, with another expression too vulgar to mention. To this the colored woman responded, "I am no more a liar than you are." This expression, from a negro wench, as they called her, was so intolerable, that the white women grabbed up several clubs and leaped in the door, using the most filthy language in the vocabulary of indecency. They had not yet observed me as being on the premises. But at this juncture, I rose up, met them at the door, and cried out, "Halt!" Said they, "Who are you?" "A United States Officer," was my reply. "Well, are you going to allow that negro to give us impudence?" "You gave her impudence first," was my reply. "What, we give a negro impudence! We want you to know we are white, and are your superiors. You are our inferior, much less she." "Well," said I, "All of you put together would not make the equal of my wife, and I have yet to hear her claim superiority over me." After that, I don't know what was said, for that remark was received as such an aggravated insult, that I can only compare the noise that followed, to a gang of fice dogs holding at bay a large cur dog, with a bow-wow-wow-wow. Finally, becoming tired of their annoying music, I told them to leave or I would imprison the whole party. They then went off, and dispatched one of their party to Headquarters, to Colonel Barney, to induce him to send a file of men, and have me arrested. But the Colonel,

I believe, drove her off, and that was the end of it. I afterwards learned that they were some of the Southern aristocracy.

Next day, however, two of the same party met me on the street, and when they saw I was going to take the inside of the pavement, they gazed at me with strictured frowns, and rubbed the very palings[5] to compel me to go into the street, and give them the entire side-walk; but I returned the gazing compliment and kept on till we had effected a collision, when we both stopped and looked at each other, until they gave me the pavement. I don't think my eyes ever suffered more than when I compelled them to keep sight on those frightful faces. I shall never impose upon my eyes so again.

The second evening after my arrival, I told three young men to inform the colored people that I wanted to preach to them at night, and for that purpose, I selected a large room in the house which I occupy. I expected to see eighteen or twenty, but to my surprise, over a hundred came out. With these I had quite an interesting meeting, but to describe it would be impossible. I was in a very good talking humor, and therefore treated upon several points, and about the time I commenced referring to the dark retrocession of slavery's night, and the luminous progress of freedom's dawn, and its complete consummation in the bright day of eternal liberty and disenthralment, I tried to borrow eloquent terms from the lyric strains of the celestial hosts, and poor as was my success, yet my descantation upon freedom, liberty, and justice to all men, irrespective of color, produced the wildest excitement I ever witnessed. In order to form an idea of the scene, imagine yourself in a house where a collection of all colors, sorts, and sizes of people were gathered; some crying, some laughing, some dancing, some crazy, some drunk, some having a fit, some fighting, some kissing, some clapping hands, and some dying, &c., and

---

5. Palings are the pickets or posts of the fence between the pavement and the street.

you may glean a faint conception of the rhapsodical paroxysms and the heaving genuflections exhibited on the occasion. At the conclusion of our meeting, I announced service on the following night, in the Court House. This made many open their eyes much wider than usual, for colored people were never admitted into the Court House heretofore. However, the following night the Court House was filled to its utmost capacity with these children of infant freedom. When I told them that hereafter they would hold their services there, and on Sabbath I would preach at 11 o'clock, A.M., and also at night, and would organize an A.M.E. Church there, at 3 o'clock in the afternoon, and that, hereafter, the Court House was to be their church, the announcement was received in ecstasies of joy. What will be my success, I shall not surmise. I find that the principles of morality are at a very low ebb here, growing out of the uncultured masses upon whom hinged the prevailing sentiments of social decorum. These extraordinary characteristics, which tended to the people's popularity, and constituted the *élite* and embellished few, were based upon the number of negro boys and negro wenches possessed by the owner, and their probable procreation.

The colored people are anxious to have schools established here. They seem to have a high appreciation of the beneficial advantages of education. Notwithstanding many of the whites cannot read, there is a recognized power in an educational ideal exceedingly marvelous for the limited capacity hitherto allowed to their intellectual development. Several have asked me if my wife would not come and teach them if I sent for her, but I told them it was nearly three months since I had heard from my wife, and if she should be detained as long as my letters and papers have been on the way, it would require six months to get here.

This place is destined to become famous, in consequence of its suitability as a rendezvous for the slaves of the adjacent counties. The coast guards having been removed, leaves unobstructed every road, except those leading to Wilmington. It is of easy access to the escaping fugitives from several large farms. Thus they are coming in by droves, sometimes fifteen or twenty in a gang, some of whom are pitiful looking creatures. Oh, how the foul curse of slavery has blighted the natural greatness of my race! It has not only depressed and horror-streaked the should-be glowing countenances of thousands, but it has almost transformed many into inhuman appearance. There were two men came in night before last, and had I met either by myself, I should have run for my life,—supposing him to be the devil. But what capped all was, when I commenced to converse with them, one seemed to be intelligent, and I could not imagine where he kept his intelligence, for I could see no place in his head to keep it; but it was there, and could not be counteracted.

We have enlisted several men whom I think will make splendid soldiers, and the work goes on finely. I intended to have sent you our address since the reorganization of our corps, but we are so divided by temporary detachments, that I hardly know how we do stand. My regiment, I think, belongs to the 1st Brigade, 1st Division, 25th Army Corps, but being now detached and twisted up, our old address had better be continued, until we are properly arranged.

   Yours very truly,
   H.M.T.

## "*Army Correspondence*"

(*The Christian Recorder,* March 4, 1865)

*Smithville, N.C., Feb. 11, 1865.*

Mr. Editor:—Since I last wrote to you from this place things have undergone some transitions which I trust will tend to the progress of society here. The infamous Yankee hatred so strongly cherished by our secesh neighbors, is melting down in elementary proportions before the warmhearted and philanthropic endeavors of our gallant soldiers to transform the lethargical inertness of their southern customs into that lively interest so characteristic of northern energy. As an evidence of this, boats can be seen daily plowing the waters in every direction, while wagons are driven, horses are ridden, mules are freighted, cows milked, dogs bark, cats mew, &c. Besides, churches, theatres, and ballrooms are being fitted up. I am trying to establish a religious nucleus around which to gather the religious and moral, and the soldiers (white) are fixing up a hall for theatrical performances, as several are well versed in the science of theaters, while the more vulgar and ignorant class are getting ready to hop and squat on the ballroom floor.

We have a great many hard-looking customers here called southern belles, who generally keep themselves rather retired from the raw-boned and bloody-handed Yankees, and I believe the boys intend to try and get them outdoors once more before the world ends. I have been rather more fortunate than the rest; being a sort of lay-low preacher, I have had the pleasure of addressing a few large audiences, which has caused great slaughter among the fowls, if nothing else. Every evening I am out to tea, and nearly every day to dinner, and somehow these North Carolina chickens will get in my way at every invited meal, and I have such a dislike for them that I most unmercifully devour them wherever I find them.

Last Sabbath afternoon I had the inestimable pleasure of organizing the first A.M.E. Church in the state of North Carolina. I selected the courthouse as my church, where I preached at 11 o'clock and at night, and laid the claims of my Church before them in the afternoon. After the bell was rung at 11 o'clock, several of the natives (white) came to the door and saw this colored brother occupying the judge's stand, and took with a polite leaving. I inquired after service, of the colored people, why the white people left. Was it because I was so ugly? They said no; but it was preaching enough for them to see a negro occupying the platform in their courthouse. That sight alone was as much gospel as they could swallow in one week, and to receive any more would be murder.

Our afternoon service was not so well attended, in consequence of the bell not being rung, but to those who came out I tried to speak at some length, holding the discipline of the A.M.E. Church in one hand, and the discipline of the M.E. Church South in the other, reading and commenting from both. After concluding my remarks I sat down to await their action in the case, as to accepting our Church, or remaining in the Southern; but no action was taken further than the leading men coming forward and saying, "Here, take my name." This they continued to do until thirty came forward, each thanking God that the light had come. And during the week a large number have come to me requesting their names recorded among those received last Sabbath, as they were not at church on the occasion. I learn there are not more than fifty pious persons in the town, and many of them had back-slidden in consequence of no care being taken of them. They had not met a class for four years, nor heard of a prayer-meeting for the same length of time, and every sermon was a speech on slavery. They tell me here that one southern minister had the spunk to preach that the north would whip, for slavery was a curse, and God would subdue it or suffer every southern man to be killed, and that he was not even arrested, much less shot or hung. But as regards our church here, I am certain that every person holding membership in the M.E. Church South will, at the first opportunity, give in their names. I have been trying to find one of the brethren whom I could license to take charge in the event I am called away, but a competent one I shall fail to find. Oh, what a field for some young man looking to the ministerial position! Here might he study, teach and preach, receiving both the blessings of God and the endless thanks of a grateful people, till his capacities were developed to their full maturity and strength.

Recruiting in this department goes on finely. We have enlisted several hale, stalwart-looking fellows, whom we think will fill their places nobly. One man wants his gun now, so he can get to killing right off; he declares a louse shall not move his big toe where he goes along, and that nits had better keep silent. The colored people are coming in from all quarters, even from plantations one hundred and fifty miles in the country. Three women came in the other night who had traveled through woods for a hundred miles. Several rebels have endeavored to block up the roads and bridges, but all to no purpose. Still they come. Report says many have been caught and killed. Some who succeed in getting in tell frightful tales about their narrow escapes. One man, who was pursued for several hours by the rebel kidnappers, arrived here a few mornings ago very ill. The circumstances are as follows: since my arrival here I have been acting as a one-horse doctor, in recommending castor oil, Epsom salts, and a few army pills for every kind of disease a person has; so a few mornings ago I was called to bestow my surgical skill on a man who had been terribly chased in his attempt to get within our lines. I consequently hastened to his quarters and put him through a rigid examination. I found him lying just at the point of time, looking for every moment to be the next [*sic*]. He had an awful pain upon his appetite, his stomach pulse beat very slowly; his eyes exhibited signs of a previous fright, and his heart seemed to throb under a reactionary impulse of joy on his reception into the Yankee lines. With this knowledge of his case I was enabled to console his friends, and pronounce his condition quite hopeful. I then turned to my assistant surgeon (the cook), and recommended that he (the man) be given a heavy dose of fat meat and hard tack, and that his insides be well bathed with warm coffee or tea, and that he be furnished with the floor and as much sleep as could be packed in a twenty-four hour measure. The next time I saw the gentleman he had recovered, and had come around to enlist as a U.S. soldier. But I must confess that I was offered a case this morning too hard for me. I was hailed by a boy while going to breakfast, who told me his mother wanted me to come there immediately. I inquired the object and was informed she had been badly beaten. I hastened there and found her lying on a bench, with a most frightful gash cut on her forehead, about three inches long and apparently the entire depth of the flesh. She was covered with blood, yet nothing excited me so much as to learn that her own daughter had inflicted this wound. I did not regard the blood nor the wound any thing at all, but what startled me was the idea of it being done by the hand of her own daughter, and she a young woman, and that it was the result of being hissed on by some white women who were afraid to attempt it themselves. There was a young man there from Baltimore, who loaded his gun to shoot the daughter, but she was concealed by some of her white backers. The lady's wounds, however, were attended to by one of our army surgeons, and the daughter will be seen to also.

We hear great rumors of peace being declared through lip communication; how true this is I am not able to say, for we get no newspapers here. I have only seen two newspapers this year. I neither get *Recorders*, *Anglos*, letters, nor hear any thing from the northern world, only some stray tales, which fly by sometimes and a part of which, I suspect, is false. I hear more of what is going on north from the colored people who come in our lines, than from any other source. So far as news is concerned a man might as well be in the penitentiary, though I hope it will soon be better. But referring to peace again, I pray that it may soon come, for I have seen just as many men killed as I wish to. Likely, for one, I am casehardened to death, as men generally get to be; for when I am tired I had rather much sleep a night in a house with dead people than living, because the dead don't bother me by either talking, laughing, or walking about, and a man can rest quietly, yet feel that he has company. But for all, I must say, to walk over a field covered with dead and wounded men, is no pleasant sight. God, grant that peace may speedily arrive, upon honorable terms.

I have the honor to be your most obedient servant,
H.M.T.

## "*Army Correspondence*"

(*The Christian Recorder*, March 18, 1865)

*Headquarters Recruiting Department,*
*Twenty-Fifth Army Corps.*
*Smithville, N.C., February 24, 1865.*

Mr. Editor:—Likely I have never witnessed a day in which more pleasing streams of intelligence ran (all at the same time) into my soul than I have to-day: Having a few days ago received nearly two months' mail, which I had been deprived of on account of our military movements; and having received between seventy-five and eighty papers, over which, for the last two days and nights, I have been poring; and having been astounded at the progressive developments which are fast rolling the colored race to the harbor of their God-given rights, the port where unbiased justice and eternal equity will pavilion them from the ruthless fangs of slavery and all its accursed retinue; and having yesterday received the intelligence of the fall of Charleston, S.C., and to-day of the fall of Wilmington, N.C., I can scarcely tell how to tender that profound debt of gratitude to the God of all favors, which one must impulsively feel who is endeavoring to devote his time, talents, and life to the accomplishment of these very objects.

Our military successes, however, have not so much surprised me, for I know that the divine principles of our side must prevail. But the solution of that sublimely wrought mathematical problem which has been cut out and stamped upon the frontispiece of American prejudice, by the admission of Rock, as a practitioner, at the nation's highest bar of jurisprudence; Garnet to the Congressional chamber, to proclaim those eternal truths, pure and unadulterated, which have been trampled down by the oligarchical fanatics of human tyranny for many years; Matthews to the captaincy of a battery; and to crown the golden, yea, diamond statue, the passage of the constitutional amendment, which wipes out the blot and heals the hideous canker which, for many years, has preyed upon our beloved land.[6] This enactment ensures and guarantees freedom and equality to the human race, irrespective of [*text missing*]. Would to God I could find words [*text missing*] express my joy and thankfulness [*text missing*] blessings to our race.[7] But as I am deprived of such prerogatives, I must be contented to use the language of an old colored lady yesterday, viz.: "Thanky, Jesus; O, Jesus, thanky, thanky, thanky!" These words were not uttered grandiloquently, but eloquently and impressively, coming from a heart which felt the force of every thank she gave. The negro ascends higher and higher, notwithstanding the exertions of the democratic parasites, in Congress or elsewhere, to the contrary, for which God be eternally thanked.

---

6. J. S. Rock was admitted to the bar February 1, 1865, and was the first black lawyer to argue a case in front of the Supreme Court. Henry Highland Garnet (1815–82), a prominent black abolitionist, was the first black man to deliver a sermon in the House of Representatives, on February 12, 1865. William D. Matthews (1827–1906) served as de facto captain of the 1st Kansas Colored Infantry, though he was refused an actual commission when the battery entered active federal service due to his race (Roger D. Cunningham, *The Black Citizen-Soldiers of Kansas, 1864–1901* [Columbia and London: University of Missouri Press], 20). The Thirteenth Amendment to the Constitution abolishing slavery passed, 121–24, on January 31, 1865.

7. The corner of the page is torn off. Unfortunately, the Mother Bethel A.M.E. Church copy is the only extant copy of this issue.

I was highly pleased to learn that Rev. James Lynch had taken Andrew Chapel, at Savannah, Georgia, into the A.M.E. Church. This is a splendid church and has a fine congregation, and it is not the only church in that state that will be benefited by uniting with us. Brother Lynch, though quite young, is very enterprising, and through his indefatigable and untiring zeal and energy, is accomplishing a great work in that portion of the Lord's vineyard.

Being shrewd, active, and possessing a high degree of natural sagacity, and an industrial vigilance equally commendable, James Lynch stands high among colored clergymen. If not presumptuous, I would respectfully hint to our worthy bishops, that it would be more conducive to the interests of our church to transfer some of its most talented ministers to these great southern fields, as the work to be done here is very extensive and requires able men to accomplish it.

I am sorry that it was not my privilege to accompany my regiment to Wilmington; being on recruiting service, I am left thirty miles in the rear. I hope some one will give the details of the affair. I simply know that Wilmington has fallen.[8] How much fighting was done, or how many prisoners were taken I have not learned. I hope to see the place, however, in a few days. This place is daily growing in importance. A great many sick have been brought here, and it may, in fact, be called a hospital town. I am very glad to see a certain Episcopal church turned into a hospital, which has been hitherto closed. The use of said church was asked, solicited, both by myself and a certain white chaplain; each of us wanted it for our respective purposes; but we were politely informed by our post commander that if we would see the trustees (rebels), and get their permission, we could use it, otherwise he did not care to open it. I am not prepared to give his reasons, yet I am satisfied they were sufficient. But it is now quite

---

8. The Battle of Wilmington was fought February 11–22, 1865, effectively shutting down the Confederacy's last major port and completing the Union blockade.

as profitably employed, for when General Schofield landed his troops here, he opened it, regardless of trustees or any one else, and made a hospital of it for the accommodation of our sick and wounded soldiers.

This is a famous place for balls. They are the acknowledged order of public and private association. The people dance to make acquaintances; dance to court; dance to get married; dance every night in the week for a fashion, and take a private dance on Sabbath for a rarity, and if they have no violin (or fiddle, as they call it), one fellow steps out, whistles, sings, or hums, and pats his feet (heels and toes going at the same time), claps his hands, beats his breast, and other like gesticulations, which he will probably keep up for half an hour. During this time the assembled crowd becomes enraged at their feet, and in order to vent their spleen, both men and women will stamp, kick, scrape, and knock their heels and toes over the floor, so cruelly that a more civilized person could not but feel sorry for them, especially where most of the persons were barefooted. And yet this same vulgar fun is countenanced in more enlightened parts of the country, and among what we sometimes style *big fish* and *upper tens*.[9] It is certainly a mystery how ladies and gentlemen can take pleasure in leaving their comfortable homes for the purpose of engaging in such outlandish pastimes. But some evil genius or false prophet prompts them to it. Many of our churches are cursed with the same moral miasma. Talk about having a revival, without cutting similar capers, is regular nonsense. But let a person get a little animated, fall down and roll over awhile, kick a few shins, crawl under a dozen benches, spring upon his feet, knock some innocent person on the nose and set it bleeding, then, squeal and kiss (or buss) around for a while, and the work is all done; whereas, if the individual had claimed justification under more quiet circumstances, its legitimacy would have

---

9. Upper tens are the "upper ten thousand"—i.e., the elite. The writer Nathaniel Parker Willis first used the phrase in 1852, referring to the upper echelons of New York society.

been doubted. O, that people could learn that "without faith it is impossible to please God!"[10]

The *Recorder* of February 4th contains an article written by a lady in the west, which contains a song, entitled "The Children's Freedmen Song,"[11] which seemed so appropriate to those just

---

10. Heb. 11:6.
11. The song appeared in a letter titled "Items from the West," written by a correspondent from Iowa named "Martha." Sung to the tune of the "Battle Hymn of the Republic" (which was, in turn, inspired by the song "John Brown's Body"), the lyrics are as follows:

> Free! we are free! with a wild and happy cry,
> We children, in our gladness, are shouting far and high.
> Free! we are free! oh, let the tidings fly:
>    We are free to-day!
> Glory, glory, hallelujah,
> Glory, glory, hallelujah,
> Glory, glory, hallelujah,
>    We are free to-day!
> Free from the fetters that bound our fathers low,
> Free from the wretchedness our weeping mothers know,
> Free from the auction block, with all its shame and woe;
>    We are free to-day!
> Free! we are free! now all shall be repaid,
> The cravings of the hungry mind, with knowledge shall be stayed,
> And ignorance no longer bind the soul for glory made.
>    We are free to-day!
> Free! we are free! though dusky be the skin,
> Pure may be the spirit that God has put within,
> For Jesus has redeemed it from misery and sin.
>    We are free to-day!
> God bless the President, who signed the freedom bill!
> God bless the Christian hearts, who pray for freedom still
> And praises be to God above, by whose most blessed will
>    We are free to-day!

emerging from the chains of slavery that I proposed to teach our recruits how to sing it. Could the author of those verses have seen those slave-driven recruits endeavoring to tune their voices to the music of the song, and have seen them shake their heads when the words portrayed their previously forlorn and unhappy condition, she would have felt herself amply recompensed for the time and labor bestowed upon her poetic production.

Lieutenant Holmes, of our regiment, a noble specimen of that part of American humanity, whose progressive sentiments keep pace with the philanthropic revolutions of the country, has been appointed by the General to command the troops now being enlisted. It is sufficient to say that the motto of Lieutenant Holmes is, "Push the Negro forward." My esteem for all that is gentlemanly and dignified lies between him and Lieutenant Bishop, our noble and efficient adjutant.[12] The principles possessed by these two officers will clothe them with honor, while hundreds filling equally high positions will squirt out a foppish existence and die, without leaving a footprint upon the sands of time.

H.M.T.

## "Army Correspondence"

(*The Christian Recorder,* March 25, 1865)

*Smithville, N.C.,*
*Feb. 29th, 1865.*

Mr. Editor:—The necrological records are daily augmented in our various hospitals. Our sick are passing from the thresholds of time into eternity's boundless limits, in rapid succession. Truly is

---

12. An adjutant is a staff officer, an aide-de-camp.

the Roman adage verified, "*Infinita est multitudo morborum.*" And truly is this broad earth *one great necropolis!* O death, thou foul enemy of man, whose ravaging scythe neither spared the sages of antiquity, the world-renowned heroes of modern years, nor remits the prey of thy austere vengeance upon the sons of freedom! when, O when will thy wrath be assuaged, and thine anger appeased? Did you not hear that soldier day before yesterday, while passing through your cold, chilly, and ceremented hands, say, "Well, Death's got me at last. I will soon be gone. Please write to my dear wife. Tell her William lives no more. Give my five little children their father's dying kiss. Tell her also, to raise them the best way she can with her scanty means, and to teach them to fear their God, and love their country"? O Death! thou unrelenting foe of all that live! is thy pity incompressible? Hast thou grown callous to the sighs and anguish which follow in the wake of thy mortal march? Is there no sympathy in the bowels of thy compassion? There seems to be none. But you are inclined to be rather exultant in your daring feats. You boast of not only killing a man, who is a soldier, husband, and father, regardless of his country's needs, or his wife and children's sympathy, but in process of time you threaten them with the same terrible danger. You say, "Yes, when I get ready, I will kill wife and children, too." Never mind, Death! you may ride on in glorious pomp and destructive conquest, but your proud career will have an end.

Have you forgotten the morning, when your arm hung palsied at your side, and your brandished dagger was knocked from the iron grip of your infernal grasp by the sledge hammer of divine omnipotence?—when a single ray of light from Heaven's gleaming legate sent a terror-stricken paralysis through the bravest hearts of the Roman guard, and when Jesus rose from His sepulchral confinement and walked to Galilee before your face? Death, I know that you remember it.

Now let me tell you something, which [you should] also remember. These noble heroes whom you are slaughtering, while carrying the message of constitutional liberty to the long enslaved children of oppression, will only rest awhile from their labors, during which time their children will boast, and laud their gallant fathers to the skies. Their deeds, the cause in which they died, and motives which prompted them, will constitute more glory and honor for their children than ancestral royalty ever could, and it will be transmitted from generation to generation.

At the end of time, O death! thy dagger, bloody with the gore of billions of hearts, shall be snatched from thy ruthless hands, and those heroes, who have fallen upon many battle-fields, died in many hospitals for want of proper care, and have sacrificed their lives for all that is dear to man on earth, will rise before your face, to recount the fruits of their labors, and join in the chorus of the anthem, for ever to sing, "*The world is redeemed, the slaves are free.*"

Having had a little more leisure time than usual, I have been devoting it to reading James McCosh's great work on *Divine Government, Physical and Moral*, &c., which work cannot be too highly esteemed.[13] I have also examined our new discipline, which contains some of the most egregious blunders I ever saw in a book of its size.[14] Several amendments, which were offered and passed

---

13. Turner refers to James McCosh's *Method of Divine Government, Physical and Moral* (1850), which went through five editions by 1856. A philosopher in the Scottish common-sense tradition, McCosh (1811–94) came to the United States in 1868 to become the president of what is now known as Princeton University. He served as president until 1888, and taught philosophy until his death; the university's English department is housed in the hall named after him.
14. Turner is referring to the A.M.E. Church's official document outlining church practices and governance procedures.

during the session of the last General Conference, and which appear in the minutes of the General Conference, were either left out, mutilated, or changed to a worse form than its relative bearing was before. There ought to be a committee appointed, *upon the conduct of the discipline,* with power to send for papers and persons, and correct these blunders, for unless such a course be adopted, there will always be a similar state of things. But I suppose if the matter were investigated, it would appear that Brother Weaver had all the work to do, just about the time he had all the various Conferences to visit, which compelled him to leave it in the hands of some one else, and thus it was managed, while the actual committee did nothing. I do not say that this was the case, but I do say the discipline is very defective.

The rebels in this vicinity are trying to stipulate terms with their former slaves, which will, to some extent, perpetuate the institution now broken up by the Yankee influx. The farmers, especially, are offering them the use of their present homes (slave huts), and the use of their horses, wagons, lands, and other farming utensils, which they may work or use, by giving them their owners one third of their income, while they (the slaves) keep two thirds. This ingenious trickery is designed to keep the old master fat doing nothing, making the Yankees believe "dis old nigga no wants to leave massa," and for the purpose of fizzling them out of all their claims upon the real estate. Many of them in the country have accepted the proposition, and are now working under the new diplomatic stipulation.

I would suggest the propriety to the colored politicians north, of investigating that momentous subject, EMIGRATION, very thoroughly. It is not my intention, as one, to enter any political arena, pro or con, for if my life should be spared to serve three years in the army, I think I shall have done my share, unless undeveloped emergencies should demand more. But finding that subject is being, of late, very much spoken of, and very thoroughly canvassed by some of the army *petit-maîtres*, and knowing also that there is a large sum of money in the treasury, for emigration purposes, and that certain sharpers can't get hold of it, unless they revive this subject, it behooves the thinking part of our race to begin to look that bull in the eye. I have noticed several references to it of late in the speeches of able men. No one need presume it is forgotten. As soon as this rebellion is over, it will be the chief topic in every legislative department, from Congress down to town councils. Therefore, it would be wise in our colored counselors to read all the history bearing upon such subjects, and to furnish themselves with such analogical facts, as will fully prepare them to rebut or defend the question, with that ability which command respect at least, be they historical, ethnological, or philosophical arguments.

There are scores of geological relics or specimens here, which would give large scope for the play of some scientific mind. A few days ago, I was thinking how proud I would feel if I only possessed the rare attainments of Professor Solomon G. Brown, of Smithsonian notoriety.[15] With his massive intellect and scientific lore, I could travel from strata to strata, and number the epochs while ages swept by, counting time's revolving cycles from the very morn of creation. The scientific field, though little thought on, must yet engross the attention of our aspiring young men. It will yet be seen that it affords a greater arena to mental

---

15. Solomon G. Brown (1829–1906), born free in Washington, D.C., and self-educated, was the first African American employed by the Smithsonian Institution, where he worked from 1852 to 1906. While he was not a "professor" per se, he worked closely with the first three secretaries of the institution, and eventually was trusted with the preparation of maps and drawings, which he used when he gave illustrated natural history lectures that became well known in the Washington area.

development than any other, theology excepted. Those great beacon lights, who have popularized it for many years, are falling, one by one. In 1864 the firmament of science was robbed of five of her brightest stars, viz.: Struve, Silliman, Hitchcock, Merian, and Dr. Bache.[16] Their places must be filled. Will not some black boy endeavor to fill one? I think there will be one, at least, who will try. I should not be surprised, yet, to hear that Solomon G. Brown had laid bare some scientific problem, or phased it, at least, with a theory far in advance of any of the already stereotyped definitions.[17] Be that, however, as it may, there is ample room—science is not half exhausted, and our wisest men are still boys at school.

The non-acceptance of rebel money with us has caused the rebels to resort to their gold and silver. I verily believe, if it were possible to establish a store here at the present time, as much specie could be gathered in as in former days. Indeed, I am astonished to see so much. Many of these rebels, I am informed, actually have bags of silver and gold.

The people are daily passing and re-passing from here to Wilmington. But Turner has to sit here. With all my ardent desires to see that city, I can't go without the General's permission,

---

16. Friedrich Georg Wilhelm von Struve (Russian astronomer, b. 1793); Benjamin Silliman (American chemist, b. 1779); Edward Hitchock (American geologist and third president of Amherst College, b. 1793); and Franklin Bache (Philadelphia physician and great-grandson of Benjamin Franklin, b. 1792), all died in 1864. Henry W. Merian (b. 1839), an engineer on the ironclad *Weehawken*, actually died on December 6, 1863, when his ship went down off the coast of Charleston, South Carolina.
17. When Turner refers to "stereotyped definitions," he means definitions that have become accepted, fixed in scientific discourse. The notion of "stereotype" as an oversimplification or caricature did not come into use until the early 1920s.

and he is on the other side of Wilmington. But Lieutenant Holmes is gone, and I trust that he will bring an order relieving me from this one-horse town.

Very truly,

H. M. Turner.

## "Wilmington Correspondence"

(*The Christian Recorder*, April 1, 1865)

Mr. Editor:—After trying to preach to nearly six thousand persons on Sabbath afternoon, I galloped my horse into Wilmington for the purpose of attending night service there, in the splendid church which was recently received into our connection by Chaplain Hunter. After stabling my horse, I immediately proceeded to the church, where I found one of the finest churches in the city, filled with an audience equally interesting. Rev. Brother Hood, of the A.M.E. Zion Church, was preaching, and Hunter was sitting in his rear.[18]

After looking over the church a few moments, as this was my first visit, I then threw my head back to listen to Brother Hood. He preached a splendid sermon, which was highly appreciated by civilians and officers. After he concluded, I treated the subject of education a short time, and thus ended our meeting.

Next morning I learned that Brother Hood was here for the purpose of forming the Methodist congregations, and that Chaplain

---

18. In many ways, the career of James Walker Hood (1831–1918) paralleled that of Turner. He was a long-time bishop of the A.M.E. Zion Church, the founder and editor of the denominational newspaper, *The Star of Zion*, and was the author of *One Hundred Years of the African Methodist Episcopal Zion Church: Or, The Centennial of African Methodism* (New York: A.M.E. Zion Book Concern, 1895).

Hunter was holding on to his claims. My heart sank within me immediately, for I could anticipate the troubles which would follow.

During the day I met Brothers Hood and Hunter, with whom I conversed freely on their respective claims; Hunter contending that he had received the people, and procured for them military protection from General Schofield, and should not be interfered with; and Hood contending that Hunter was a chaplain in the army, and had no business interfering with civil matters, that the Zion Church had a conference in North Carolina and had resolved to hold their next session in Wilmington, and that he felt in duty bound to press his claims on the people.

While Hunter estimated the value of his right by virtue of the men slaughtered in his regiment in taking the place, doubting the possibility of holding Conference there without the aid of the military. But it is needless to refer to the arguments of these two men, suffice it to say, that from Sabbath night till Tuesday morning I heard and saw enough to sicken any man.

These two men conversed with me separately, and it will be understood that I did not feel any disagreeableness from the fact of their wrangling, for I know they were familiar with the circumstances connected with the matter. But what hurt me was, the citizens began to inquire of me how this difference existed.

Now, the idea of these two connections preaching the same gospel, believing the same doctrine, differing only on episcopacy, coming here among an innocent people to create a church schism, is a burning shame.

I am not finding fault with either Hood or Hunter. I am disposed to condemn neither for their connectional zeal. Both are right in trying to build up their respective connections; but the blame lies in the existence of the two organizations. As one of God's feeble instruments I tried to my utmost to unite these two churches, foreseeing this evil. I wrote and spoke upon it prior to the meeting of our last General Conference, at which I drew up and offered a set of resolutions that I thought no one could object to. These resolutions met the free endorsement of Superintendent Clinton, and several distinguished divines in both churches. But having to leave the General Conference for the army before they decided upon the proposition of uniting, I was informed they had agreed upon terms of partial unity, till informed better by Brother Hood.

According to his definition we stand upon the same uncertain base that the last General Conference found us. If that be a fact, I am much mistaken, for I positively thought something was effected in the convention held between the two connections; but if it be a fact, in the name of all that is dear to our religion, let the better thinking men rise in their great might and pity and break down that wicked partition.

The Conference will soon begin to meet, and as I shall not be at any of its sessions, as we will move in a few hours for some point in the middle of the state where terrible battles may have to be fought, and where I, for one, may fall in death, I feel it due the cause of my race and humanity to make this request. But as for one, I shall never quarrel with any body, relative to churches or theological technicalities, unless some one besides a Methodist assails my faith; then I may try to vindicate my religious policy. But I expect to quarrel with these two connections until they unite. Rather than destroy the unity of the Southern Methodists, I would prefer seeing the Bethel Church absorbed in the Zion ten times. I am for unity, at all hazards; and these brethren whom I learned threw firebrands in that convention which assembled for that purpose had better repent in sackcloth and ashes.

Let us unite at once, and stop this connectional fizzling henceforth and forever. I know there is not a minister in either church but would vote for it, could they witness what I do daily, and if the ministers will agree, the people will say nothing against it; they will be glad to see it: some timber-head might jabber a little, who can't appreciate its advantages, but God will soon kill him off.

Well, I must pack up and get ready to march; I learn that we are going to start for Goldsboro, where we may have to fight a great battle. However, be that as it may, try, friends of God and man, to unite the Zion and Bethel Churches.

Please excuse this writing, for all are in a bustle now.

Yours truly,

Chaplain H. M. Turner.

## "Army Correspondence by Chaplain Turner"
(*The Christian Recorder*, April 15, 1865)

*Headquarters 1st U.S.C.T*
*Fort Raison Depot.*
*March 28, '65.*

Mr. Editor:—I would have written a few days sooner, but for the fact that a thieving scoundrel, under the clandestine cover of night, came, and, with roguish hands, stole one of my horses, valued at $200. But as this dirty wretch has been overtaken, and my mind relieved by the return of my servant's horse, I trust I can now frame myself into writing humor sufficiently to throw a few facts together for the benefit of the many friends who are ever anxious to know our whereabouts.

On the morning of the 16th of March, at the command to march, we broke camp; and all portable comforts were girded on by the soldiers, and lashed to horses, or packed in wagons by the officers.

Every thing being in readiness, we marched out of camp, and halted for a few hours, at no great distance, in the woods, and near the pontoon bridge which was laid across the Northeast River.

Shortly afterwards, General Terry and staff rode past, making a splendid appearance. Then followed the 2d Division of the 24th Corps (white), after which our division (1st Division 25th Corps, colored), followed in pursuit. I might say that the whole of General Terry's command left. It will be understood that General Terry commands the brave troops who first came to attack Fort Fisher, with a view to its speedy reduction.

These forces were made up of the 1st Division of the 25th Army Corps (colored), and the 2d Division of the 24th Army Corps (white). The colored troops were commanded by Brevet Major-General Payne, and the white troops by Brevet Major-General Ames. The chief command is vested in the intrepid Major-General Terry.

Since the capture of Wilmington, General Terry's command has been lying at Northeast Station, about ten miles above Wilmington. However, the white troops having passed, my regiment led the advance of our division. Soon after crossing the river, we passed an extensive line of rebel works, which they had hastily evacuated upon hearing that Sherman was about to cut off their retreat.

Shortly after taking up our line of march, we were informed that our destination was Goldsboro. Consequently our march was continued for several days. Many incidents took place on the march of an amusing character, and also some which were quite saddening. But whatever was disagreeable was borne with the usual liveliness of our men. Passing through an extensive rebel country was a new thing to our soldiers: therefore, for the first few days, the inhabitants fared quite well. But afterwards, the white soldiers commenced the ransacking policy, which the colored troops had been rather reluctant to engage in; but as we were now considered a part of Sherman's army, and as they were accustomed to relieving the rebels of whatever they desired, our soldiers thought they would follow their example. So every one who had any desire for the foraging fun (we call it foraging), went at it in earnest.

The advance was led each day by a different division—one day by the white, and the next day by the colored. And I must say for the colored soldiers that they manifested more feeling for the rebels than did the white soldiers. When the white soldiers were in the advance, they would leave comparatively nothing—taking the last bit of meat, and every chicken, hog, sheep, cow, or horse upon the premises, and hurling the most bitter maledictions upon them if they dared to utter a word. But the colored soldiers, in several instances to my own knowledge, would leave some, and tell the rebel women to hide it if they could, or the white soldiers would take it all when they came along. Sometimes they would shout—

"Stop, boys! you have got enough now. Leave the poor creatures something to eat!" and like expressions.

But the white soldiers would excuse themselves by telling the rebel women and men (when the men were there), "If we don't take all, the colored boys will; so we might just as well take it now!"

There was one infamous old rebel who lived at Renanville, named Herron, who, however, fared very badly with the colored troops. He was a mean old wretch. He owned three hundred slaves, and treated them like brutes—yes, worse than brutes. It was on Sabbath, the 19th inst., when we arrived there, and as Providence would have it, we halted to rest and eat dinner.

Seeing his splendid mansion standing near the road, our boys made for it, and soon learned that he had just released a colored woman from irons, which had been kept on her for several days. Upon hearing of this and sundry other overt acts of cruelty committed by him on his slaves, the boys grew incensed, and they utterly destroyed every thing on the place. They gutted his mansion of some of the finest furniture in the world. With an axe they shattered his piano, bureaus, sideboards, tore his fine carpet to pieces, and gave what they did not destroy to his slaves—and on his speaking rather saucily to one of the boys, he was sent headlong to the floor by a blow across the mouth, his downward tendency being materially accelerated by an application of boot-leather to his "latter end." I heard afterwards that the white soldiers burned his houses to the ground; but whether they did so or not, I cannot say. But this much I do know—that I have seen numbers of the finest houses turned into ashes.

Oh, that I could have been a Hercules, that I might have carried off some of the fine mansions, with all their gaudy furniture. How rich I would be now! But I was not. When the rich owners would use insulting language, we let fire do its work of destruction. A few hours only are necessary to turn what cost years of toil into smoke and ashes.

During our entire march from Wilmington until we met Sherman, there was only one Union flag displayed by a citizen to our forces. His house was well protected. Neither soldiers nor officers would touch a cob. It was remarkable, too, to hear how impudently some of the rebel women would talk. Yet their loose-hung tongues in almost every instance brought them into trouble.

One very fine-looking lady, residing in a small village which we passed through, ran out of her house door, and bleated very loudly to a certain officer—

"Keep your negroes out of my yard!"

The officer said nothing, but passed on—but such a shower of "blessings" as the negroes heaped upon her devoted head would have well nigh aroused the dead from their graves. Such a string of expletives, I presume, never before greeted the ears of such a haughty Southern goddess.

I must now stop, for here comes marching orders.

\* \* \*

Having left Harrison Depot, and marched about fifteen miles, I now resume my correspondence with you.

As I was writing about the contemptibleness of several white women, I regard it needless to use their vulgar parlance, but simply to state that their repeated insults were almost in every instance visited with their just reward. I am sorry to state, however, that some of Sherman's men took their revenge in quite a disgraceful manner.

Among the amusing scenes which transpired was when our army came to fordable streams, which was often the case. Some streams through which we were obliged to wade would take the men up to their arms. Each brigade would generally halt for a short time prior to crossing, so as to be prepared for it. Some would simply hang their cartridge boxes on their bayonets, and plunge in with a cheerful but vociferous yell—while others would dismember pantaloons and drawers, and others still strip entirely naked, and swing their clothes over their heads—and amid all kinds of expressions and laughable utterances ever conceived by the genius of mirth, like some monstrous brood of liberated ducks, our brave boys would wake to the water as naturally as a beaver—wading through water, mud, and slop. This was indeed but an every-day occurrence.

So far as provisions are concerned, we found them in the greatest abundance. I even rode up to a fodder stack, and commenced pulling out some for my horse, when hams, sides, and shoulders of bacon fell out in such rapid succession that I thought I was mistaken in the place. Suffice it to say that our whole army, fifteen thousand strong, found enough and to throw away while passing through the enemy's territory. Honey itself was plentiful; for on passing several houses we found bee hives in any quantity—and these little fellows with all their stings were not proof against the voracity of our soldiers. One fellow would pick up a bee gum[19] on his shoulder and

---

19. A bee gum is a beehive, the name being derived from the hollow gum trees in which they were often built.

run like fury, while a dozen more would charge on the honeycomb with their bayonets, and the bees would pour out and blacken the air with numbers.

By this time the fellow carrying the gum would dash it down and run his bayonet or hand in, take out a pretty good piece of comb, and then *leave* like a streak of greased lighting, with apparently ten thousand enraged bees darting around his head. And by the time one brigade would pass, all the bee gums on the place would be robbed, and something less than twenty millions of bees intent on vengeance flying in every direction, stinging or trying to sting every thing they saw. And while in this pleasant mood, the remainder of our army would have to run the gauntlet past them—and you may be sure that men, horses, dogs or whatever passed by, were politely and *smartly* accosted by these gentlemen. But those who were stung by the maddened bees seemed to enjoy the joke quite as well as the more fortunate ones who laughed at them.

The colored people, too, were peculiarly interesting, and sometimes gave vent to expressions and acts which were quite amusing. Some would clap their hands and say, "The Yankees have come! the Yankees have come!" Others would say, "Are you the Yankees?" Upon our replying in the affirmative, they would roll their white eyeballs up to heaven, and, in the most pathetic strain, would say, "Oh, Jesus, you have answered my prayer at last! Thankee, thankee, Jesus."

Others would cry out, "I have been looking for you many years, and God told me you were coming to possess the land; and now here you are."

Others again would commence venting their revengeful desires by telling of their hardships and the cruelty of their owners, and wanting us to revenge them immediately.

But I must pass on. It was on the 20th inst. when we first came within hearing of General Sherman. His big guns sounding some eighteen miles distant told us we were nearing the great champion.

Our army was much fatigued, and every one felt quite exhausted, until the sound of his artillery gave us new life. We all longed to be there. The consequence was that we now marched more swiftly, and took longer strides.

At ten o'clock on the following day we came to where a part of Sherman's army had passed and saw for the first time a portion of his brave cavalry. And here we just began to learn what destruction was. We thought our men had been doing outrageously, but now we were convinced that we were all good fellows. Houses were burnt, and the fences for miles on both sides of the road demolished. Corn-cribs, smoke-houses and dairies were emptied of their contents—and if, perchance, a house was left standing at all, on entering it, one might find an aged white man, some white women, and a few children (formerly very rich), standing in the door, with watery eyes and haggard faces, and every thing either carried off or broken to pieces. Even the garments of women and children were destroyed, except what they had on their backs when the Yankees came to the house. The condition of the roads beggars description. Added to this was the woods on fire as far around us as the eye could reach.

Besides the children, turkeys, hogs, sheep, goats, cows, mules, horses, and all such things, for fifteen miles on either side, had disappeared. But that distance I do not think is sufficient, although I was so informed; for I saw some of Sherman's raiders come in, who told me they had been thirty miles off. However, to resume my story. We continued to follow the road so badly desolated by Sherman's army, until we arrived at the edge of the Neuse River. There General Terry halted his army, and we all commenced to prepare such quarters as we could rest awhile in. But it was not long before big guns began to tell us that Sherman and Johnson were only five miles away, and were measuring each other's strength.

All the afternoon and part of the night, amid a heavy falling rain, did the terrific roar of cannon and musketry keep up an unbroken clamor, while deadly missiles flew thick and terrible regardless of whom they might injure. Never did I hear such musketry before, except at Petersburg on the night of the 18th of June, 1864, when Grant and Lee, with more than fifty thousand men on each side, were kicking up a dust over that doomed city. During the night, however, Sherman drove the rebels across the river, but did not cross at the same place. So General Terry, with Sherman's pontoon corps, succeeded in laying two pontoon bridges over the Neuse River, up near where our troops were encamped. After the bridges were prepared, two brigades (1st and 2d) of our division were sent to hold them against any possible attack from the rebel side.

Having crossed the river, we soon had ourselves well fortified within a circle ranging about three hundred yards from the pontoon bridges. Here we lay quite secure from any rebel disturbance, except what opposition was offered to foraging parties, who were frequently driven in by the rebels, who were swarming on the road leading to Smithfield. Several times were our venturesome foragers driven within our undaunted lines.

During this time two corps of Sherman's great army passed over the bridges, and came through our works, en route to Goldsboro. This was a sight equally novel to both. We all desired to see Sherman's men, and they were anxious to see colored soldiers, particularly the colored heroes of Petersburg, as they called us. Therefore you may be sure they were not passing long before our boys thronged each side of the road. There they had a full view of Sherman's celebrated army. Soldiers without shoes, ragged and dirty, came by thousands. Bronzed faces and tangled hair were so common, that it was hard to tell if some were white. Their guns, instead of being clean and bright like ours, were rusty and dirty. They wore all sorts of hats, many of them looking like nests of confusion. Some of their officers were dressed the same as privates, many having no shoulder straps. Some of their generals looked worse than our second lieutenants. Sometimes a soldier would pass with his shirt-tail out, walking as large as a prince. About this time, here comes the rear of the corps. Now, look out for the rubbish—wagons in great numbers, pack mules, buggies, carriages, ambulances, and droves of colored men, women, and children.

I must say, and I say it with no prejudice whatever, that luck (if the word be admissible) has had much to do with the popularity of Sherman's celebrated army. I believe I estimate the value of its services, as highly as any one, but I do not regard it as *the* army of America. That is all I will now say, wait and see for yourself. So much for Sherman's army. After it had passed and gone to Goldsboro, our men went out foraging every day, each day contending with the rebels. I can't refer to any of our fights now, as the mail is about to leave.

H.M.T.

## "Army Correspondence"
(*The Christian Recorder,* May 6, 1865)

Warsaw, N.C.,
April 5th, 1865.

Mr. Editor:—At the close of my last letter, I had just commenced treating on the attack we sustained from the rebels on the 24th ult. As I was saying, having fortified ourselves north of the Neuse River so as to protect the pontoon bridges from any rebel interruption, we sent out foraging parties daily, who acted as scouts and also helped to keep our men and animals supplied.

The first day a few white soldiers went out in a rather straggling manner, and were captured by the rebels on the road leading to

Smithfield. On the following day the Division Battalion of sharpshooters encountered the enemy on the same road, in larger force. But the next day (the 24th), the rebels prepared to meet this party of Yankees, who walked so recklessly about upon their sacred soil. About ten o'clock, a company or two went out again, but had not proceeded far before the rebels halted them, and soon the roar of the cannon, in deafening reverberations, told us they meant fight. After exchanging several musket shots our men came back within our works, yet no one seemed in the least alarmed, as our men had made them fall back before leaving. Our camps were still full of life, and every thing went on as usual. About three o'clock, the rebels, expecting our return, came down the road, concealing a large force under cover of the woods, and began to annoy our pickets. Consequently, a few detachments were sent out to support them. They had not gone further than three hundred yards from our works before they met the rebel force. Our pickets by this time, however, had considerably aroused our attention, by an increased musket fire, and, joining the detachments sent to their support, resolved to question the rebels' authority for visiting our quarters, which they seemed to have in contemplation.

 A few volleys from our men, which were promptly responded to by the rebels, prepared every body in our lines for the war gauntlet. Our works teemed with *smoked* Yankees (as the rebels call us), while before them stood our pickets and detachment, contending with the rebel advance. I am sorry to say, a few volleys soon made the men of a certain regiment leave our detachment in front, and fall behind their works, which only left one of our companies and a few men of the 6th United States Colored Troops, to skirmish with a force quadrupling their number.[20] However, the brave boys of the

---

20. Turner is implying that the white regiment (the 2nd Division of the 24th Army Corps, commanded by Brevet Maj.-Gen. Ames) retreated and

1st Regiment, who have never given way in any skirmish, nor in nine battles, nor have ever failed to take any works they charged, and who have the confidence of every general in our corps, were there, and they stood firm, while the rebels poured the most galling fire into them that I ever saw poured into so few men in my life, and it is well known, I have seen war wonders. And there they continued to stand until the rebels began to fire grape into their ranks, when orders were sent them to come in, so as [to] get out of the way of our artillery, and allow us the same chance to fire grape at them.

The conduct of our boys on that occasion elicited the praise of thousands. But the bravery of my regiment has long since ceased to be a question, therefore, it is needless to rehearse it. And while the boys would rather die than lose their reputation, they are well aware that their good name has cost them severely. For they will be picked out of 20,000 colored troops to assume a risk, when others will lie around in camp.

Returning to the subject, our detachment, as I stated above, only came in to give room to our artillery. By this time the rebel artillery was in such position as to shell our camps very easily, and awful were the whizzing bombs which they for awhile hurled into our midst. They cut men in half, and pieces from exploded shells killed and wounded several. My tent happened to be in direct range of their artillery, and three or four bombs passed through and over my quarters. In a terrible state of excitement, I raised up to ascertain if they were really in earnest. At that moment, here came another. I then bargained with my feet and legs to carry my body away from that place, which they did in a hurry. The soldiers saw me running through the field in search of safer quarters, and, instead of looking out for the bursting shells, all began to laugh at the

---

left the fighting up to the colored troops of Turner's regiment.

chaplain. But the chaplain, preferring a good run to a bad stand, charged out of range as bravely as his soldiers generally charge in, which enabled him to bury the killed with divine service, instead of being buried with it himself. The rebels, however, dared not approach our works, though they had many invitations, for our men were constantly saying, Come on! Come on! But the rebels thought the colored Yankees were too willing, so they stayed away for spite, and well they did. Had they attempted to enter our lines, such a slaughter would have never been witnessed. Even as it was, we would have killed three to their one, had it not been for their shelling us, not because the rebels exhibited signs of cowardice at all, but because they overshot our men. The rebels numbered twelve hundred at least, while our detachment numbered less than one hundred. However, our artillery soon silenced theirs, and thus ended the engagement.

Shortly after, orders came to pack up and march, which we did, camping a few miles south of the Neuse River, which place we also left next morning, and marched for Faison Station, on the Wilmington and Goldsboro Railroad, en route to this point. We had to march again through a portion of country trodden a week before by Sherman's army. Here every thing wore the garb of desolation, portraying evidences of adversity's most awful sweep, raging in exterminating fury and shrouding every thing in the habiliments of utter waste.

Finally, reaching Faison Station, we went into camp with the understanding that we were to rest for several weeks. Upon this information we all commenced to prepare quarters for a long rest, but by the time we got our quarters done, and all things arranged for a few weeks' respite, our regiment was ordered to break camp and proceed to Warsaw, to guard that post, which we did with great glee, as we all thought it indicated some local duty. Arriving here about two o'clock at night, we made our beds on the ground, and went to sleep. Next morning opened up to our vision a little village. The news of black Yankees being here soon spread through the adjacent country, which has been ever since bringing in hundreds of contrabands to this place.

On Sabbath I had the large Baptist church opened, which holds about eight hundred persons, and preached at eleven o'clock, and my inestimable armor bearer Rev. John Hames at three, and myself again at night. A description of the day's proceedings would consume more time than I have now to spare. At all our services, however, the church has been far too small to hold the people. But owing to my heavy responsibilities, and incessant labors, I am compelled to transfer the most of the preaching to Brother Hames and Rev. Edgar Stephenson, both of whom are known as non-commissioned chaplains, by virtue of their being (by my own appointment) my assistants. Brother Hames is a member of the A.M.E. Church, lives in Washington City, is a splendid preacher, mighty in prayer, excellent at singing, obedient to orders, always at work, and wields a moral influence throughout the regiment, that will tell for good in years to come. Besides, wherever he goes he establishes prayer meeting and preaching places so rapidly and successfully, that I am often surprised. Had Brother Hames a better education, he would be one of earth's great men. Brother Stephenson lives in Alexandria, Va., is a member of the A.M.E. Church, a good man, good character, ordinary, preacher, charming in prayer, sings well, but not very feelingly, reads well, writes some, obedient to orders, thinking nothing impossible for the people of God, and is an assiduous laborer in and out of the regiment. No one can imagine the pleasure it often gives me, while engaged in my labors, to have Hames on one side and Stephenson on the other, for each one knows his side.

Every thing has gone off finely, except a little misunderstanding which created some excitement yesterday among our soldiers, growing out of some adjustment of contraband affairs by some of our officers. But as these people have been placed in my charge, every thing is as smooth as ever.

Will not some of the friends of humanity collect at least 1,000 copies of President Lincoln's Emancipation Proclamation, and forward to my address. Send also any Congressional enactments bearing upon the freedom of the slaves. I want no abolition speeches, but legal documents. I only wish I had 5,000 copies. If some of our Tract Societies would circulate that Proclamation through the South, it would accomplish far more good than some of their tracts, which are too often looked at and thrown aside.

I know it has become quite popular for soldiers and young ladies to correspond on the subject of marriage, yet strangers to each other. But those three young ladies who have been writing to me, complimenting my letters to the *Recorder,* and desiring to correspond on the subject of matrimony, will allow me to inform them, that I am a married man; besides, if they could see me, they would not want me, for I am as ugly as Old Harry, have a woolly head, face scarred with small pox, big feet, bowed shanks, and I can't walk, but have to hobble (my horse threw me the other day). And if I were not married, and ever so attractive, I have no time to waste upon such trashy matters now. I am not able to answer one third of the letters received relating to important business. Before me now lie nineteen letters, which ought to be replied to. I have six sheets of paper, four envelopes, and two postage stamps, and those I begged from my soldiers.

The news has just arrived that five of our soldiers who were on guard at Faison's Mill have been killed by the rebel cavalry, who dashed in and took them by surprise.

*Ten Minutes Later.*

I have just been out to see Penny, of Company K., whose left fingers are shot off, and has a ball in his head. He is covered with blood, and reports all killed but himself, and he was left for dead by the rebels after having his pockets searched. I think his case is beyond recovery. There is great excitement among our men. One company has left to look for the rebels, and woe be unto the wretches if found.

## "Army Correspondence"
(*The Christian Recorder,* May 6, 1865)

Headquarters 1st U.S.C.T.,
Raleigh, N.C.,
April 17th, 1865.

Mr. Editor:— I must be content to sketch out a short synopsis of our route from Warsaw to this place. Sunday morning, the 9th inst., orders to march came early in the morning, every thing being in a bustle to be ready at the shortest time possible. The news spread with inconceivable rapidity among the inhabitants of the place. The whites were evidently glad on the reception of such intelligence, while the colored were sorrowful, chagrined, and despondent. Men, women, and children had come for miles from the adjacent country, to find freedom and patriotism under our flag. Six or seven hundred of these, at least, were women and children in a state of nudity, and without any means of support. To this class especially I had issued government rations, supplied them with house room, and protected in the best manner possible. But they were not the only recipients of this favor. Several white ladies and slave oligarchs were glad to enter my office in the same humiliating custom which they formerly would have expected from me, and ask for a permit to draw from the government, whining under a pretended vengeance they would like to inflict upon their southern degraders. I know that was all fudge, but it satisfied me to see them crouching before me, and I a negro. But I am leaving the subject.

The news having spread that we were going to leave, the colored people became wonderfully excited. There were hundreds of children who could not walk, women in the same fix, and vast numbers thought it impracticable to attempt to follow us into the middle of the state, and to remain there was thought to be death, for the scouts of the rebel Wheeler were expected in as soon as we left, who would kill and destroy them without mercy.[21] To describe the scene produced by our departure would be too solemn, if time and space permitted. Suffice it to say, many were the tears shed, many sorrowful hearts bled. Vast numbers followed us at every risk, and others started for Wilmington, where they all are. God alone knows I was compelled to evade their sight as much as possible, to be relieved of such words as these, "Chaplain, what shall I do? where can we go? will you come back?" &c. But amid it all we marched off about nine o'clock, followed by an immense concourse of colored and white. And thus we continued, resting at intervals, till we arrived at Faison's Depot, ten miles up the railroad. Here we joined our brigade, and in rejoining that, joined our corps, which was rendezvousing from its scattered fragments preparatory to our move upon this place.

Early Monday morning, 10th inst., the drums beat, trumpets were blown, tents struck, horses saddled and geared, and soon the long line of soldiers, marching to the cheering music of the bands, told Faison's Depot farewell, but told Raleigh to look out, for the Yankees were coming.

As we marched out of our respective camps, cheer after cheer went up, and deafening huzzas rang far and wide. And thus we continued all day, passing through a country hostile to us from

---

21. Gen. Joseph ("Fighting Joe") Wheeler (1836–1906), one of the Confederacy's most storied commanders, led the cavalry of the Army of Tennessee. Decades later, the now-elderly general would return to the front in both the Spanish-American War (1898) and the Philippine-America War (1899–1902).

every consideration, but at the same time possessing many things which were quite friendly, such as meat, chickens, turkeys, molasses, and a great many things which our boys knew how to make use of. We will not stop here to speak of the many transpiring occurrences which attended our march. Though much was very visible, especially where justice seemed to be paying off some of these old slave-holding rascals in their own coin. In the afternoon of the 11th inst., we arrived and marched through the battleground of Generals Sherman and Johnston, where they fought at Bentonville, on the 19th ult.[22] This was an interesting spot to our corps, as we were out in the fight at the time, though we were close to the place. The rebel General Johnston had thrown up a line of works near the road where Sherman had to pass, to stop his audacious march, but the same audacity which had led Sherman thus far, led him to stop and throw up a triple line of works in Johnston's face, and run him away. I was struck with the difference between Sherman's and Johnston's engineering. Though Johnston had been there some time before the arrival of Sherman, yet he only had one line of defenses prepared, and not one of flanking works, while Sherman in one night built three lines within two hundred yards of Johnston's main works, and had his flanks all prepared in the best manner imaginable. If Johnston's military genius as displayed at Bentonville constitutes him a great general, then I know I am a greater one (General Turner). The battleground being in the woods, the trees were in many places riddled with balls. I was amused at one tree, through which seven cannon balls had passed, yet it continued to stand. That tree must have been a rebel. Be that as it may, however, the tree seems to say, "I won't

---

22. The Battle of Bentonville (March 19–21, 1865) was the final encounter between Gen. William Tecumseh Sherman and Gen. Joseph E. Johnston. Johnston would surrender to Sherman on April 26, following Lee's surrender to Grant at Appomattox Court House on April 9.

fall." Other trees had every limb shot off without materially injuring the trunk, while several graves told us, here lie the victims of treason's foul curse.

Passing on to notice further, we halted on the 12th inst., we being in a valley to eat dinner, amid the most quiet time we had witnessed on our march, the main army being on the roadside. All at once a terrible musket fire broke out, and such cheering I never heard. This excited us; the Colonel formed the regiment in great haste, preparing for a battle. I mounted my horse and sped toward the firing to learn the result. They told me General Lee had surrendered. Back I went to spread the news, and no sooner was it announced than the most vociferous shouts were given; soldiers ran, jumped up, turned over; officers hugged each other, clasped their hands, &c. And all day long, from that time, would regiments and brigades cheer, shout, whoop, shoot guns, while companies join and whistle Yankee Doodle and Hail Columbia, until I wished every mouth was crammed full of mush to stop the noise. I had rather hear cannon fire, than to hear 50,000 men get to hallooing. Cannons will stop some time, but men seem never to know what stop means.

Finally, drawing near to Raleigh, we began to form junctions with the various columns of Sherman's army.

About nine o'clock, Thursday morning, 13th inst., General Kilpatrick entered Raleigh with his cavalry, closely followed by the 15th Corps.[23] The rebel Wheeler's cavalry retreated before him. One rebel lingered behind and shot at General Kilpatrick, expecting his horse would save him, but our men caught him and hung

---

23. Brig. Gen. Hugh Judson Kilpatrick (1836–81), known for his fearlessness and recklessness in battle as well as his womanizing ways, served under Sherman during both the March to the Sea and the Carolinas campaign.

him immediately. He was brave, though. He said he didn't care a d—n what we did with him, and you may be sure our men did not care, since he did not. But our entrance into Raleigh I know will be fully delineated by the northern papers. Therefore, I regard it needless to speak of it in detail. I presume, also, that the *Herald*, ere this reaches you, will have the topography of the city so well mapped off, that a description in that respect would also be useless. Our corps having gone into camp near the city, I was soon in town looking around at the place. Finding some Methodists in my perambulation, I began to inquire of the state of the churches. One gentleman referred me to a Mr. Henry Hunter. I went to his house, made his acquaintance, and to my great surprise, found myself among the relatives of Chaplain W. H. Hunter. His wife, Minerva Hunter, is an aunt of the chaplain's. Her nine children, Eleanor Hinton, Cela Jefferis, and Patsy Turner are married, and Cinthia, Sarah, Henry, Elliot, and George Hunter are single. I am proud to say, this family is as nice a family as can be found in the state. They are clean, intelligent, quick, and stylish. Brother Henry Hunter is one of the oldest leaders, and is regarded as a pillar of the church. Sunday, the 16th inst., we had decided upon attending church, but in consequence of the colored Methodist church being both dirty and lousy, in consequence of the rebels having made a hospital of it, for whenever a rebel stays two hours, you may expect lice, the colored people rented an old shop, which would hold about 1,200 persons.

Here I preached in the morning, and Rev. J. H. Payne, in the afternoon; after which I received the leaders, 14; stewards, 7; members, 450 or 500; and a fine sumptuous church, and large lot, all paid for, into the A.M.E. Church, and a finer-looking audience I have never seen than I found in Raleigh, N.C. I had to congratulate them several times on their appearance, manners, customs, habits, rules, and social regulations. Though one-half, if not two-thirds, of the colored people are mulattoes, yet there is evidently a higher moral status among them than is usual in this state.

This morning I licensed one preacher and one exhorter, which was the first thing of the kind in a generation of years.

But I know you want me to stop. I forget I am writing so much. This I must say, however: there were great fears here last night. The soldiers threaten to avenge the death of President Lincoln on the citizens. I will refer to that next time.

  H.M.T.


## "Army Correspondence"
(*The Christian Recorder*, May 27, 1865)

*Goldsboro, N.C.*
*May 15th, 1865.*

Mr. Editor:—Having seen that your columns were gorged with correspondence, I have become somewhat delinquent in what I hitherto regarded as a duty, obligatory under the most pressing circumstances, which was to keep up a weekly communication with the *Recorder*.[24] Ever since you raised the *Recorder* from its sepulchral confinement, I have endeavored to support you and your measures for its perpetuation, to the best of my ability. And now, as the paper has become indispensable to the public, and is daily growing in its wide-spreading interests, thus bringing to its aid the patronage of the best minds, both as subscribers and literary contributors, I feel that the time has nearly if not entirely

---

24. No issue from May 13, 1865, is extant, but it is unlikely that Turner published a column in that issue given his comment here. No column appeared in the May 20 issue.

arrived, when acuter minds and abler pens can be substituted for mine.

I have been often told, under the subterfuge of a dry joke, that my letters to the *Recorder,* for the last five years, were written in view of personal aggrandizement. But unfortunately for them, these parties were generally composed of that fastidiously squeamish class of persons, who have neither the ability nor the moral courage to encounter public criticism, and for whom I care no more than I do for the cackle of a hen, or the braying of a mule. I would have to pull straws to decide which I hate the most, the devil or these self-conceited timber-heads. One is the bane of hell, the other is the plague of earth, and you might as well try to get honey out of a horse-shoe, or music out of an elephant, as to try to get any good out of either. I make these remarks regardless whether there are any preachers guilty of the act or not. But it is a lamentable fact, that in the very crisis that demands all the energies, gifts, attainments, natural or acquired, and every other qualification tending to give fitness and suitability, in shaping public sentiment, developing the capacities of the contrabands, moralizing our soldiers, whose unbridled lives for the past four years have almost hurled them headlong into the vortex of irrevocable profanity, vulgarity, and impoliteness, that men who would disdain to be called foolish will idle away their abilities straining at gnats and swallowing camels. But for fear I may be somewhat flaw-eyed too, and disposed to hatch molehills into mountains, let us turn to another subject.

About the 29th ult., our division left Raleigh, N.C., and took up our march for Goldsboro. Passing leisurely through the country, we had a pleasant time observing things under their more natural exhibitions, than when we were proceeding towards Raleigh; for on our march there, it was next to impossible to see a male rebel, as they were mostly concealed in the woods. But on our return to Goldsboro, the men had come out of their private retreats, and could be seen standing in their yards, and sitting in their piazzas.

Arriving at Smithfield, we found the bridge burned, and Sherman's pontoons all removed; thus subjecting us to the very disagreeable necessity of wading the river, which in some places was chin deep, but as this had become a familiar job, those who had no horses went in clothed or nude, just as they chose to take it. I was much amused to see the secesh women, watching, with the utmost intensity, thousands of our soldiers in a state of nudity. I suppose they desired to see whether these audacious Yankees were really men, made like other men, or if they were a set of varmints. So they thronged the windows, porticos, and yards, in the finest attire imaginable. Our brave boys would disrobe themselves, hang their garments upon their bayonets, and through the water they would come, walk up the street, and seem to say to the feminine gazers, "Yes, though naked, we are your masters."

Shortly after our arrival in Smithfield, one of our sergeants called my attention to a colored lady, whose child a rebel woman had hid. I immediately started for her sacred premises, and having entered her piazza, in company with the sergeant, colored woman, and a few others, the following conversation ensued:

"Have you got this woman's child?"

"No! her master carried it off."

"Where is her master, as you call him?"

"He is gone into the country."

"What did he carry the child away for?"

"Because he wanted to."

"Did he not know the child belonged to this woman?"

"Yes! But if it is her child, it is his negro. You Yankees have a heap of impudence. What are you meddling with our negroes for? You may think the South is conquered, because she has surrendered to superior numbers. But, sir, you are sadly mistaken."

"Stop, stop!" I replied, "I don't want any more of your rebel parlance. You are not too good to be hung, and you had better dry up, or you might get a rope around your neck in short order."

At this stage of our dialogue, one of the general's staff rode up, and she began to tell him a long story about me, weaving in a lie here, and a lie there. But he soon silenced her by saying:

"O, well! he has a right to say what he thinks proper! Madam, I want to know why this child is not given up?"

So she proceeded to chit-chat the subject with him, and having heard as much as my stomach could digest at once, said I to the officer, "It is reported that the child is hid in town, but she says her husband has taken it into the country. I now propose, as he has five children standing here, that we take one to be held as a hostage, until the colored child is returned to its mother." The words had hardly left my mouth, before such a running, crying, and squealing took place among the children that my indignation melted down into laughter. The very utterance of these words frightened the poor children nearly to death, and made the mother tremble. At this juncture, learning that the general had taken the matter in hand, I left. But look at the inconsistency: they could not feel the colored woman's grief, yet when the same pill was offered to them, they were frightened into fits. To have taken one of their children would have been pronounced, by the slave oligarchs, an act of fiendish cruelty, but for them to perpetrate the same crime on a poor colored woman, was only an inconsiderable circumstance. If a few of our Northern slave advocates had the tables thus turned upon them, it would materially change the tone of some of their brutal sophistry, as well as morally improve that remonstrating gibberish too often used to stay the designs of an administration whose ultimate purpose seems to be the upbuilding of a depressed people.

Having, however, arrived at Goldsboro, the 2d Brigade (General Duncan's) was assigned to duty in that city, while the others were placed in such positions as the state of things required. My regiment went into camp on the suburbs of the town, where they still remain.

Goldsboro is said to contain about 1,200 inhabitants, two-thirds of whom are colored. There are several fine buildings in the place, encircled by spacious yards, shade trees, flower gardens, &c. The houses built especially for the colored population stand far back in the rear, which makes the principal approach to them through massa's front gate, enabling him, in other days, to sit back in his big arm chair and propound all the interrogations which might suit his fancy, before letting you pass. But thank God, those days are now numbered among passed events. When these colored dignitaries, known as United States soldiers, step by in Uncle Sam's paraphernalia, the only sentence that greets their ears is an invitation to take a seat.

This being a city from which numerous railroads branch out, it has become the rendezvous of returning rebel soldiers. The cars, for the past few weeks, have been thronged with them, from the armies of Johnson and Lee, presenting in their appearance, every imaginable aspect, from ragamuffins to ten-toed dandies. Some strut around town, assuming as much air as an old turkey gobbler with a dozen gills. Down street a party will start, who were once officers, wearing, as a waning memorial, the dying vestige of a played-out confederacy, in the shape of an ideal uniform. But they proceed only a short distance before they meet another party of gentlemen, whose black faces seem to glisten in the rays of the sun, their caps whirled over on one side of their heads, burning the rebels' own narcotic, under the appellation of segars, and puffing in dense fumigations, with heads thrown back and eyes elevated so high that they seem to say, I wouldn't look down, if I knew I were wading through greenbacks. The rebel party steps to one side, and onward goes the negro van, looking neither to the right or left. But the rebel party stops, and looks back at these magic lords, swaggering on in their exultant conquest, and seems to be musing as to whether they are actually in another world, or whether this one is turned wrong side out, until they finally resume their equilibrium.

I am happy to inform you that Chaplain Hunter has begun, and is carrying on, a great work in this city. His regiment having been assigned to do provost duty, and having his quarters in the courthouse, he is in a favorable situation to use his gifts and graces among our people. He has, therefore, taken possession of the Methodist Church, formerly used by the white congregation, except the gallery, which was appropriated to the colored, and in it has commenced a school, which numbers nearly four hundred. It is entirely taught by the chaplain and several young men of his regiment. And, although it has only been in existence two weeks, it is better conducted than many I have seen in two years. There are few men who take more pride in training children than Chaplain Hunter; besides, his extensive experience peculiarly fits him for this work.

There is also a glorious revival of religion going on in the same church, which is also under the auspices of the Chaplain. I have given him all the assistance I could under the circumstances, but shall lay claim to no part of his glorious reward, when God pays off his laborers in the coin of eternal life. The altar is nightly thronged with penitent souls seeking the pearl of great price.

Rev. Dr. Deems, of the M.E. Church South, called upon the chaplain yesterday, to ascertain the relation of this church to its former conference, and to see if the chaplain intended to hold on to it. I did not hear the conversation entirely, but heard enough to satisfy myself of the fact that the chaplain, in the most humorous manner, and with that significant air of dignity which is so peculiar to him, looked the late exponent of Southern rights in the face, and in the mildest language possible, wrote out his epitaphical dirge, and sung the funeral ditty quite chagrin[ed]ly, to the once pompous, but now blighted chop-fallen of fancied imagination. If I were Dr. Deems, I would inform Jefferson Davis about Hunter's conduct and have my revenge, if I had to climb a greasy pole, or swallow a Bologna sausage.

Large crowds of soldiers are leaving daily on furloughs, but it is unpleasant for many to be compelled to go without money. My regiment has received no pay for ten months. I cannot help finding some fault with the government about this. If our soldiers were paid regularly, they would not grieve so often about their wives re-marrying, and claiming as an excuse that they were compelled by actual necessity. While I do not regard it as any apology at all, but if any thing, an aggravation of their disgraceful treachery, for which no soldier should receive an apology, nor pardon the wretches, if they were to shed enough bloody tears to wash Mount Vesuvius from its burning crater to its cindered base, yet these long intervals between pay days subjects our gallant heroes and their families to a thousand inconveniences. But I do not think the chief authorities are at fault in the matter. I believe it is the oversight of paymasters.

H.M.T.

## "Army Correspondence"

(*The Christian Recorder,* June 10, 1865)

Headquarters 1st Regt. U.S.C.T.,
Goldsboro, N.C.,
May 25, 1865.

Mr. Editor:—Living, as we are, in a dispensation pregnant with events, and pending with immortal issues, the expansive mind, amid the scenes and vicissitudes engaging its miraculous progress, seems ever and anon to be trying to balance itself like a ship rocked to and fro by the uncertain waves of an angry ocean, yet helmed with fear, doubt, and timid apprehension. Was ever earth swept before by such a varied succession of revolutionizing eventualities as now spread themselves before the astonished gaze of mankind, even to those who have looked and waited with breathless suspense for the dawn of brighter days, much less the crude, ideal, and corporeally-formed minds of that retrogressive class who live and die in the masquerade of their own selfish propensities? Nothing less than some magic scroll, indented by the touch of some ancient demi-god or semi-devil, and worked by the invisible and fantastic force of a superstitious agency, could have embodied and broadcastly scattered revelations so joyful to-day, and so appalling to-morrow. That seemingly drastic and rejuvenescent tree, which but yesterday stood studded with inflorescent charms so enrapturing to the eye, to-day bends under a blighting curse and wears the black drapery of blasting death, to the ghastly horror of the same spectator. Such divergent extremities to meet in one panoramic view, the startled observer, in the same train, and managed by the same God, adjusted by the same Providence, tending to the same ends, and consummating the same great, grand, and noble object, makes this (all things considered) one of the greatest epochs known since the world began.

Weighty and forcible analogies might be adduced to bear out the above remarks, if argument were necessary. But as these fluctuating transitions stand out in such unclouded glare, and as political changes and diplomatic mutabilities all seem to loom up with an operating agency, through forces marshaled under such divine display, that the idea rises so sublimely grand, and ravishes all human conception so transcendently, that to attempt a practical illustration would be like trying to recognize a single gem amid the glitter of ten thousand.

So we will omit to specify much of interest in the grand wheel of progression, for the ultimate conclusion of all must lead to the fact, that the instrumentalities which seemingly are so heterogeneously at work, and are so diametrically opposite in their character, are convergently tending to the glorious and benign consummation of justice, right, and equity upon an eternal bastion immovably irresistible. Consequently the startled beholder looks on in astonished wonder at the mysterious providence of God in events, like a complicated machine diverse in its parts, yet belted in mercy, and webbed with a singular and significant conglutination.

But suppose we leave this train of ideas, and turn to occurrences actually transpiring, as they are much more interesting at this time than our metaphysical ramblings could be made, however gaudy or florid their adornment.

Only a few weeks ago we were at Warsaw Depot, where I had quarters in a house with an old man and his son-in-law, both of whom had always been slaves. The old gentleman was rather antipathetically disposed towards the flogging fun, and consequently had spent about one-third of his life in the woods, bidding defiance to slave-hunters, negro hounds, or any other scheme they might try to catch him with. But after we went there and assured him of his freedom, and had left, several rebels went through that vicinity, beating the colored people and making them resume their former servitude. So one, with his natural sense of lordship, well armed and equipped, rode around to this old gentleman's home, and after a ventilation of orders and threats, the old man (Uncle Bill Hill) and his son-in-law nabbed him, took his gun, pistol, home, and tied him with ropes, and marched him on a double quick, some ten miles to our troops, and then accompanied him to Goldsboro, where the general received the scamp and paid the old man the highest compliment.

This is not the only instance, by far, where the colored people are giving evidence of commendable manhood. That innate principle guarantied to all men by their Creator, is fast quickening into life ,and rising from the slumber that has shrouded them for many ages;

and when once the impulsive race of color has regained its natural promptings and aspirations, woe be to those who would dare to desecrate the sanctity of their rights by intruding their selfish and diabolical schemes to thwart, through force or any ambidextrous treachery, the ends and ultimate designs of God in their creation.

There are a great many deaths in and around Goldsboro; the principal portion of whom are citizens. The most prevalent disease appears to be a physical prostration, growing out of a want of vegetable food. Sherman's army, while recuperating in this place, destroyed every vestige of vegetation, and burned every fence surrounding the gardens, fields, &c. Many, however, are at work trying to reestablish those horticultural institutions which have been disorganized by the pillage (as the secessionists call it) of Sherman's army, who, I trust, will be able, in a few weeks, to supply all necessary demands; but at present there is a terrible state of scarcity.

I must, with much regret, say that white troops are not fit to garrison the country, because there is not one in twenty who will do justice to the colored man. If there were no prejudice growing out of color, it would be quite different. But many, I am sorry to say, will curse, threaten, and, as I learn, even whip colored persons, where they think they will escape detection, to gratify some "secesh belle," or to keep the good will of some Southerner who can keep a sumptuous table. I have been told, over and over, by colored persons that they were never treated more cruelly, than they were by some of the white Yankees. But the colored troops treat the colored [sic] troops respectfully, and have nothing to do with the whites at all. Besides, the white people here prefer the colored troops, from the fact that they are respectful and orderly, and are not rambling through their houses, nor troublesome to their wives and daughters, &c.; neither do they stand by the wayside to taunt or blackguard those who are passing, as I have heard the whites do. Some of these disorderly white soldiers passed through here a few days since and forgot where they were. They soon commenced their habitual custom, by cursing the negroes. Some of the colored soldiers came up and began to return the cursing compliment, which much enraged the white soldiers; a fist-fight ensued, which lasted some time, and resulted in knocking several down, and placing the whole party under negro guards. There is seldom any disturbance where colored soldiers are guarding a place; but with the whites there is an endless bow-wow over and about some great big nothing.

There was a Union meeting held in this place a few days ago, which brought together some of the hardest-looking men I ever beheld. They came in from the adjacent country, representing its various districts in the capacity of delegates. Their speeches were quite patriotic, however, and savored of a willingness to abide the consequences of laws repugnant to their former institutions.

Thousands of poor white people are coming in town daily, and drawing rations. Women come from forty miles off, traveling for days to and from the town, to find something to eat. Others take the advantage of this benevolence on the part of the government to traffic, and satisfy their roguish ambition by whining for rations, and then speculating with them.

But, as I am bothered so, I cannot write, owing to so many calls, I will stop for this time.

    H.M.T.

*Chapter Five*

# *Roanoke Island*

*(June 24, 1865–August 5, 1865)*

AFTER THE WAR, the Union troops that remained in the South became, in Edwin S. Redkey's words, "the only official government in the ex-Confederate states."[1] Because the term of enlistment in the army was customarily three years, many white soldiers were mustered out at war's end. However, because most of the black troops enlisted after emancipation, the majority of black troops were expected to continue their service. Thus a large number of black troops, in an ironic twist, became the keepers of those who were once their masters. Others were put in charge of camps and colonies made up of freed slaves, like the Roanoke Island Freedmen's Colony, off the coast of North Carolina, where Turner's regiment was sent in early June 1865.

The Roanoke Island settlement, like many of the freedmen's camps, formed somewhat organically after Union troops occupied

---

1. Edwin S. Redkey, ed., *A Grand Army of Black Men: Letters from African-American Soldiers in the U.S. Army 1861–1865* (Cambridge: Cambridge University Press, 1992), 161.

the island after the Battle of Roanoke Island in February 1862. The island attracted slaves from the island as well as from northeast North Carolina, and initially, the settlement was largely organized and run by the escaped slaves themselves.[2] By January 1865 there were about 18,000 freedmen in Union-controlled eastern North Carolina; 3,091 of these were encamped on the island.[3] Most camps were meant to be temporary, and conditions were primitive, if not downright deplorable. The Roanoke settlement was significantly more livable than most, in large part because it was intended to be permanent. The colony was laid out on a grid on the northwestern corner of the island. Each family was given a two-hundred by two-hundred-foot piece of land, nearly an acre, on which to build a house and plant a garden. For the Rev. Horace James, chaplain of the 25th Massachusetts, who was assigned to run the Freedmen's Colony in 1863, "there was an important distinction between a camp and a colony: a camp provided a safe temporary haven for former slaves, while a colony offered the opportunity to mold a permanent community," intended to be made up of the families of freedmen soldiers.[4]

James recruited teachers, mostly from the American Missionary Association, to establish schools on the island. However, the vicissitudes of war, as well as the ambivalent racial attitudes of the military leaders under whom James served, made the future success of the colony tenuous. Soldiers of the U.S.C.T., as well as those left on the island, complained of their treatment. Some were impressed into work crews for local construction projects, most notably, the canal at Dutch Gap; others worked without receiving pay. In one particularly disturbing instance, residents of the colony reported

---

2. Patricia C. Click, *A Time Full of Trial: The Roanoke Island Freedman's Colony, 1862–1867* (Chapel Hill: University of North Carolina Press, 2002), 32–36.
3. Click, *Time Full of Trial*, 11.
4. Click, *Time Full of Trial*, 12–13.

that they had been accosted and restrained by members of the colony's (white) theatrical troupe, who cut off their hair to make wigs for their "minstrel chorus."[5]

By the time Turner arrived on the island with the 1st U.S.C.T. in June 1865, the colony was on the verge of revolt. Holland Streeter, appointed by James to be superintendent of the island, had apparently been selling the rations intended for the freedmen (many of whom were families of black enlisted soldiers and thus guaranteed protection by the government). Col. John H. Holman, commander of the 1st U.S.C.T., found the island in a state of "gross mismanagement," and wrote to the head of the Freedmen's Bureau that the inhabitants of the island had "lost all confidence in the persons appointed to conduct their affairs. . . . There is a great degree of corruption and disonesty."[6] In July 1865, Streeter was tried and convicted by a military commission for embezzlement, fraud, and "cruel treatment to the colored women under his care."[7]

Turner's letters from Roanoke portray the colony at a critical point between success and failure. In his last letter, he writes, "I do not expect a high state of things, in this day at most; it will be impossible for the present generation to become wonders of the world. Nothing more than a partial state of civilization and moral attainment can be hoped for by the most sanguine." While praising the efforts of Horace James and his missionary colleagues for their attempts to educate and literally civilize the freedmen, he also argued that it was up to the educated black man to perform this function. "About him the most incredulous would have no doubt," he wrote; neither would blacks be swayed by the demagoguery of "oily-tongued slaveocrats" or bribed with offers of "sumptuous tables, fine chambers," or "attractive misses." Most of all, because he

---

5. Click, *Time Full of Trial*, 125.
6. Qtd. in Click, *Time Full of Trial*, 144.
7. Qtd. in Click, *Time Full of Trial*, 147.

Fig. 5. Col. John H. Holman, 1st U.S.C.T. United Military Army Military History Institute.

would be welcomed into the social spaces of blacks—their "homes, weddings, parties, promenades," he would have a greater "influence and personal identification" with the freedmen than whites could ever achieve.

Turner clearly presented himself as an example of one of these "cultural missionaries." He also used the advantages of his military post to engage in actual missionary activity on behalf of the A.M.E. Church. However, despite the army's efforts, as well as those of the other philanthropists and missionaries who came to the island, the Roanoke colony failed. In large part its failure was caused by confusion over land ownership, for after the government promised the freedmen title to the land of former slaveholders, President Johnson refused to bestow the property without compensation. Since the freedmen had no capital to begin with that would enable them to purchase this property, they found it nearly if not absolutely impossible to buy and maintain their farms. Attempts to establish manufacturing on the island also failed. The colony was officially dissolved in March 1867; within a few short years, hardly any traces remained of the settlement.

\* \* \*

## "Army Correspondence by Chaplain Turner"
(*The Christian Recorder,* June 24, 1865)

*Headquarters 1st U.S.C.T.*
*Roanoke Island*
*June 14, '65.*

Mr. Editor:—On the 3d instant our division was aroused from its quiet slumbers by dashing orderlies galloping in every direction, with marching orders. Thus we were all soon in a great stir, getting ready to leave Goldsboro, where we had rested pleasantly for several weeks. Our entire division having been assigned to coast duty, in consequence of an idea cherished by the commanding general that colored troops are better adapted to the climate on the sea coast in hot weather than white troops, therefore, the three brigades were respectively assigned as follows:—

First Brigade, consisting of 1st, 30th and 107th U.S.C.T., to Morehead City and vicinity, while my (1st) regiment came to Roanoke Island.

Second Brigade, consisting of 4th, 5th, and 39th U.S.C.T., were assigned to New Bern and vicinity.

Third Brigade, consisting of the 6th, 37th, and 27th U.S.C.T., went to Wilmington and vicinity.

We left Goldsboro, to the displeasure of all parties, both white and colored being opposed to our going.

Taking the cars, we arrived in New Bern on the afternoon of the same day. Shortly after my arrival, I was met by the Rev. Mr. Hood, of the Zion church, who offered me the comforts of his house and extended me a most cordial welcome to the city. I went to his house, stayed all night, tried to preach in his splendid church, and had a pleasant time generally. Mrs. Hood is a beautiful lady, very prepossessing, highly cultivated, and reflects honor upon the parsonage. I admire Brother Hood's taste in selecting a partner very much; for ministers generally pick and choose a great deal, and then marry the most homely ladies. I find Brother Hood a strong advocate for union between our two connections. He informed me that the name proposed for our connection after its union is the United African Methodist Episcopal Church. I would suggest that its name be simply, United Methodist Episcopal Church.

I suppose some will think I have fallen a devotee to the sophistry of Brother Lynch.[8] But as he is recognized as the champion of

---

8. Turner is referring to his friend and fellow A.M.E. Church minister,

that theory, I acknowledge myself a devotee to his irrefutable arguments; for it is destined to popularize him, if it takes fifty years—though I have no idea that he ever presumed on such a thing as popularity in his advocacy of the subject. I make those assertions for him. I believe not only the African Church, but all other religious and moral institutions designated by local terms, are destined to die out. That little word "unity" is going to eat up and annihilate, in God's own good time, every other phrase or sentence expressing man's upward march. All others will be but dry stubble before the hungry flames.[9]

Roanoke Island is a very nice place, healthy, salubrious, and full of living resources. There has been a system of fraud going on here for some time with contraband stores, provisions, &c. Colonel J. H. Holman has put several under arrest, and black things are coming to light which would startle you. Government agents here seem to have been making their own money, while the freed people were undergoing a practical course of starvation. But the hero of the fighting 1st U.S.C.T. is making every thing within a hundred square miles tremble, if the least guilt is apparent. Those who are innocent are in great suspense, fearing that some one will call their names.

Several colored men, who have been working in the Commissary Department since General Burnside took the place nearly three years ago, have been arrested and put under guard, while white agents have been sent to New Bern and elsewhere under negro guards. I should not be surprised if some colonels are arrested and brought to trial. Roanoke Island being a sort of out-of-the-way place, parties have been doing as they pleased. There are about

---

James Lynch (1839–72) who advocated that the word "African" be dropped from the denomination name. Acting on this conviction, Lynch eventually left the A.M.E. Church to join the M.E. Church (Stephen Ward Angell, *Bishop Henry McNeal Turner*, 48).

9. Isa. 5:24; Obad. 1:18.

four thousand colored people here, of whom I shall speak hereafter. My work is so great now, that I will have to give you short notes.
H.M.T.

## "Army Correspondence"

(*The Christian Recorder*, July 1, 1865)

Headquarters 1st U.S.C.T.,
Roanoke Island, N.C.,
June 23, '65.

Mr. Editor:—Since my arrival here, the duties devolving upon me are so weighty and responsible that I can rarely find enough of spare moments to write any thing, especially those connected with the post office. Prior to the war there had been no mail base established here, owing to the exorbitant price asked by the boat line plying between Norfolk and New Bern, N.C.; consequently, all mail matters yet are partially conveyed through military channels. Still, we have a provisional post-office, which supplies at least five thousand citizens exclusive of the military forces. So, on our arrival here, our gallant colonel (precious for his many virtues) requested me to take charge of this office, the duties of which nearly absorb all my time.

So great has been the change of affairs on this island that I would be at a loss for a starting point, were I to attempt a detailed narrative of things now, contrasted with them when we first landed.

We found thousands of colored people on the eve of starvation, while the parties authorized by the government to issue rations were cheating, stealing, and defrauding them of their lawful subsistence. We found hundreds of colored men with scraps of paper in their pockets as the only reward for one and two years' work, performed under the promise of being paid by the government, while the money had been actually drawn, and lavished upon the greasy carcasses of lazy thieves and their accomplices. But I forbear to tell more. However, Colonel John H. Holman, of the 1st U.S.C.T., is ferreting out matters as fast as possible, and could send in a long list of impeachments, though I do not think he will strain every point, but simply make examples of the most prominent parties.

I also found the post-office in a miserable condition, and have given out a large quantity of letters which have been lying here for months. But things otherwise are most excellent. Thousands of colored people, formerly slaves, live on the island, each having one acre of ground allotted to the family. Most of them have found houses and excellent gardens, streets, and avenues well laid off and arranged. Fish, eggs, poultry, and such like eatables are in great abundance and exceedingly cheap.

Women are here by thousands, while men are numbered by hundreds, as a great many soldiers' wives live here. Children throng the highways and crowd the schools, and still they clamor for more; while fleas and mosquitoes rove by the million, thus keeping up a terrible scratching all day and night, for they make no allowance for company whatever. I find my fingernails very useful here both for digging and scratching.

The prevailing religions on the island consist of Methodists and Baptists. The Methodists are under the auspices of the Zion brethren, and the Baptists are not disposed to claim relation to any organized body whatever, but are simply Baptists. They have two or three churches of their own with colored pastors, but none are ordained; still they baptize and marry with as much boldness as if properly authorized, though Rev. William A. Green, Chaplain of the 37th U.S.C.T., will not allow them to do so in his presence.

Chaplain Green is a Baptist minister from Boston, Mass. Most of the Baptists here have those old worn-out ideas still, that you must go under the waters before you are right; while a more liberal-thinking portion regard true Christian fidelity as the standard of moral rectitude only. They are very orderly in their worship, observing Christian decorum in its high sense of appreciation.

I have only visited, though, one church of each denomination. The Methodist Church, which I visited twice unobserved by the members, appeared to worship under a lower class of ideas, or to entertain a much cruder conception of God and the plan of salvation, than the Baptists. Hell-fire, brimstone, damnation, black smoke, hot lead, &c., appeared to be presented by the speaker as man's highest incentive to serve God, while the milder and yet more powerful message of Jesus was thoughtlessly passed by; that, of course, formed the key to their class of ideas. But, oh! what zeal and determination they manifest in their efforts to serve God! I have to admire it as much as I admire the soldiers' prayer meeting in my regiment. I have repeatedly stood and looked at my soldiers, when holding their prayer meetings, until I cried like a child, standing out under heaven's broad canopy singing and praying in the most inclement weather, water drenching them, and running in streams beneath their feet; yet they would stand with twenty or forty in a gang, and their voices, clear in singing and impressively loud in prayer, never seemed to quiver or break its euphony. I never see them do thus without shedding tears, yet I have seen them repeatedly. I remember once looking toward heaven and saying, almost unconsciously, "O rain, that meeting (pointing to the place where the soldiers were praying) defies thy falling torrents!"

I was struck by a remark made recently by a gentleman:—

"Do you hear those negroes over yonder making all that fuss," said he.

"Yes," was the reply.

"Well," said he, "some of those same ignorant fuss-makers will be living with God in peace, when such fellows as you and I will be scrambling all over hell."

The uncouthness of the phrase did not in the least detract from the genuine meaning with which it was pregnant. However meager our moral and devotional conception may be of the intrinsic truths of the Bible, those who embrace them with an undeviating determination draw out a signal majesty from them whose reactionary power will be felt and improved upon by the most hardhearted sinner.

I sustained quite a disappointment a few days since by a flank movement by Rev. Brother Hood, of the Zion Church. Some fifty miles above here lies a little town, on the edge of the sound, called Edenton. The colored people there have a splendid Methodist Church, given to them several years ago by the whites. Hearing of it, I made several inquiries, and finally came in possession of the most flattering accounts regarding my prospects in taking it into the A.M.E. Church. I therefore surveyed my ground, or, in short, counted my chickens by hearing of the eggs, supposing that it would take a small corps only to carry that point. I proposed to send Rev. John Hames with one division to engage them and draw their fire, so as to ascertain their strength and discover their topography. Afterwards I would come with the remainder of the corps and carry every thing by storm.

The day having arrived for the boat to leave (as one only runs there once in two or three weeks), I was expecting the first division to go forward. But ere the boat steamed off, I looked, and lo! there stood General Hood armed to the teeth, with all his veteran force ready, and intent upon the capture of Edenton, after a forced march from New Bern of nearly a hundred miles. So, like the man who lost his rabbit, I solaced myself by pronouncing Edenton, church and people all, dry meat, and poor at best. But General Hood, not deterred by such trivial considerations in the least, went in, carried the place, left it well garrisoned, and returned yesterday, exultant in the glory of his conquest, and no one was more ready than I to lavish upon him my highest congratulation, and when I go there now, I shall compliment them as highly as if I had taken them. But at the same time, had I even surmised General Hood had any idea of the place, I would have been there before, yet I shall never wrangle, by the help of God, with a Zion brother.

This letter being too long already, I must stop.

H.M.T.

## "Army Correspondence"
(*The Christian Recorder,* July 22, 1865)

*Headquarters, 1st U.S.C.T.*
*Roanoke Island, N.C.,*
*July 7th, 1865.*

Mr. Editor:—The extreme sultriness and heat of the weather has for several days past palsied all my efforts to throw together a correspondence.

The 5th of July was surpassingly warm. The oldest inhabitants of this place speak of it as being one of the warmest days witnessed here for many years. In the shade the thermometer stood at 104 degrees. This kind of weather, as you are aware, is by no means agreeable to brain work. Though I suppose you will smile to yourself and say, "Where is the brain work about such letters as you write?" Well, I can only say as a reply, if they will pass for good nonsense, I shall regard myself as rewarded, for good nonsense is not unfrequently appreciated as our most interesting literature.

Roanoke Island is still the theater of many interesting incidents. Every imaginable phase of character, every question having for its color scoundrelism or virtue, however hatched with uncertainties through the phantasmascope of suspicion or seen in the vulgar revelry of the unconsciounable audacious, are ever and anon before the bar of adjustment.

A strong, athletic young man is not satisfied with being granted the loan of a horse by the post commander; but if the horse should back his ears, and look rather earnestly at the fellow seeking to astride a lazy carcass upon his back, he will stop, and in a maze of deliberation, return to headquarters and report the disagreeable looking features of the horse. It is nothing uncommon to have reports of dogs barking, and such trivial affairs, handed in at headquarters.

Colonel Holman, however, listens to them all, passes judgment upon them, and the parties respectfully retire.

But here is a circumstance to which I most respectfully invite your attention. The narrative runs as follows: Near Edenton (a place about one hundred miles from this island) lives an old rich slaveholder who, in the days of southern rights, wielded an immense power in that community, or in other words, he was one of the lords of the land.

He visited Wilmington about twelve years ago, and there saw a very handsome mulatto girl, or rather lady, around whom his licentious affections clustered. Thus, she was bought, and conveyed to his country mansion, and admitted to the lofty honors of sacred concubinage. In that very wholesome situation she has remained ever since, giving birth to six children, all illegitimate production of purchased connection. Providentially, both of these individuals had business before the colonel, and during the investigation the colonel's attention was called to their mode of living. The matter was referred to the chaplain for counsel and advice, as it was a subject of morality, who decided with the colonel that he should marry her at once. But he (the slave holder) could not see the point; he showed many reasons why it would not do to marry a colored woman in this part of the country. He argued skillfully in the false logic generally produced by slaveowners; finally, he was dismissed, and left with an exultant sense of his victory over Yankee morality.

Colonel Holman, after weighing the matter again, sent for me, and finding the parties already there, rose upon his feet, and commenced as follows: "Sir," looking at the slave-owner, "I have talked to you as a brother and friend: you have had this woman twelve years acting as your wife; she, in the sacred honesty of a lady, has in return given to you, your country, and your God, six children: you brought her away from her home, her relations, and friends, as a man would convey his wife; you have also devoured the flower of her youth, and torn from her cheeks the flush beauties of maidenhood; you have reaped and consumed these charms which God gave her to find a happy partner in life, and make her existence pleasant to the grave, ay! and to an eternal future. You have desecrated the sanctity of the matrimonial institution by force and unjust authority. But your day is gone: this is my day, and this great nation's day;—and as an officer of the United States, invested with power to execute justice, and carry out the proclamations of the President;—I tell you and your comrades, I tell all in my military district, such conduct shall not be tolerated. You can take your choice, either marry that woman, or endow her and her children with property sufficient to support them for life, or I will demolish every thing you have, hang, shoot, or bury you alive, before you shall turn that helpless woman and your ill-begotten children away to die, or to be fed by my country, and your property given to hellish rebels. I will hang you on the tallest tree in the state of North Carolina. You starved our prisoners to death, you cut the throats of our soldiers, and murdered in cold blood the best men God ever made, to sustain your infamous rotten oligarchy, and now, to add insult and injury, you propose to turn out your children. By the eternal God, I will sweep you all with one blast."

At this point he raised his head, and in a trembling voice said: "Colonel, you need not say any more. I can't marry Susie and stay here; but if you will give me time to dispose of my personal property, I will take her and go to the North, or to Canada and there marry her; I will sell my lower plantation, but my upper one I will hold on to."

"Well," said the colonel, "do you promise in the presence of myself and the chaplain to marry Miss Susan?"

"Yes, sir, I will; for I know it is wrong to throw her and the children away, for Suse has been a mighty good gal."

At this point we all shook hands over the prospects, and the court adjourned, to meet again when he gets ready to marry Susan and go North.

The fourth of July was very enthusiastically celebrated here. Early in the morning the coarse notes of the artillery began to proclaim its approach, and the bands broke out at several points in the sweetest melody. About ten o'clock three thousand persons had assembled before the headquarters to hear an address from the chaplain. But knowing he had made a miserable failure at Norfolk, Va., could barely muster up courage to speak, yet after he started he did better than he expected. This same speaker, a week before, made the poorest effort in Norfolk I ever heard. The evening was disposed of in prayer meetings, singing parties, shindigs, &c.

Several marriages have taken place since our arrival here, and several more are in contemplation; officers' wives are coming in from all quarters, and others are desiring leave of absence, in order to get married.

I expect soon to put my entire regiment through a course of literary drill. Several young ladies, white and colored, are coming from the North to teach in my regiment, besides two young men from New York, who will soon be here also; we allow them $50 a month; our first school will be opened on Monday. I still hope to leave my regiment with every man in it reading and writing. If I can accomplish that, I shall say to myself, Well done!

H.M.T.

## "Army Correspondence"

(*The Christian Recorder,* August 5, 1865)

Headquarters 1st U.S.C.T.,
Roanoke Island, N.C.,
July 22, '65.

Mr. Editor:—For some time I have cherished an idea which I hesitated to make public, owing to some misgivings which I had about its pre-eminent expediency. And nothing less than a profound conviction of its irrefutable utility would induce me to advocate a policy untried and vexed with prevaricable apprehensions; especially one involving, to some extent, the destiny of my people. For I hold, that this is no time to advance superficial theories wholly impracticable, or, if not so, fraught with no ultimate benefit to a race, upon whom are fixed the eyes of the world, and to whose destinies are linked the unconjectured issues of unborn millions.

The condition of the liberated people in the South has engaged the attention, and become a theme of much concern, of thousands of Northern philanthropists. Hence, the rise and liberal patronage given to such a vast number of elevating associations; for the number and variety of institutions bent upon the ultimate amelioration of the condition of the colored race in this country seems to have sprung into existence by a magic impulse, and to have spread with unrivalled celerity.

And to calculate their good: yes, the unquestionable actual good done by the Christian bestowal of teachers and books, including Bibles, Testaments, primers, spellers, daily and weekly papers, clothing of every description, and missionaries, accompanied by millions of fervent petitions to God for success and His constant, watchful care, would paralyze the most florid pen of heavenly messengers, and then the half would not be told. The progress made in that direction, first contemplated in what many thought to be a dubious project, has so affected the utility of the scheme, inaugurated in its incipiency by the precious few, that the most vacillating have become settled on that subject.

Thus, we see religious bodies of every faith and order, and even the infidel and skeptic, including humanitarians of every form, have made the colored race a central object of regard and commiseration; erecting a monument to their honor more lasting than the pyramids of Egypt.

Yet there is a broad arena of work still lying before us. Theoretical, if not practical, freedom has been secured to the colored race, and the nation pledged to its maintenance. The dying groans and crimson gore of ten thousand colored heroes, clotted in the mangled carcasses of the ball-riddled defenders of the nation's rights, ask in tones of thunder for their children's rights, at the hands of the same nation, and better that she drink hemlock and bitter gall than prove treacherous to their demands.

But all this guarantee of liberty, this superficial freedom, this dreamy idea of "do as you please," does not half cancel the debt of obligation. The societies and benevolent institutions already referred to have done much, yea, wonders. They have established several schools, but have not met the wants of our people by a hundred degrees. They have educated, and are still educating thousands, but millions have not seen their teachers yet. They have given them raiment by thousands, but millions are still clad in the coarse, tattered garments of slavery. These people, too, at least three millions of them, are without money, land, home, and houses; and many, to all noble purposes of life, are insensible. They want instruction in ordinary affairs, viz: economy, industry, and thriftiness of every species. They need to be taught the value of wealth, and to desire the acquisition of money; for I hold it to be a part of our nature to strive after this. They want to know what to do with freedom, its resources, responsibilities, liabilities, dangers and securities. It is not natural that a people who have been held as chattels for two hundred years should thoroughly comprehend the limits of freedom's empire: the scope is too large for minds so untutored to enter upon at once.

We find races, free from time immemorial, boasting of their noted ancestors and civilization, handling the tool of freedom quite injudiciously, at times, for their own interests. Then, to expect it at once from a people, for ages subjected to the most inhuman vassalage, is like trying to extort manhood of an infant. I do not expect a high state of things, in this day at most; it will be impossible for the present generation to become wonders of the world. Nothing more than a partial state of civilization and moral attainment can be hoped for by the most sanguine. But a medium state of things can be obtained by timely efforts, managed by that kind of dexterity and skill which thoroughly looks into and contemplates the necessities of a people, whose surroundings hitherto have made other minds better arbiters than their own, in matters affecting their individual and collective welfare.

As one of the bastion fulcrums to this great scheme of reformatory elevation, I would suggest and urge the propriety of the government, and all associations thus engaged, employing educated colored preachers and lecturers to travel through the South, and collect and address colored assemblies on all topics of consideration in the arena of man's sphere of action. I mean morally, economically, politically, philosophically, &c., but especially those bearing upon his industrial pursuits. I argue the peculiar fitness of the colored man for that position, because about him the most incredulous would have no doubt; neither could he be bribed by the deceptive flippancy of the oily-tongued slaveocrats, who too often becloud the understanding of the whites. No sumptuous tables, fine chambers, attractive misses, springy buggies, or swinging carriages would filch the time and labor he came to bestow, because he would find his level only among the colored race. Being accessible, too, to their huts or homes, weddings, parties, promenades, and all other social gatherings, his influence and personal identification with them would go further than the white man's.

Thus, with twenty-five colored men of good common sense and education, scattered through the South; say ten preachers and fifteen lecturers, whose entire business it would be to treat all subjects after their own manner, the moral, political, and social status of the colored race would everywhere be enhanced more towards making them good, intelligent citizens, in one year, than it would be in five, if left entirely to depend upon contingencies. There are thousands of them who cherish old slavish habits and ideas, about which they need plain talk. Even to children the most simple instructions, such as attention to personal habits, cleanliness, general deportment in conversation, domestic economy, attention to their own businesses, &c., would have a good effect.

Then, they need to be told all about virtue, chastity, honor, the value of a promise made, the contemptibleness of dishonesty and indolence. But it is useless to enumerate; suffice it to say, they need instruction in every thing, and especially the little things of life, such points of attention as thousands would never stoop to surmise.

But, some may say, why do you represent the freedmen as being more ignorant than any people I have heard of? No, that is not my intention; I claim for them superior ability. I have heard the greatest ministers and statesmen of this country, from Henry Ward Beecher and Charles Sumner down, but I have yet to hear greater eloquence than I have heard from the lips of Austin Allen, a black slave of South Carolina. In short, the ablest historian, the greatest orator, and the most skillful architect and mechanic

I have ever seen, were all slaves in the South. Having traveled through all the slave states except Texas, prior to the war, my observations have been extensive: thus I speak what I know, and the fact that one negro is smart argues the possibility of another, and another, *ad infinitum*.

But the cases referred to are such exceptions as mastered circumstances, and rose above their own level, *extraordinary projections*.

Again, if we go into cities such as Charleston, Savannah, Mobile, New Orleans, &c., and make the colored people there samples of their intellectual status, in the main, we will have no use for such arguments as I have adduced. But leave these cities, go to the cotton field, rice swamps, sugar plantations, and find, as I have found, by the hundreds, men and women fifty years old, and never five miles from some of their huts, except when they went to another farm to work. If that will not do, come here to Roanoke Island, where there are about four thousand colored people, and you will soon see the importance of my suggestion.

As this article is already too long, I must close by reasserting that twenty-five colored orators employed by the government or associations to traverse the South through, and lecture to the people on all subjects pertaining to their interest, would effect a revolution for the better, faster and more surely than any other agency or instrumentality in the circle of benevolent efforts yet engaged in it. I regard it as the one great lack, and if Congress would make an appropriation of $25,000 a year for the employment of such men, it would pay the nation quadruply; in less than five years it would yield the government an annual benefit of $100,000. The great revenue growing out of the intelligence of the people would bring to the nation inexhaustible wealth and strength.

I do not impose this as a duty upon the government, nor would I have called the government in question on the subject, had it not created a bureau claiming special interest in the freed people, and engaged white men in reforming their condition. So this is only, in my opinion, a more effective means, looking to the same end as that already in operation.

## *About the Contributors*

JEAN LEE COLE is an associate professor in the Department of English at Loyola University Maryland. She is the coeditor, with Charles Mitchell, of *The Collected Plays of Zora Neale Hurston*, and the author of *The Literary Voices of Winnifred Eaton: Redefining Ethnicity and Authenticity*.

AARON SHEEHAN-DEAN is the Eberly Family Professor of Civil War History at West Virginia University. He is the author of *Why Confederates Fought: Family and Nation in Civil War Virginia* and *The Concise Historical Atlas of the U.S. Civil War*, and coauthor of *American Horizons*.

www.ingramcontent.com/pod-product-compliance
Lightning Source LLC
Chambersburg PA
CBHW020352170426
43200CB00005B/134